IMAGES
of America

SOUTHERN INDIANA

IMAGES
of America

SOUTHERN INDIANA

Darrel Bigham

ARCADIA
PUBLISHING

ISBN 978-0-7385-0732-3

Published by Arcadia Publishing
Charleston, South Carolina

Printed in the United States of America

Library of Congress Catalog Card Number: 00106604

For all general information contact Arcadia Publishing at:
Telephone 843-853-2070
Fax 843-853-0044
E-mail sales@arcadiapublishing.com
For customer service and orders:
Toll-Free 1-888-313-2665

Visit us on the Internet at www.arcadiapublishing.com

CONTENTS

ACKNOWLEDGMENTS

Images of America: Southern Indiana evolved from a highly rewarding experience writing *Images of America: Evansville*, and from helping to produce *Images of America: New Harmony*. Members of the board of directors and friends of Historic Southern Indiana encouraged me to consider a work that would portray the HSI region. Such a work would provide not only a visual record of this special place at a distinctive moment in its history, but also a souvenir for purchase by visitors and residents alike. It would be, moreover, a source of revenue, as all royalties from the sale of this book—like *Images of America: Evansville*—are allocated to future HSI projects.

Many persons answered the call for illustrations and provided other forms of assistance in producing this book. Since the responses varied in quantity, and space and time were limited, this volume does not contain images of every community or county. Because of the size and accessibility of collections in the Evansville area, moreover, a majority of the descriptions represent southwestern Indiana. The images are nonetheless representative of the natural, cultural, and socioeconomic features of southern Indiana that HSI serves: from the gateway communities of Vincennes, Washington, Bedford, Seymour, North Vernon, and Lawrenceburg in the north to the cities and towns of the Ohio River in the south. Indiana began in this part of the state, and most of its historic sites are here.

Gina Walker in the University Archives and Special Collections Department of the Rice Library at the University of Southern Indiana was enormously helpful in providing photographs and in reproducing images sent by electronic mail or compact disk. Lyn Martin at Willard Library in Evansville was, as usual, generous with her time and support. I also wish to thank the following for providing and/or arranging for illustrations: Dusty Shultz and Mike Capps (Lincoln Boyhood National Memorial); Sally Newkirk, Lynn Rueff, and Edward Ries (New Albany); Elaine Stephenson, Marcella Beals, Pat Stroud, and Gary Roberson (Crawford County); Ron Arnold and Lars Purdue (Washington); Maxine Kruse (Bedford); John Fierst (Dubois County); Richard Day (Byron R. Lewis Historical Library, Vincennes University); Lee Rogers and Ron Grimes (Jefferson County); Bill Brockman and Fred Griffin (Corydon); Teena Ligman (Hoosier National Forest); and Ben Hubbard (Shoals and the Division of Forestry, Indiana Department of Natural Resources). Jane Reynolds, administrative assistant for HSI, helped beyond the call of duty. I am most grateful.

I would also like to acknowledge the two Ethans in my life: Ethan A. Hitchcock of Oldwick, New Jersey, my irrepressible nonagenarian father-in-law, and Ethan Hargrove Hotson of New York City, his namesake and our first grandchild, born May 5, 2000.

INTRODUCTION

This is a book about a transitional time (1910–1920) in a special place—the lower 26 counties of Indiana. In a socioeconomic and cultural sense, the 20th century was launched in this decade. For the nation, the state, and the region, by 1920 the world as we know it had begun to form, the product of the internal combustion engine and electricity, consumerism, and mass culture—formed by movies, radio, and popular magazines and newspapers. Industrial production focused on consumer goods, and advertising was now essential. The people of the United States implemented a variety of progressive reforms designed to make government more accessible and business more accountable. The income tax, the direct election of United States Senators, and the Federal Reserve System were exemplary achievements. Those who sought greater power for women were often the same who desired moral purity and social order. The implementation of women's suffrage and Prohibition occurred in the same year, 1920. The nation—a young giant—became directly involved in a war in Europe, sending two million men "over there," but in 1919–1920 chose not to join the League of Nations. But the world's financial capital was now New York City, and American business was posed to spread itself all over the globe.

This was, in fact, a transitional time for the world. People before 1914 were more often than not linked to the world of the 19th century and earlier. Theirs was an earth, for example, in which horses were omnipresent, time was determined by the sunlight and the seasons, pain and suffering were an expected lot, and monarchs predominated. Most of the 1.6 billion on the planet saw the universe as two-tiered: spiritual and material. In the West, the world was divided between civilized and uncivilized people, and white men ruled.

Hoosiers, too, were part of this fundamental shift. In the decade in which they observed their state's centennial, the percentage of those living in urban areas for the first time exceeded those in rural regions. The proportion of those working in manufacturing rose to 34 percent, while that of those in agriculture continued to plummet, to 26 percent. The percentage of those in trade and transportation almost equaled the latter. Farms continued to increase in acreage, while fewer persons lived on or owned their farms. "Scientific agriculture," promoted by the new county extension agents and the Indiana Farm Bureau, prevailed. Thanks to state legislation, the number of youth under age sixteen who worked in factories was halved. The number of working women doubled. In most cities and towns, public library systems were created, high school education expanded, and illiteracy declined. Metropolises—city centers with urbanized fringe areas—appeared. The largest by far was Indianapolis, but only one of these—Evansville—lay in southern Indiana.

In fact, the relative position of southern Indiana at the time of the centennial was vastly different from a century before. In 1816, almost all Hoosiers lived in the counties near the Ohio, but one hundred years later southern Indiana was the smallest of the three regions of the state. Among the 30 most populous cities, the region had only four: Evansville (90,000, third-ranked in Indiana), New Albany (23,000), Vincennes (17,000), and Jeffersonville, at the bottom with 10,000. Most towns and cities had had little or no growth since 1880. Evansville and Vincennes were exceptions. A number of places, in fact, had been losing population since 1900.

Despite evidence of significant change (for instance, in patterns of manufacturing), southern Indiana retained much of its 19th century character. Most people lived in rural communities or on the farm. Dominated by upper Southern culture, with a few significant German enclaves, the region led the state in illiteracy. There were only three colleges. All three Indiana counties that lacked a public library system in 1920 were in southern Indiana. The region was overwhelmingly white and intensely racist. That helped to account for the continued decline in the number of African Americans living there after 1900. Due to poor topsoil, depletion of hardwoods, and hilly topography, the economy of much of the central part of the region was poor. Many portions of the region were isolated due to the paucity of bridges and good roads. (There were no vehicular bridges over the Ohio downriver from Cincinnati until the Louisville–Clarksville connection in 1929 and the Evansville–Henderson one in 1932.) In the interior, the Wabash, White, and Whitewater rivers were barriers to the outside world. Only in 1923, for instance, was the White spanned at Hazelton, connecting Gibson and Knox counties. A state highway plan was not adopted until 1920, and hence travel by automobile in rural areas was relatively rare.

Because of geography and culture, southern Indiana retained a special quality. Each of its seven geographic regions possessed a distinctive character, whether dominated by caves and limestone quarries, coal mining, fertile farms, deep forests, or rock outcroppings. There was nothing like this in the rest of the state. The people were relatively homogeneous, retaining much of the personality of those who had founded the state.

This book about southern Indiana in this decade is divided into seven parts. The first describes, among other things, landscape, natural resources, and disasters produced by ice, floods, and wind. The second shows how the shape, size, and character of villages, towns, and cities varied. "Getting Around" comprises transit by horse and wagon, ferry, steamboat, railroad, interurban, and automobile. "Making a Living" demonstrates the many ways in which people in southern Indiana earned an income. (Quite a few of those occupations have been obsolete for a long time). The fifth part describes the infinite diversity of social interchange—pageants and rituals, schools, churches, clubs and organizations, recreation, health and medical care, and government services. "Going to War" treats the people of southern Indiana as they participated in America's first war on the European continent. And the last part, "Facing the Future," contains images of the many effects of this decade on the decades to come, from Prohibition to the movies.

One

Living with Nature

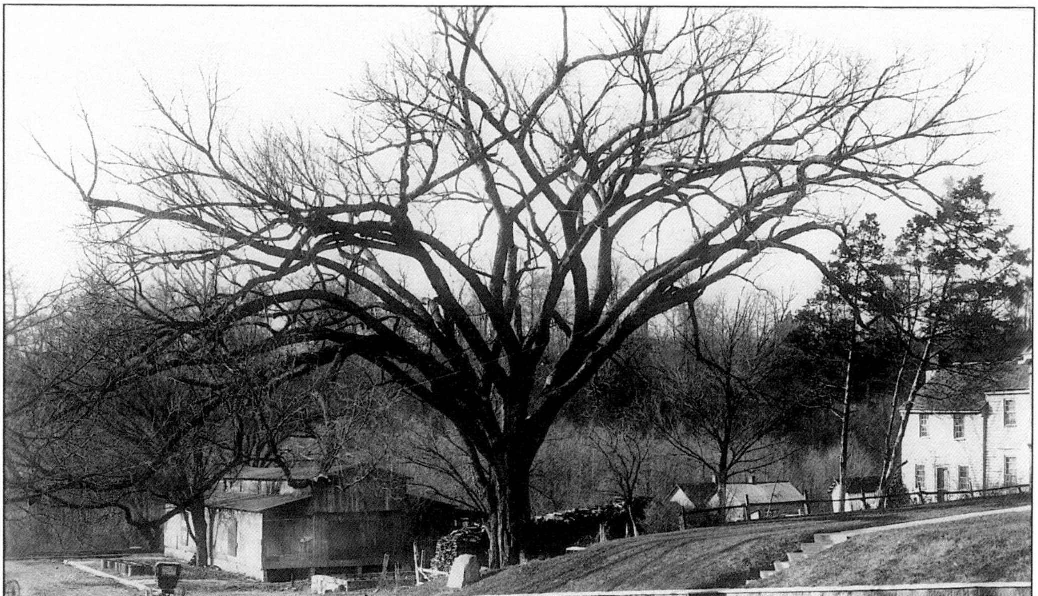

The Constitution Elm in Corydon, photographed in 1913, has special significance in Indiana history. Due to the heat, delegates to the first constitutional convention that began on June 10, 1816, met underneath it. Nineteen days later, the first constitution was completed. Dutch elm disease later destroyed the tree, but a vestige of it has been preserved as part of the Corydon Capitol State Historic Site. (Courtesy of Division of Forestry, Department of Natural Resources.)

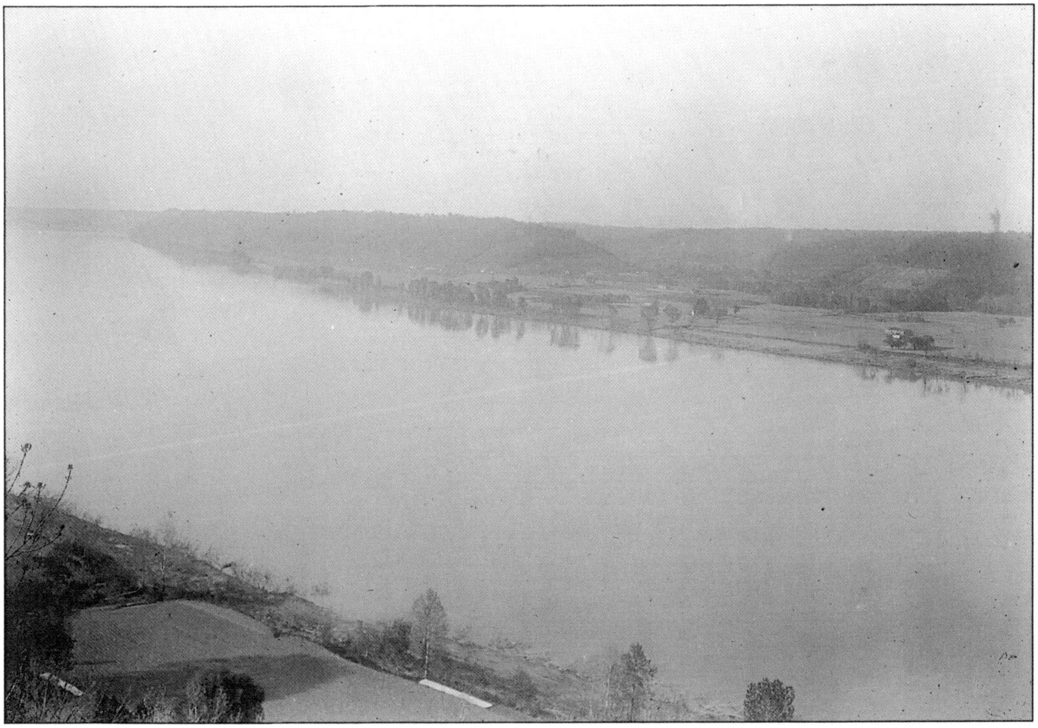

This is a view from Marble Hill, near Hanover, up and across the Ohio. Charles C. Deam took the photo late in the afternoon of May 2, 1918. (Courtesy of Division of Forestry.)

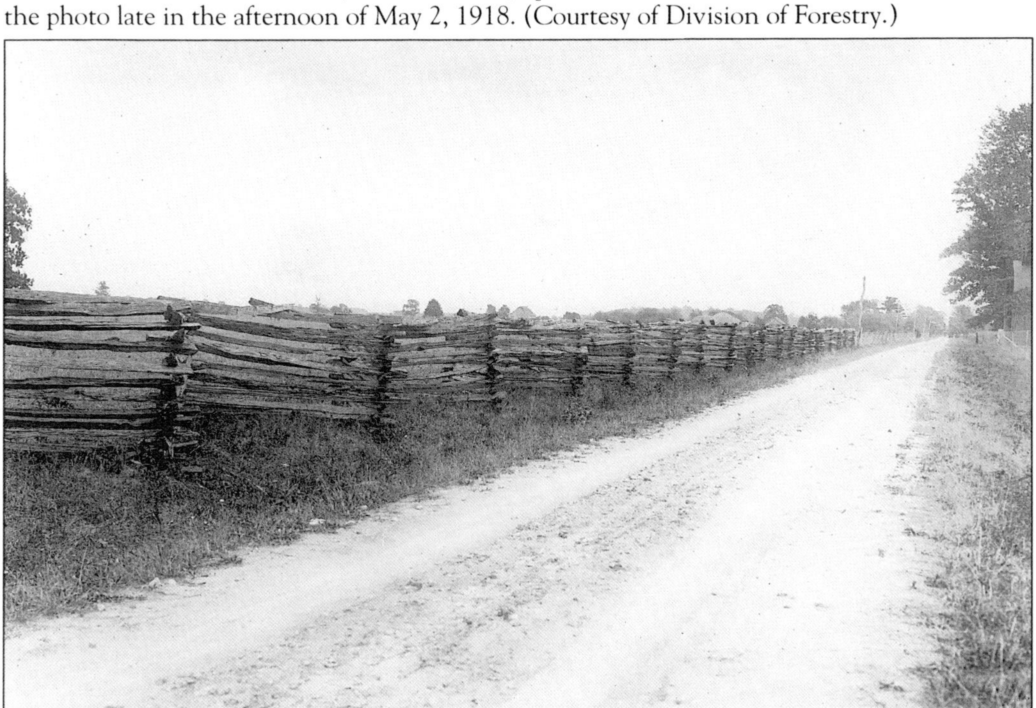

This old-fashioned rail fence was photographed two miles southeast of Milhauzen in Jennings County on the afternoon of September 20, 1919. (Courtesy of Division of Forestry.)

Charles C. Deam photographed this old cemetery in the Davis woods four and a half miles south of Salem (Washington County) on the morning of April 26, 1918. The Division of Forestry photographer noted that a tall ironwood tree, measuring 28 inches in circumference, had grown on the grave marking a death in 1845, and also that graveyard myrtle covered the entire yard. (Courtesy of Division of Forestry.)

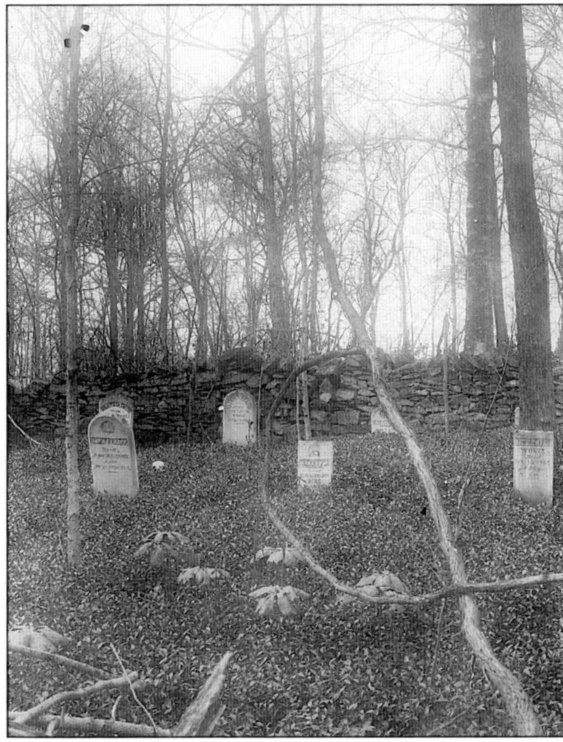

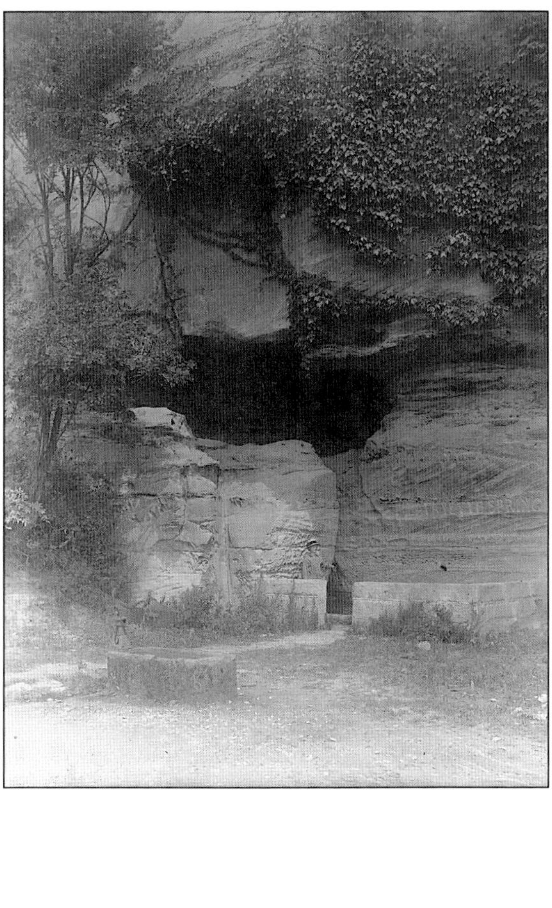

Deam also photographed Lafayette Spring, four miles east of Cannelton in Perry County, on August 13, 1919. Named for the Revolutionary War hero who visited the United States in 1825, passing by the county on the Ohio, it illustrates one of the most common geological features of the landscape in that region, the Crawford Upland. (Courtesy of Division of Forestry.)

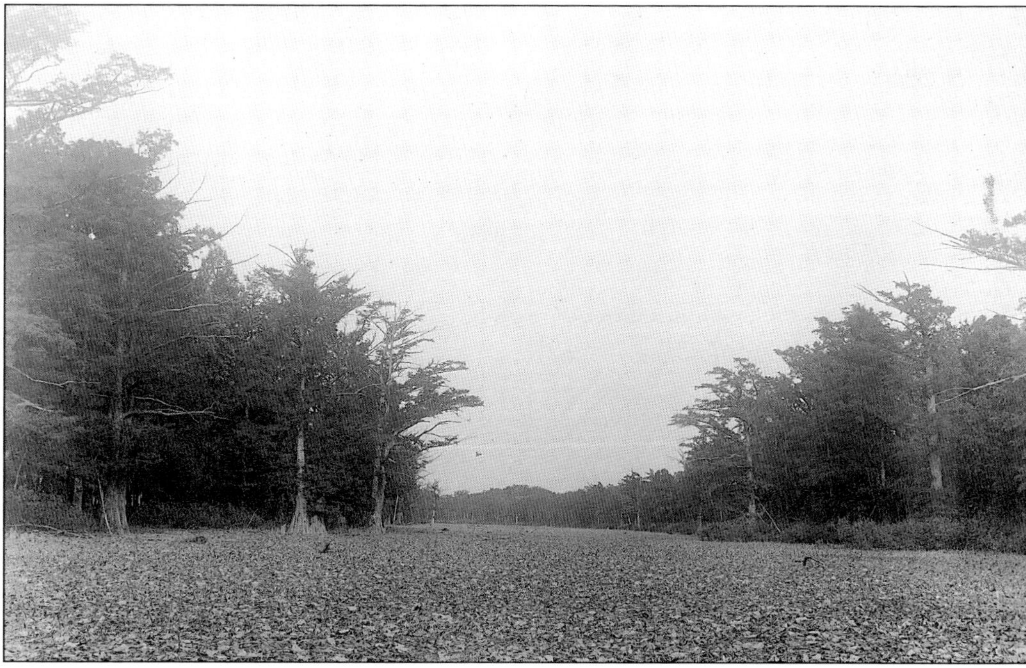

This cypress slough three miles east of Mount Vernon was dry at the time of year Charles Deam photographed it on October 14, 1917. Now a nature preserve, it illustrates some of the Deep South characteristics of flora along the lower Ohio in Vanderburgh and Posey counties. (Courtesy of Division of Forestry.)

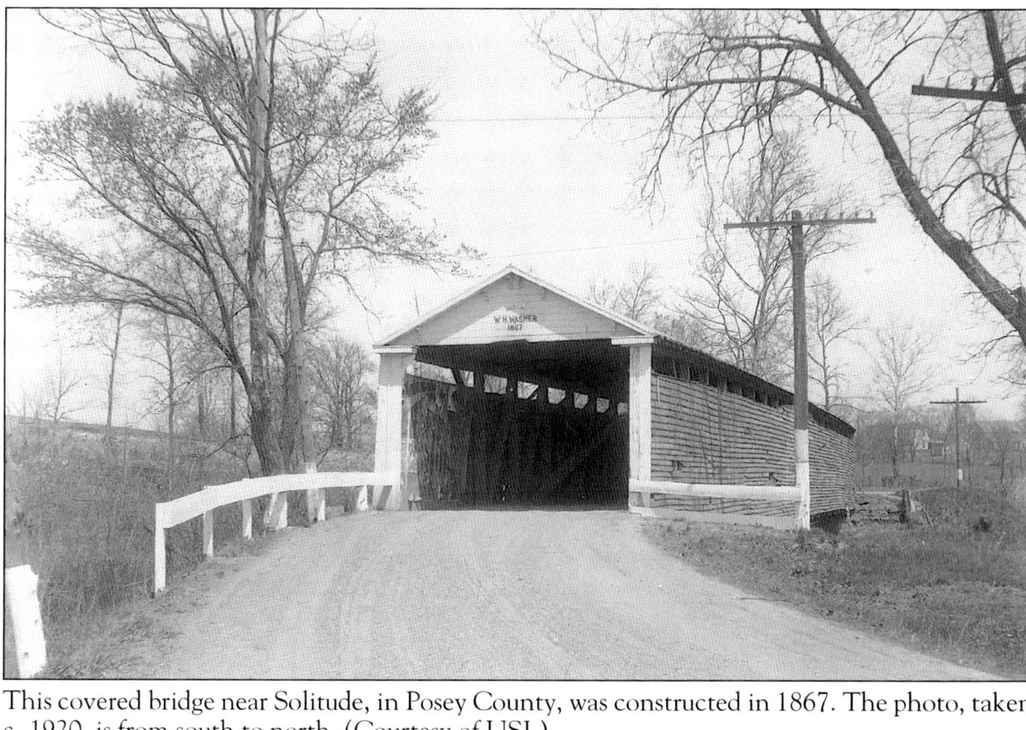

This covered bridge near Solitude, in Posey County, was constructed in 1867. The photo, taken *c.* 1920, is from south to north. (Courtesy of USI.)

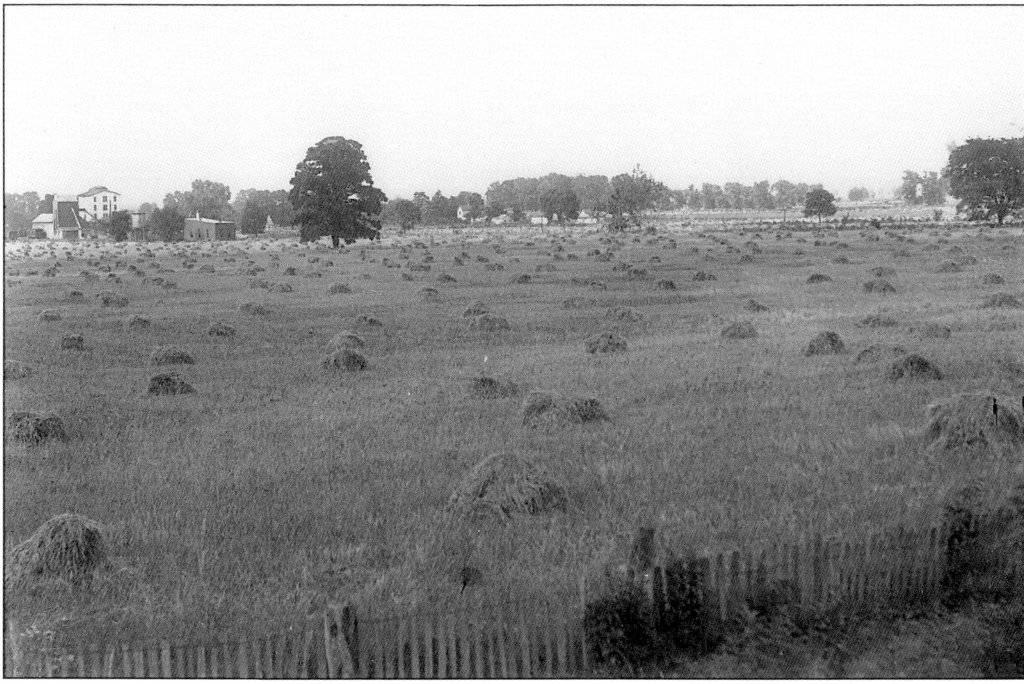

This field in Posey County, after the threshing of wheat, probably in early July, resembled countless others at the same time in southern Indiana. (Courtesy of USI.)

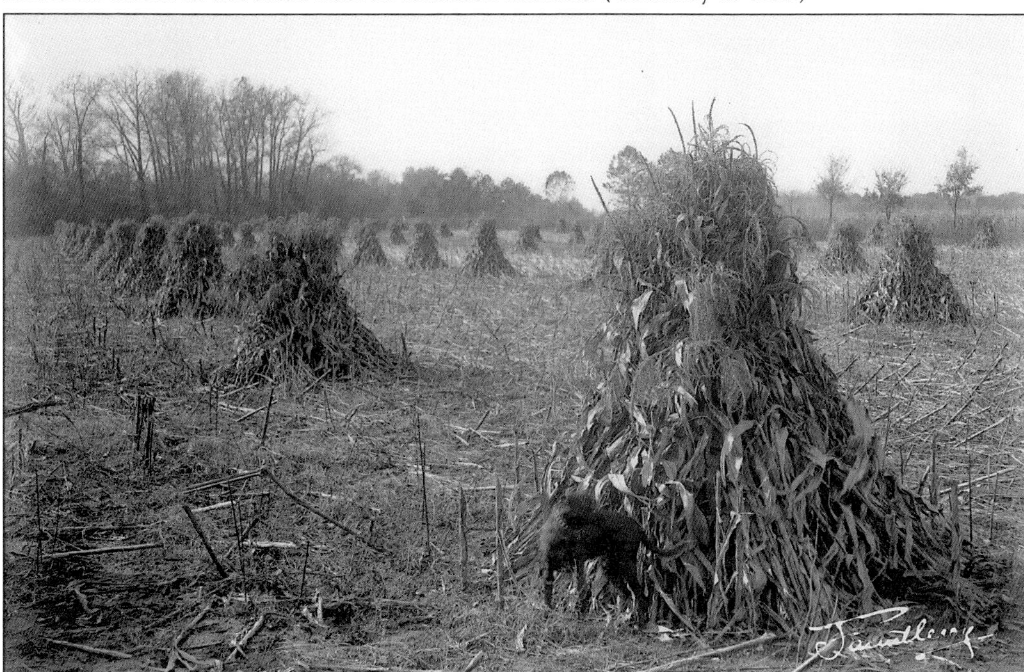

Corn though, was much more widely grown. This is a Posey County field after corn had been harvested and the stalks gathered, probably in early fall. Scenes like this would have been found in almost all parts of southern Indiana at the time. Corn and hogs were the region's—and the state's—leading agricultural products. (Courtesy of USI.)

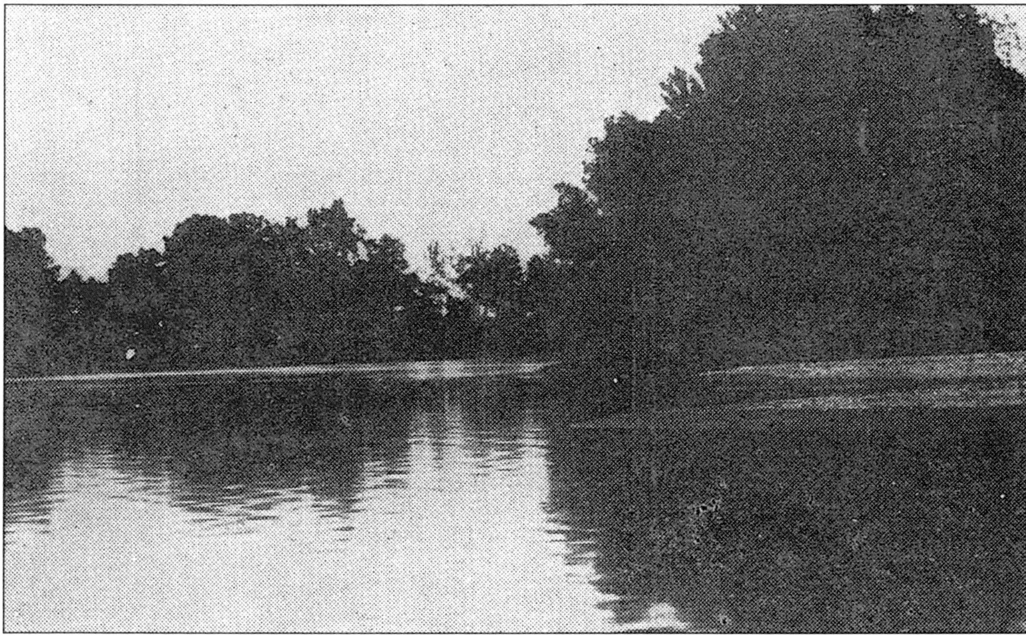

Virtually unchanged by modern times, this was White River Island, near Petersburg, in 1910. (Courtesy of Willard Library.)

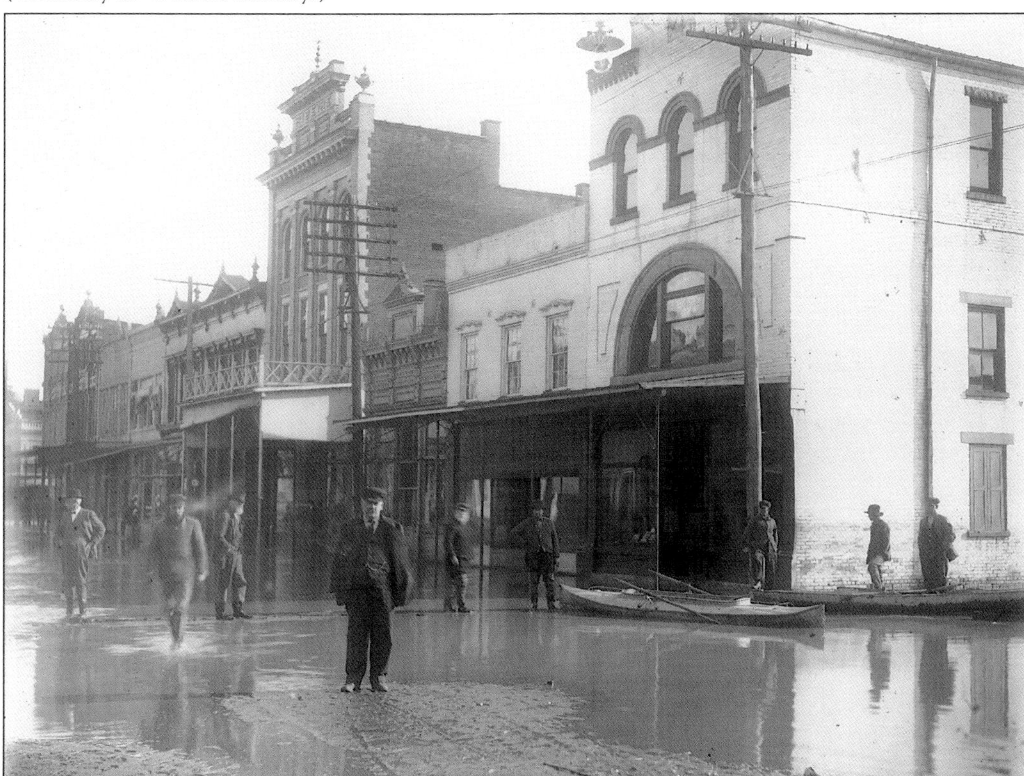

This is a scene in the center of New Harmony during the flood of March 1913. (Courtesy of USI.)

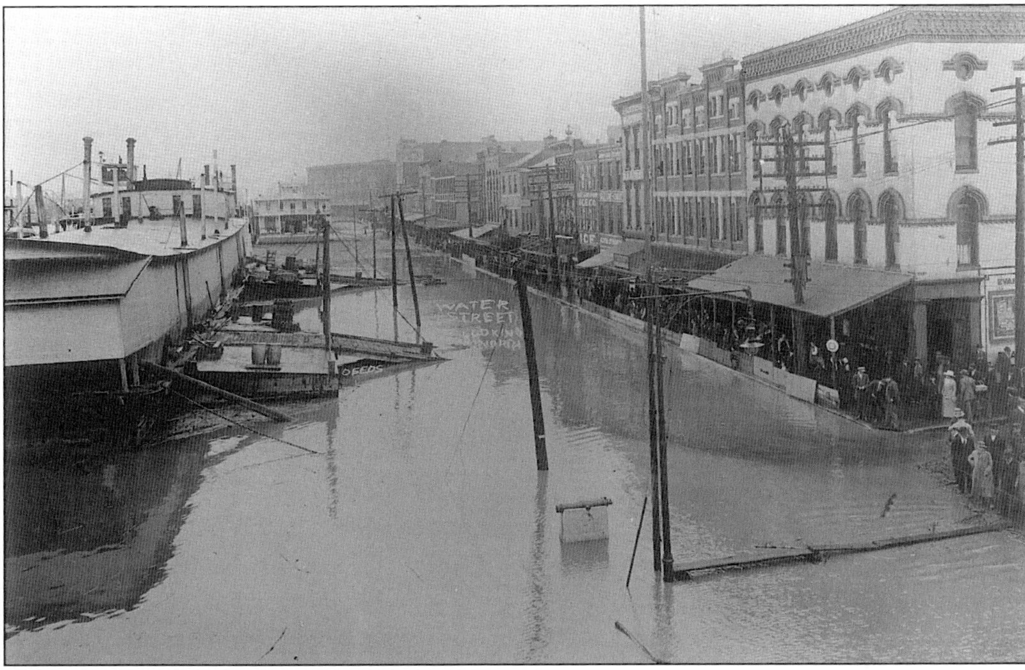

The flood of March 1913 brought the Ohio right up to the businesses along Water Street in Evansville. The only comparable flooding in the previous 50 years occurred in 1884. Neither would be nearly as devastating as the flood of January 1937, though. (Courtesy of USI.)

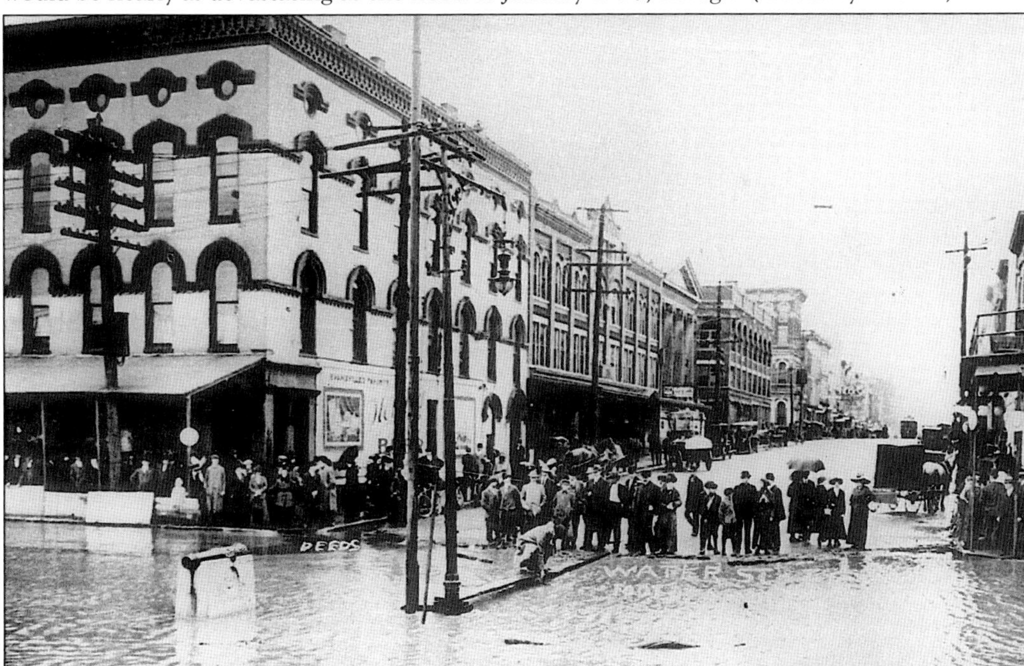

Water Street in Evansville, at the foot of Main, is shown here during the 1913 flood. The antebellum Greek Revival Old National Bank Building is the third building on the left. (Courtesy of Willard Library.)

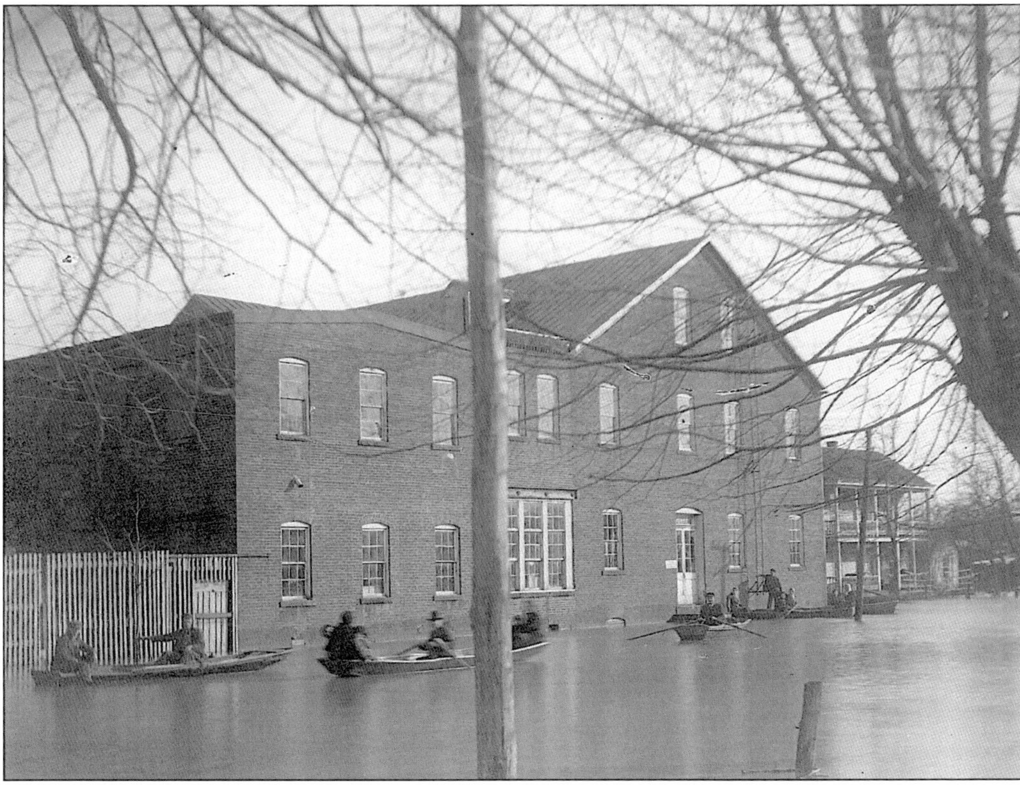

The Tell City Desk Company is shown during high water in the flood of March 1913. (Courtesy of Willard Library.)

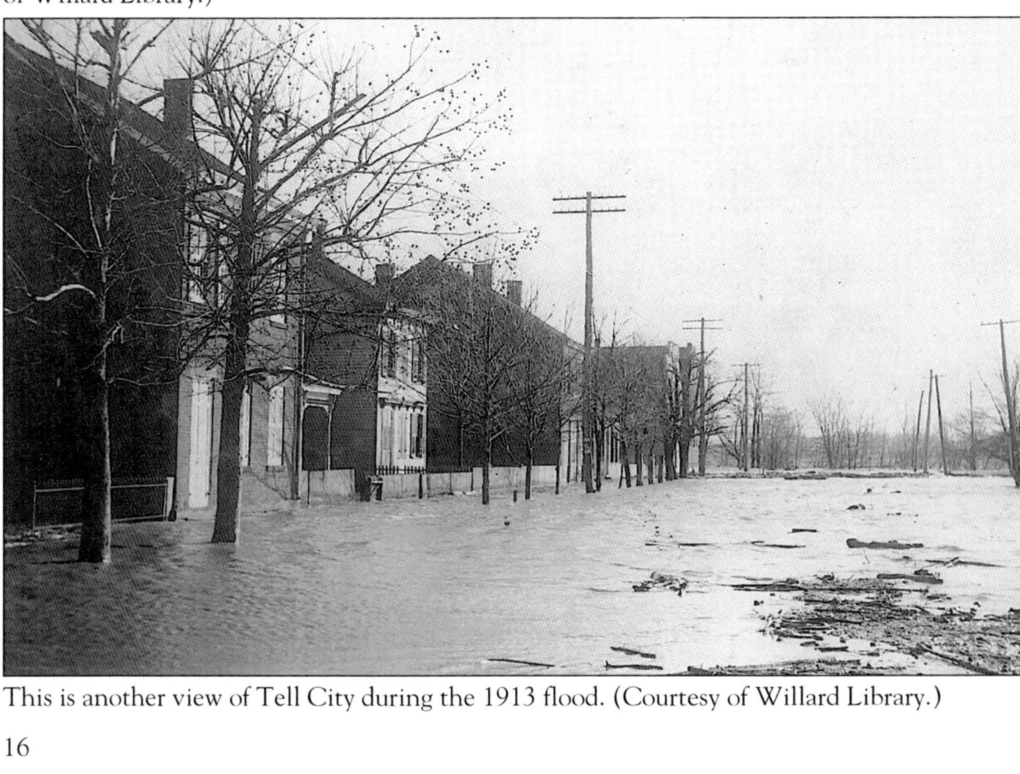

This is another view of Tell City during the 1913 flood. (Courtesy of Willard Library.)

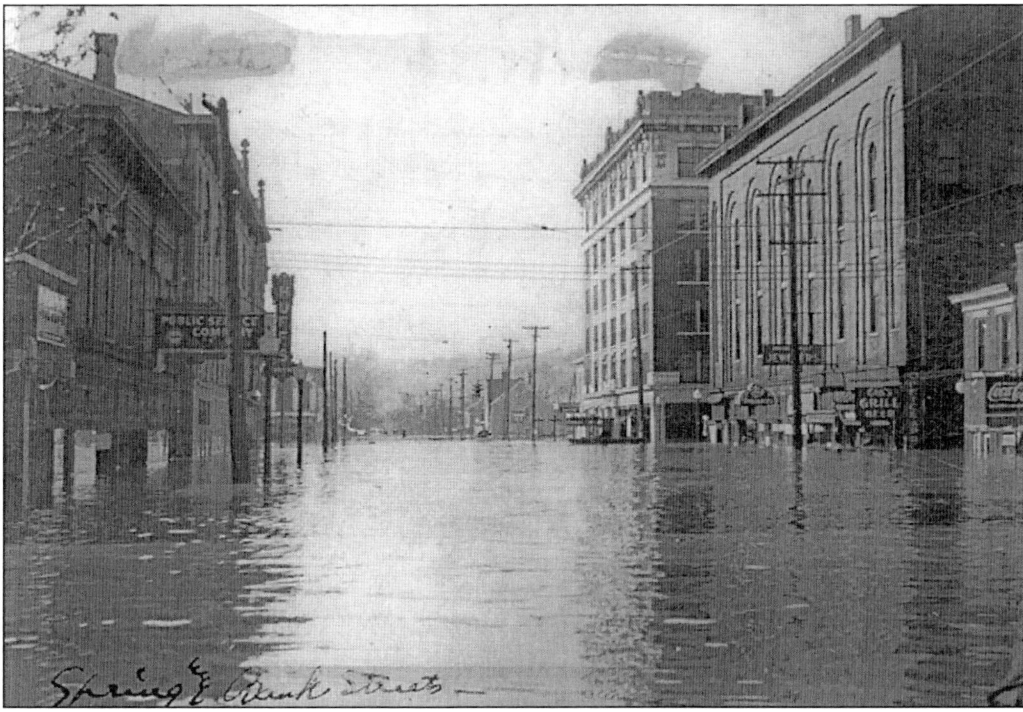

Flood waters also besieged New Albany. Shown is Pearl Street, from Spring to Market Streets. (New Albany-Floyd County Public Library.)

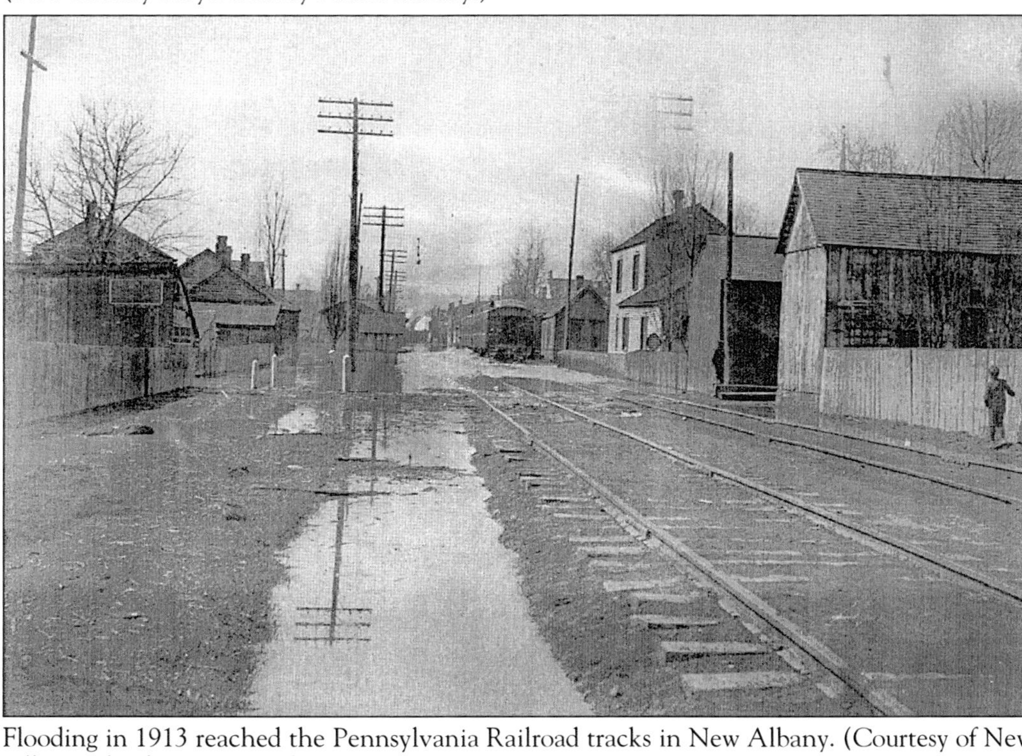

Flooding in 1913 reached the Pennsylvania Railroad tracks in New Albany. (Courtesy of New Albany-Floyd County Public Library.)

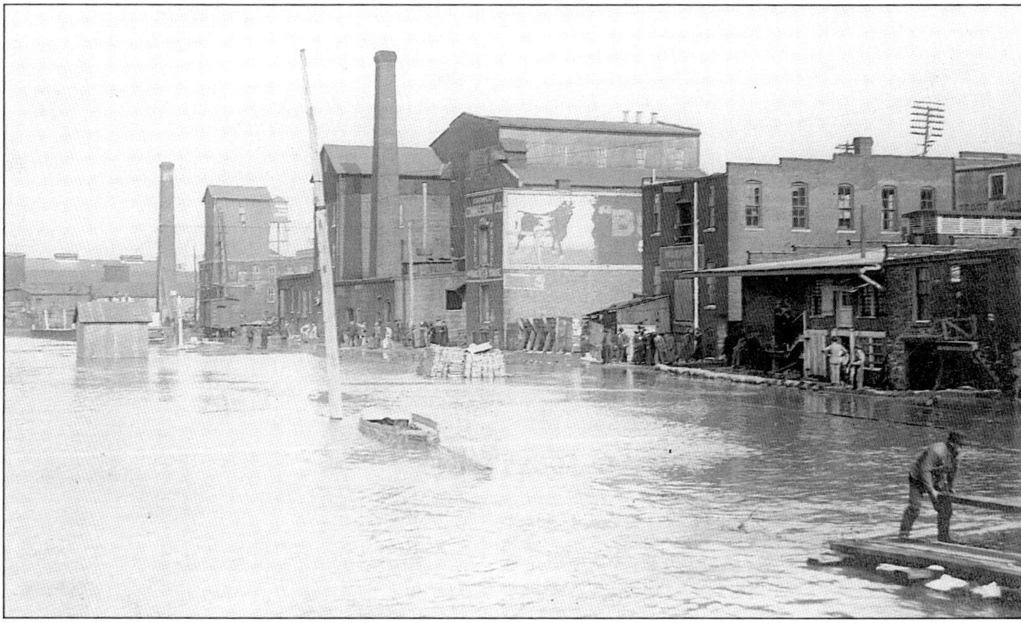

In the 1913 flood, the Wabash River washed out railroad bridges around Vincennes, making the city a peninsula. The river was about eight miles wide at one point. This photograph shows flooding north of Main Street. (Courtesy of Lewis Library.)

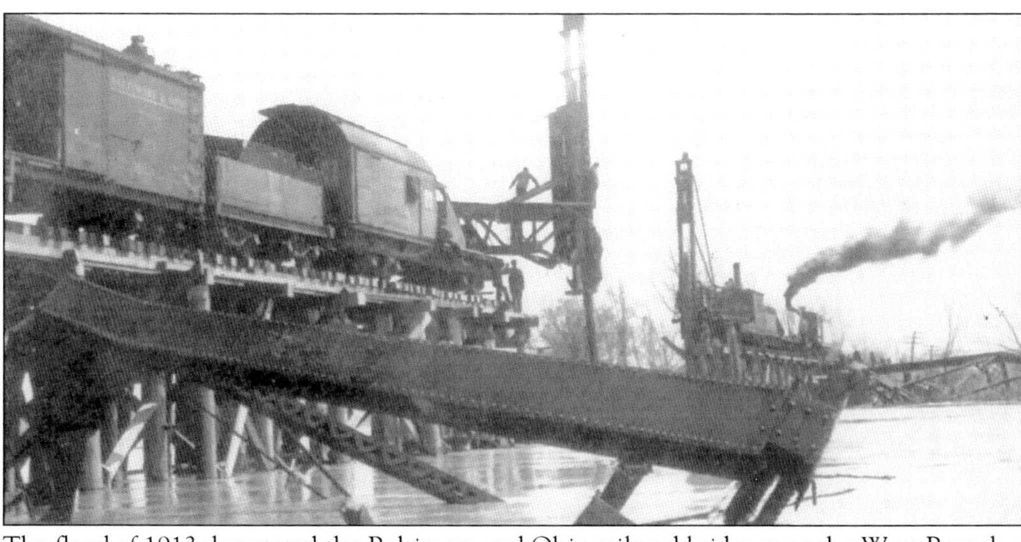

The flood of 1913 devastated the Baltimore and Ohio railroad bridge over the West Branch of the White River west of Washington. Here repair crews are shown driving pilings to replace the damaged portion of the bridge. (Courtesy of *Washington Times-Herald.)*

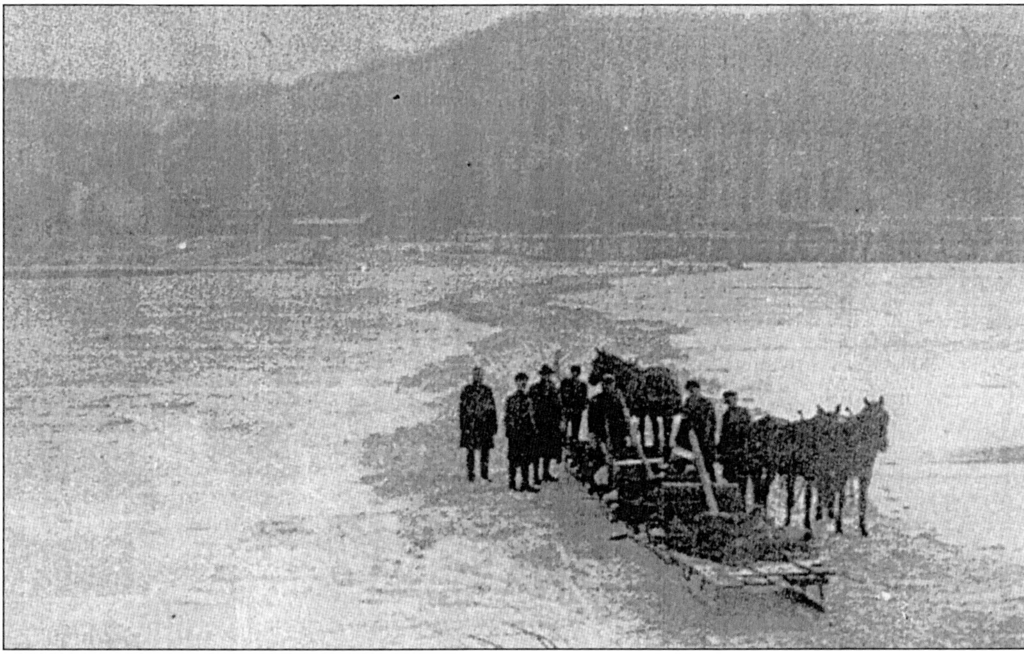

A sleigh is pictured crossing the Ohio River at Madison in January 1918. When the river froze, ferry service was halted, and crossings had to be made by horse-drawn sleigh. At the time, no bridge connected Madison with Kentucky. In fact, between the Ohio and Illinois borders, there were only a few railroad bridges—at Cincinnati, Louisville, and Evansville. (Courtesy of Jefferson County Historical Society.)

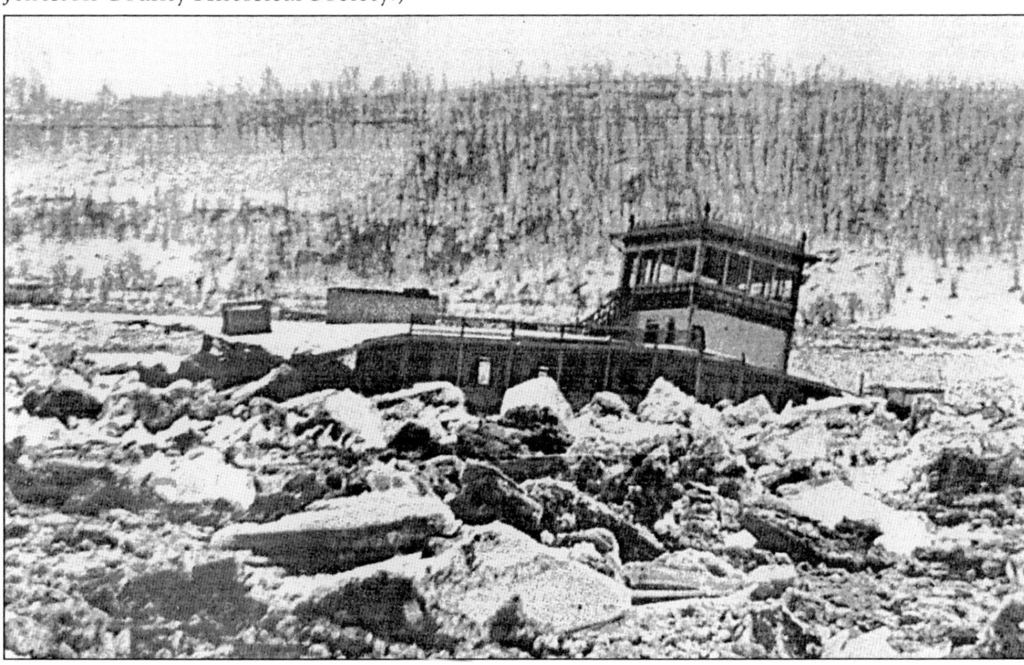

This was taken February 1, 1918, when a severe cold spell had frozen the Ohio River. Many riverboats were damaged or destroyed by the resulting ice jams. This photo shows one of the unidentified riverboats sunk at Madison. (Courtesy of Jefferson County Historical Society.)

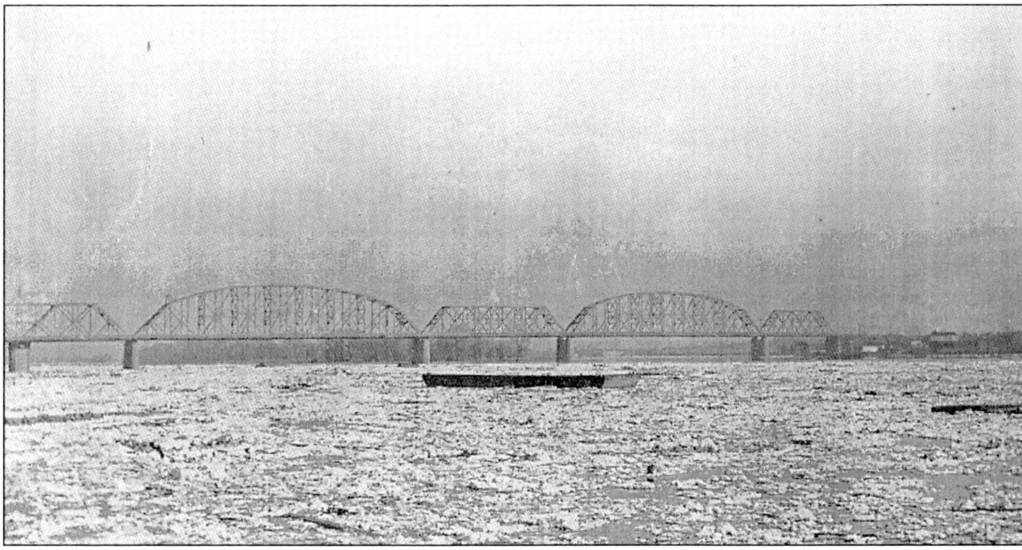

During the frigid winter of 1918, ice covered the Ohio River for many weeks. This shows the Kentucky and Indiana Railroad bridge between New Albany and Louisville on February 13, 1918, after an ice gorge broke upriver at Cincinnati. (New Albany-Floyd County Public Library.)

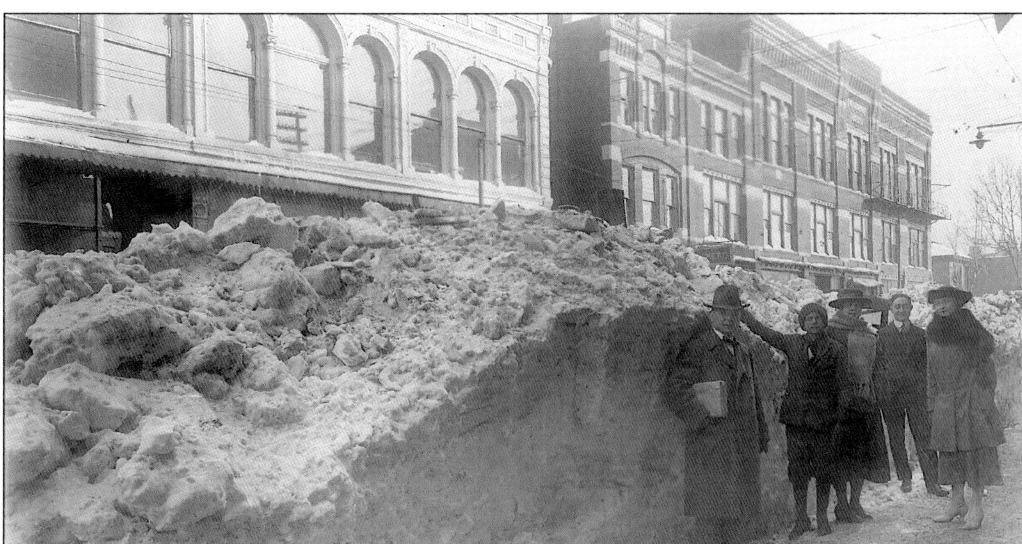

During the harsh winter of 1918, this was the scene on Fifth Street in Evansville, near the interurban station. (Courtesy of Willard Library.)

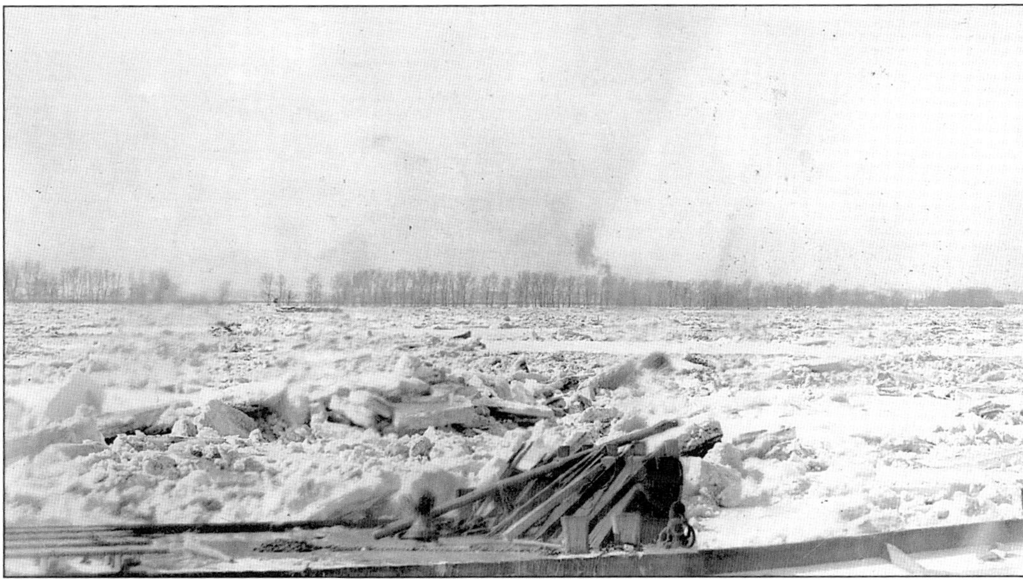

These photographs, taken by *Evansville Courier* photographer Karl Kae Knecht, document the severity of the winter of 1918. Both were taken February 4, 1918. The top, in late morning, shows the frozen Ohio upriver from Evansville. The bottom, taken at 3:30 that afternoon even farther upriver, shows the condition of the river and the ferry between Hawesville, Kentucky (foreground) and Cannelton, Indiana. (Courtesy of Willard Library.)

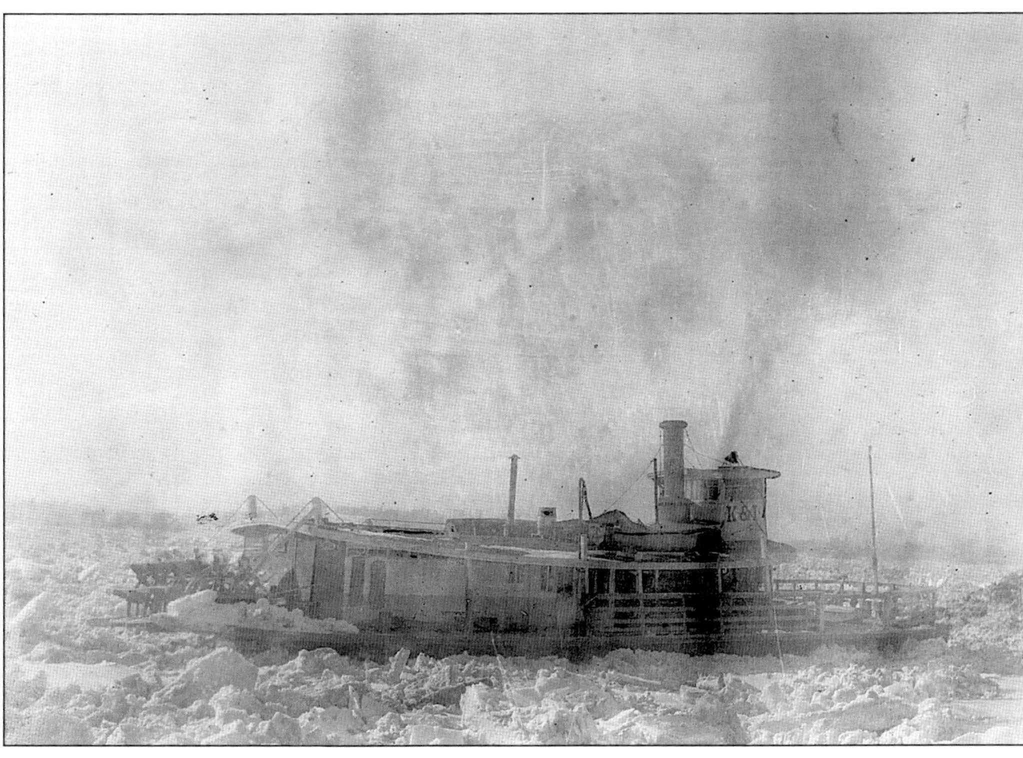

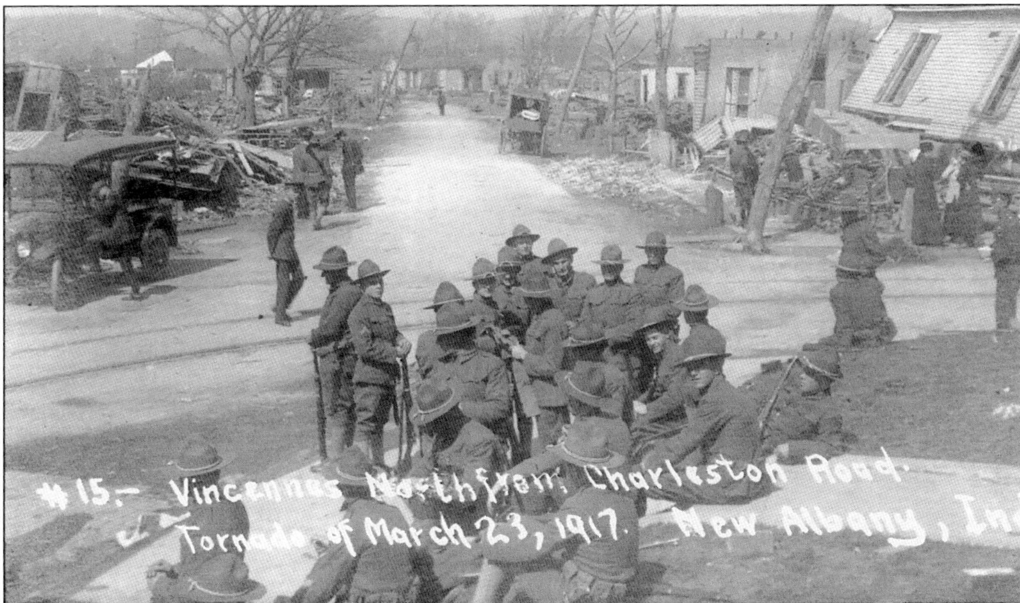

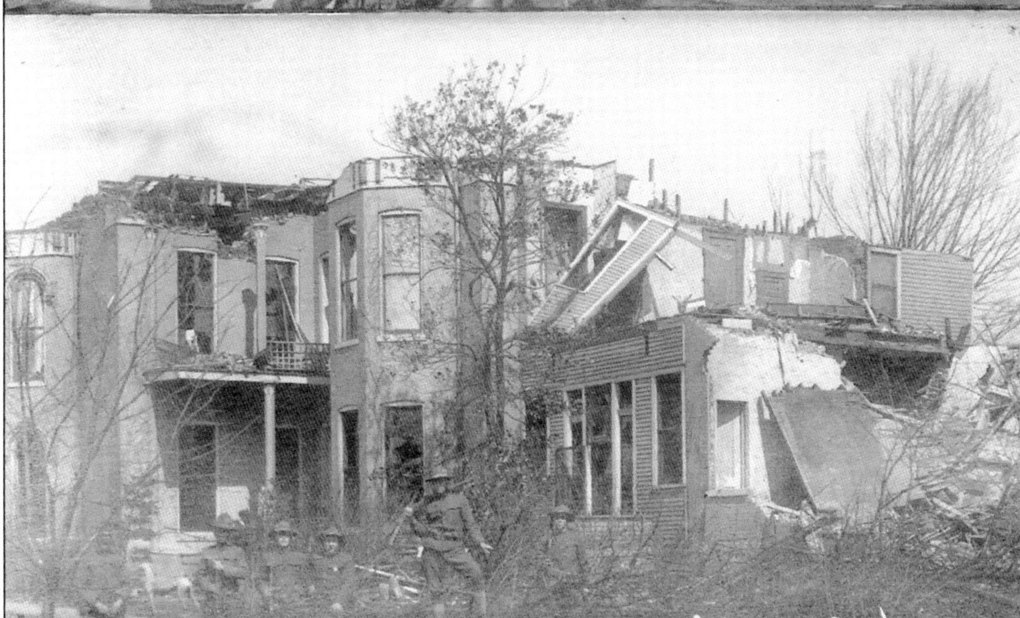

Tornadoes have been an omnipresent aspect of life in southern Indiana. This one struck New Albany and Floyd County on March 23, 1917. Shown here is damage on the Charleston Road, where National Guardsmen are assembled, and to the Depauw Apartments in the city. Despite the amount of news about the possibility of war with Germany, this event dominated the front page of March 24th papers across the state. The tornado, which hit the northeast part of the city, killed about 40 and badly injured 75. Damage was over $1.1 million. Five hundred homes were stricken; three hundred were destroyed. (Courtesy of Carnegie Center for Art and History.)

Two

BUILDING COMMUNITIES

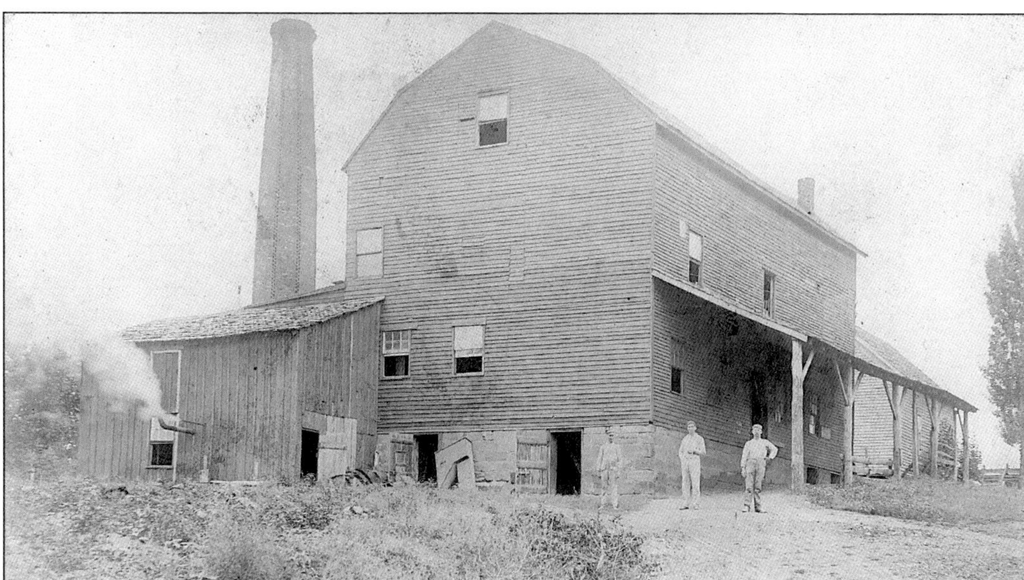

A grist or flour mill was central to the development of every village and town in southern Indiana. This is the Gentryville Mill, about 1910, in Spencer County. (Courtesy of Lincoln Boyhood National Memorial.)

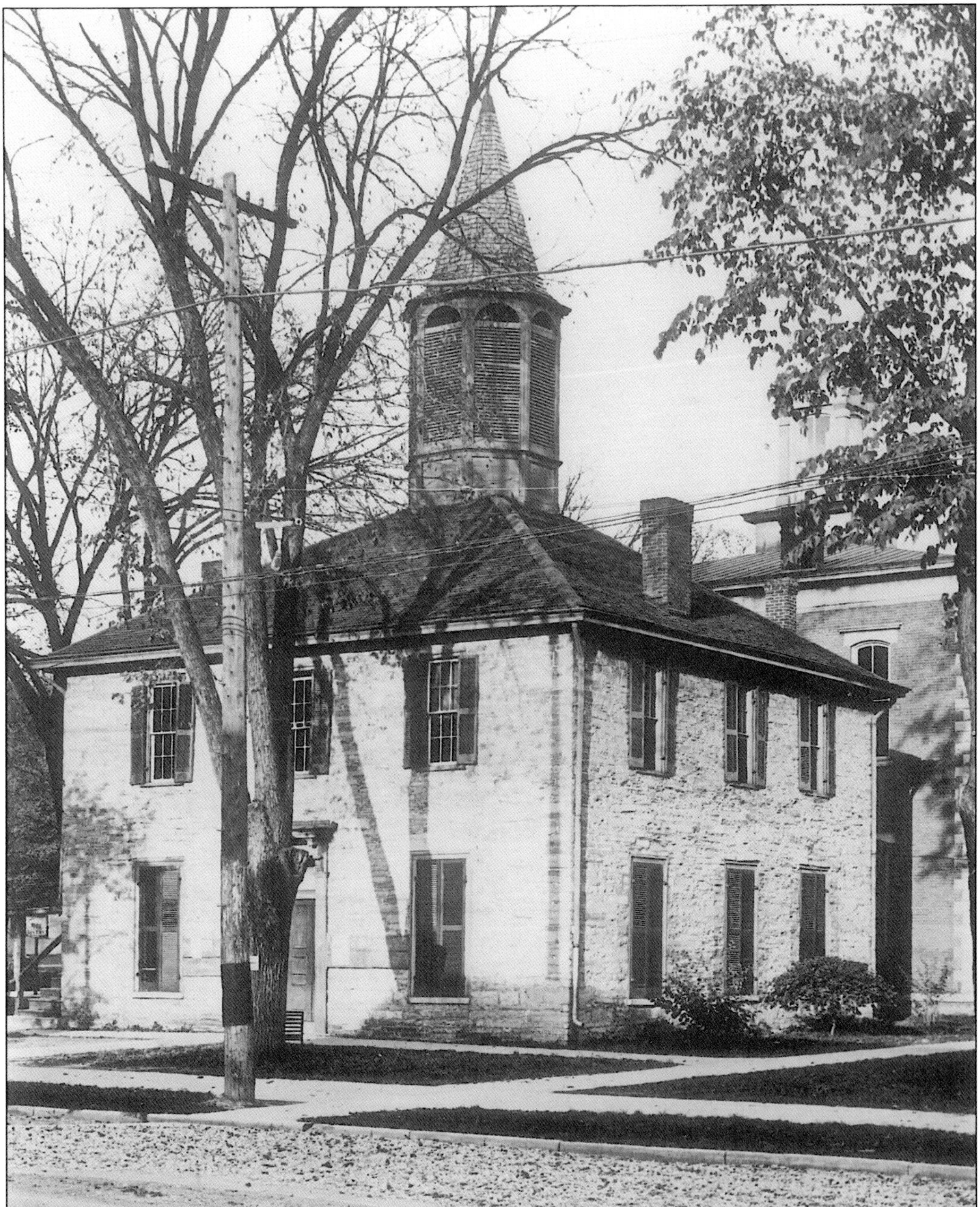

This building in Corydon served as the Indiana state capitol until 1825, when the capitol was moved to Indianapolis. Planned as a courthouse and completed after statehood in December 1816, it would revert to its original purpose after 1825. This is the way the building looked at the time of the state centennial in 1916. (Courtesy of Fred Griffin.)

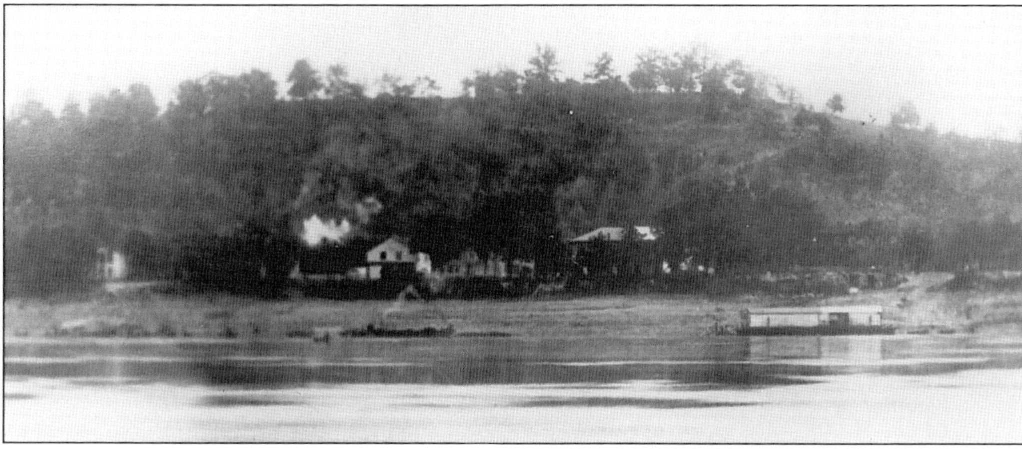

This is a rare view of the original town of Leavenworth taken from the Ohio in 1914. After the disastrous flood of 1937, the town was moved to the top of the ridge in the background. (Courtesy of Elaine Stephenson.)

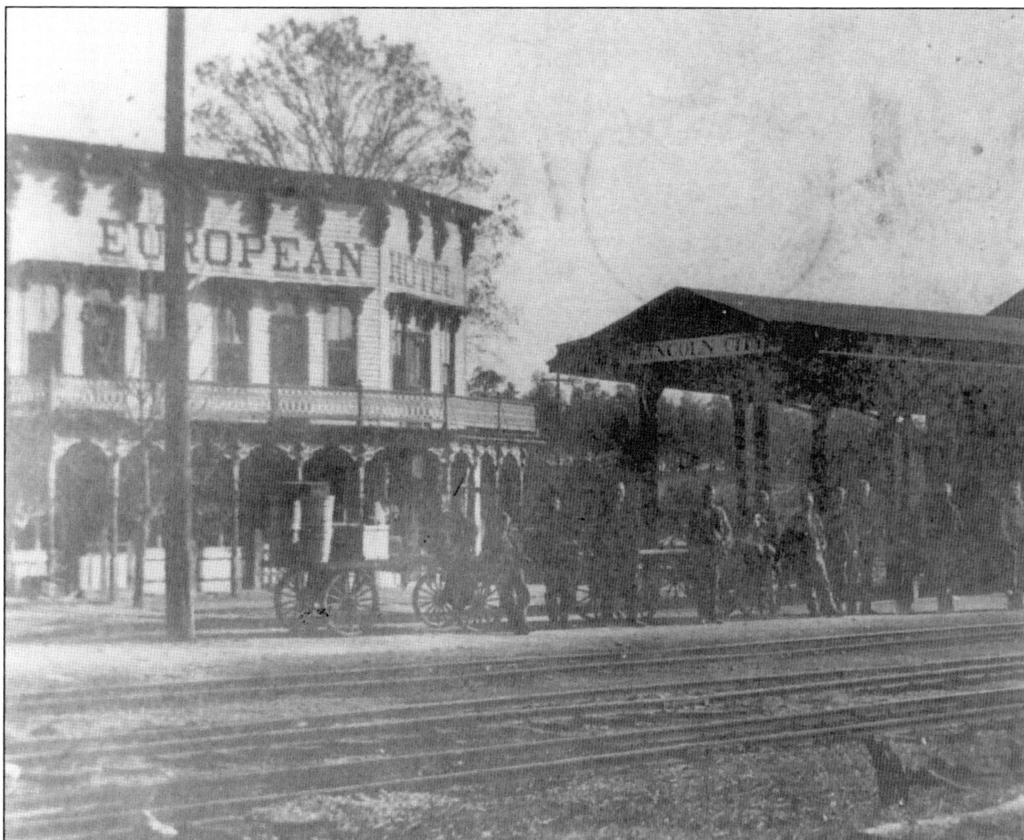

Lincoln City, named after Abraham Lincoln, who lived on a nearby homestead between 1809 and 1830, was created in the 1880s. It once had hopes of becoming a major metropolis because it lay at the junction of rail lines leading south to Rockport and Tell City, southwest to Boonville, and north to Jasper. This is its railroad station and hotel about the time of World War I. (Courtesy of Lincoln Boyhood National Memorial.)

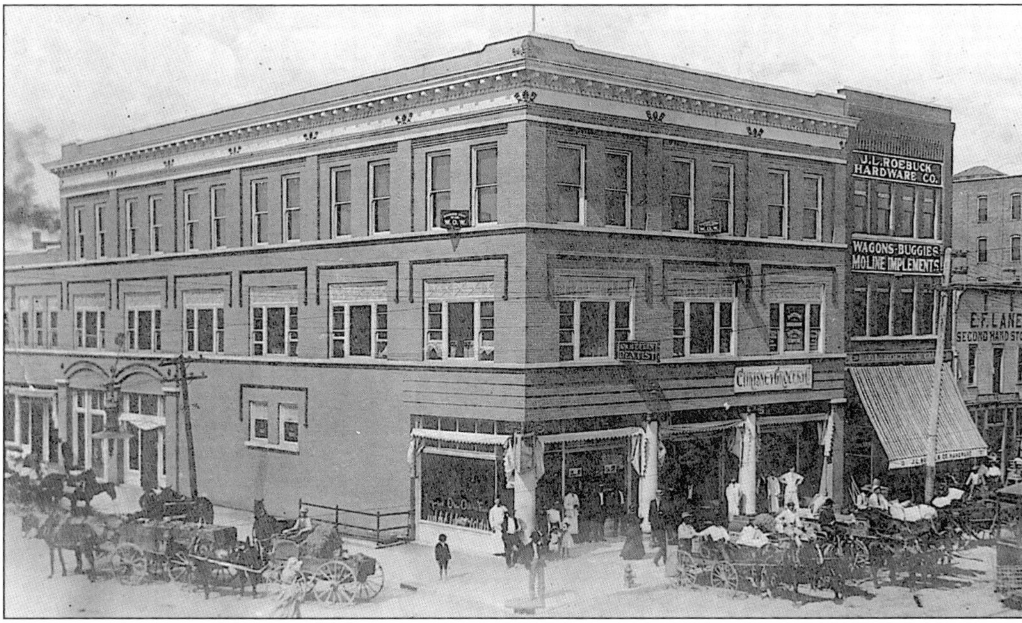

This photograph captures the changing face of downtown Boonville, county seat of Warrick County, in August 1910. Although the horse and buggy or wagon are omnipresent, a streetcar can be seen on the lower right. Main streets in America symbolized utilitarian, commercial values, or what Michael Conzen has called "republicanism, perfectionism, and domesticity." Being up-to-date was essential. (Courtesy of Willard Library.)

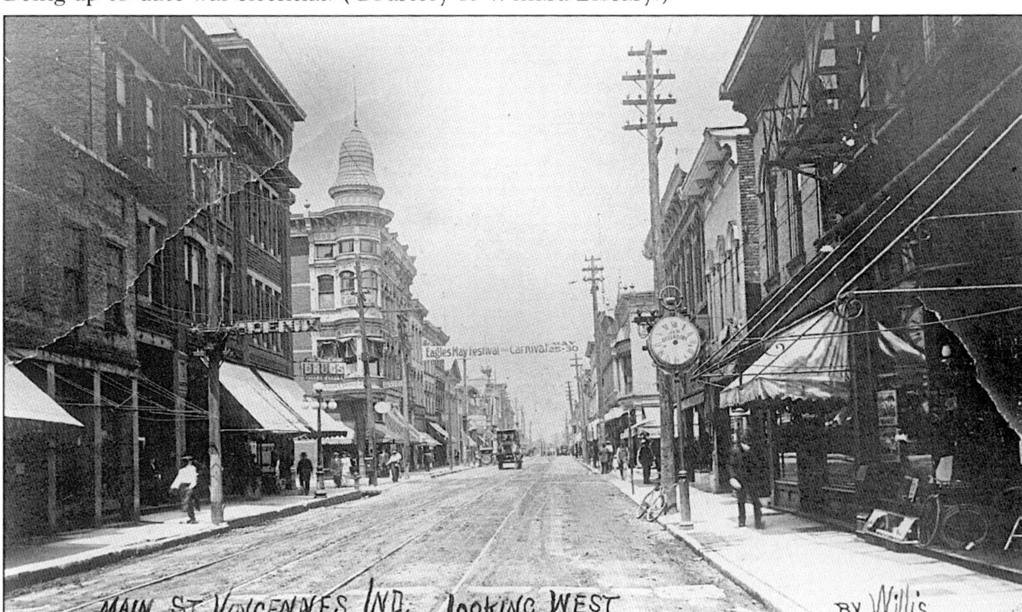

A postcard depicts Main Street in Vincennes looking west in 1914, before bricks were laid. Prior to that, the street was covered with gravel. When nearby Washington paved its main street with bricks, civic pride prompted citizens of Vincennes to do the same. Traffic was two-way, and there were two sets of trolley tracks. There were also few automobiles. (Courtesy of Lewis Library.)

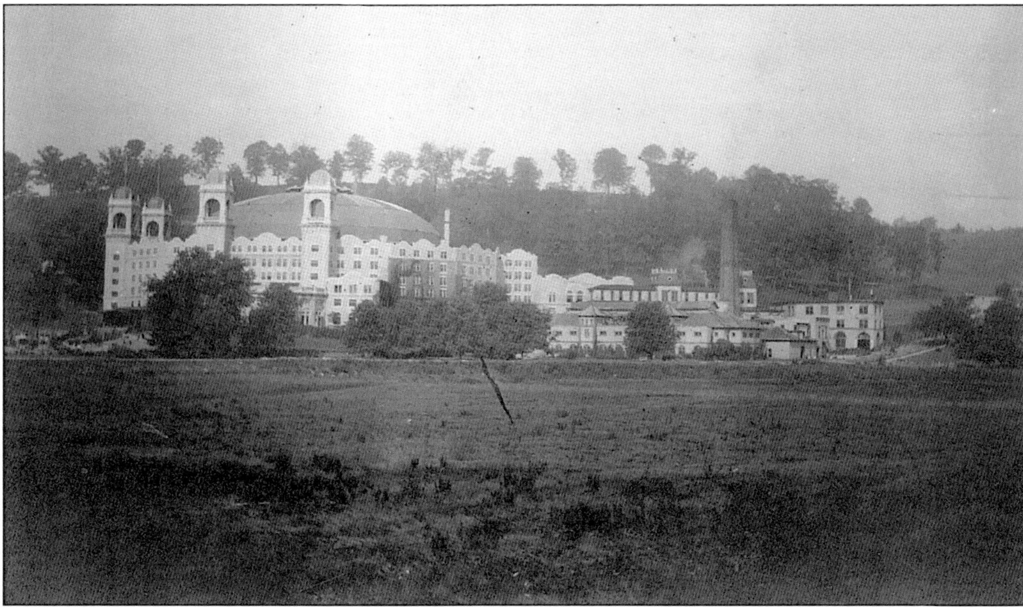

The West Baden Springs Hotel, opened in 1902, was considered the "eighth wonder of the world" because of its huge, spectacular atrium. Like its counterpart in adjoining French Lick, it had its own railroad spur and catered to the affluent seeking to "take the waters" at this Orange County spa. It is currently being restored. This photograph of the exterior was taken in 1920. (Courtesy of Willard Library.)

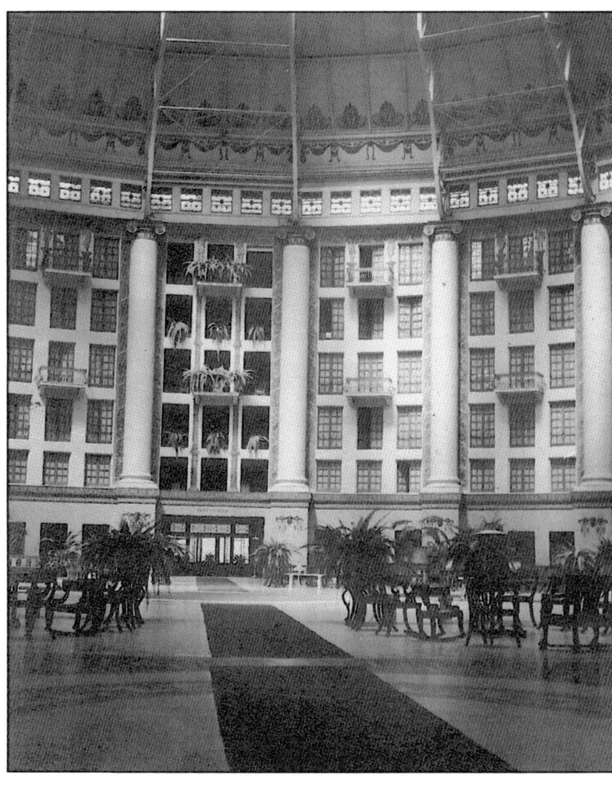

Shown here is the imposing atrium of the West Baden Springs Hotel. (Courtesy of Willard Library.)

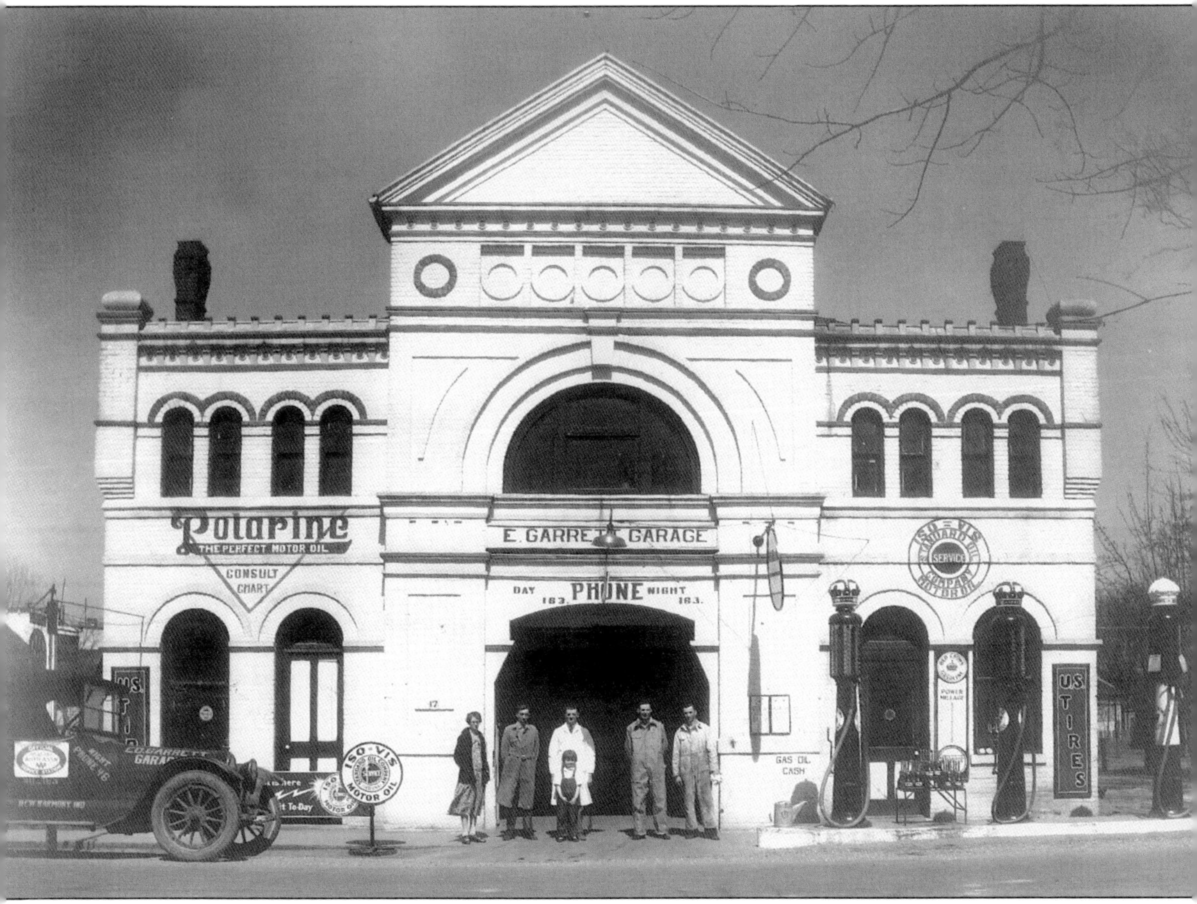

What is now the restored Thrall's Opera House in New Harmony had several previous lives. This shows the Garrett's Garage phase. (Courtesy of USI.)

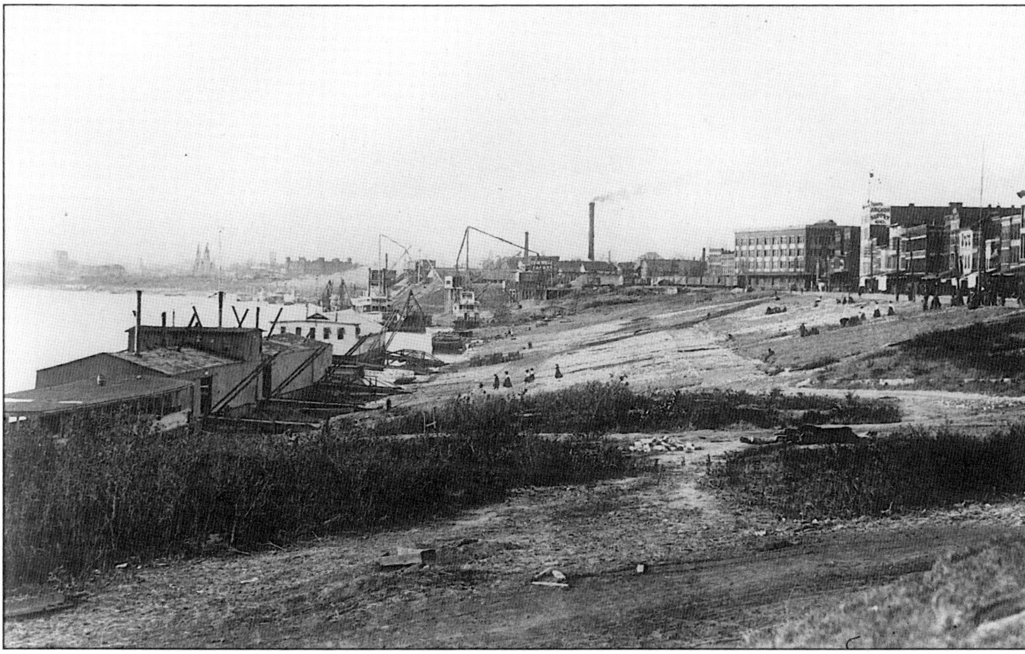

The Evansville waterfront, looking to the northwest early in the 20th century, demonstrated the continued importance of the Ohio in the city's economy. Most of the city's emerging industries—chiefly foundries and wood products—were located to the west and northwest of the riverfront. Since the city was incorporated in 1847, much investment had been made in grading and adding cobblestones. (Courtesy of USI.)

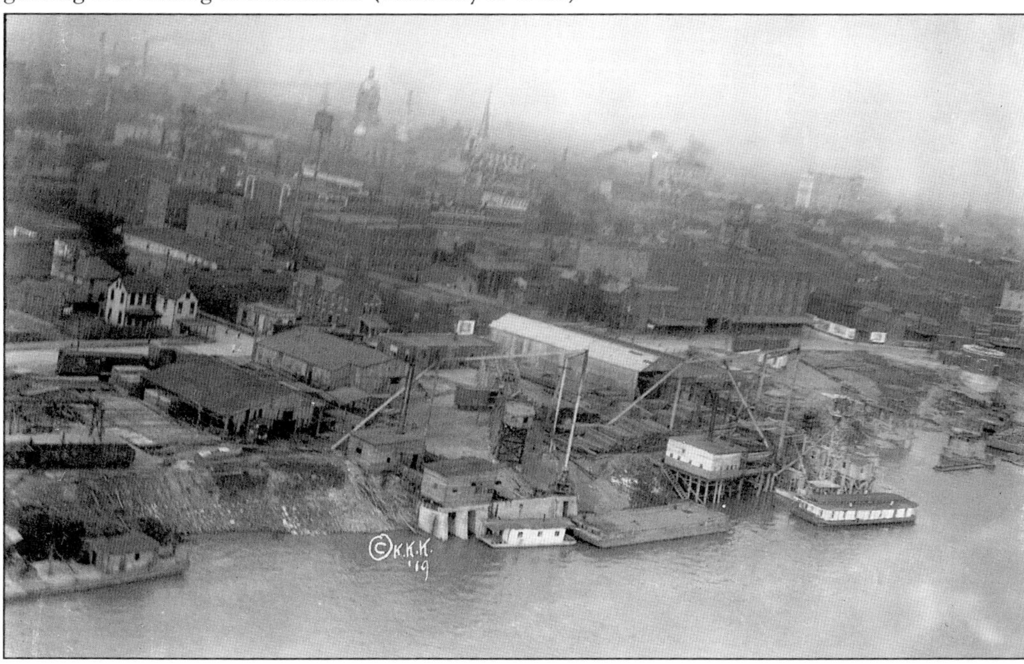

This aerial view of Evansville was probably taken by Karl Kae Knecht of the *Evansville Courier* from an NC-4 plane that stopped in the city in 1919. It documents the importance of the Ohio to this industrializing city. (Courtesy of USI.)

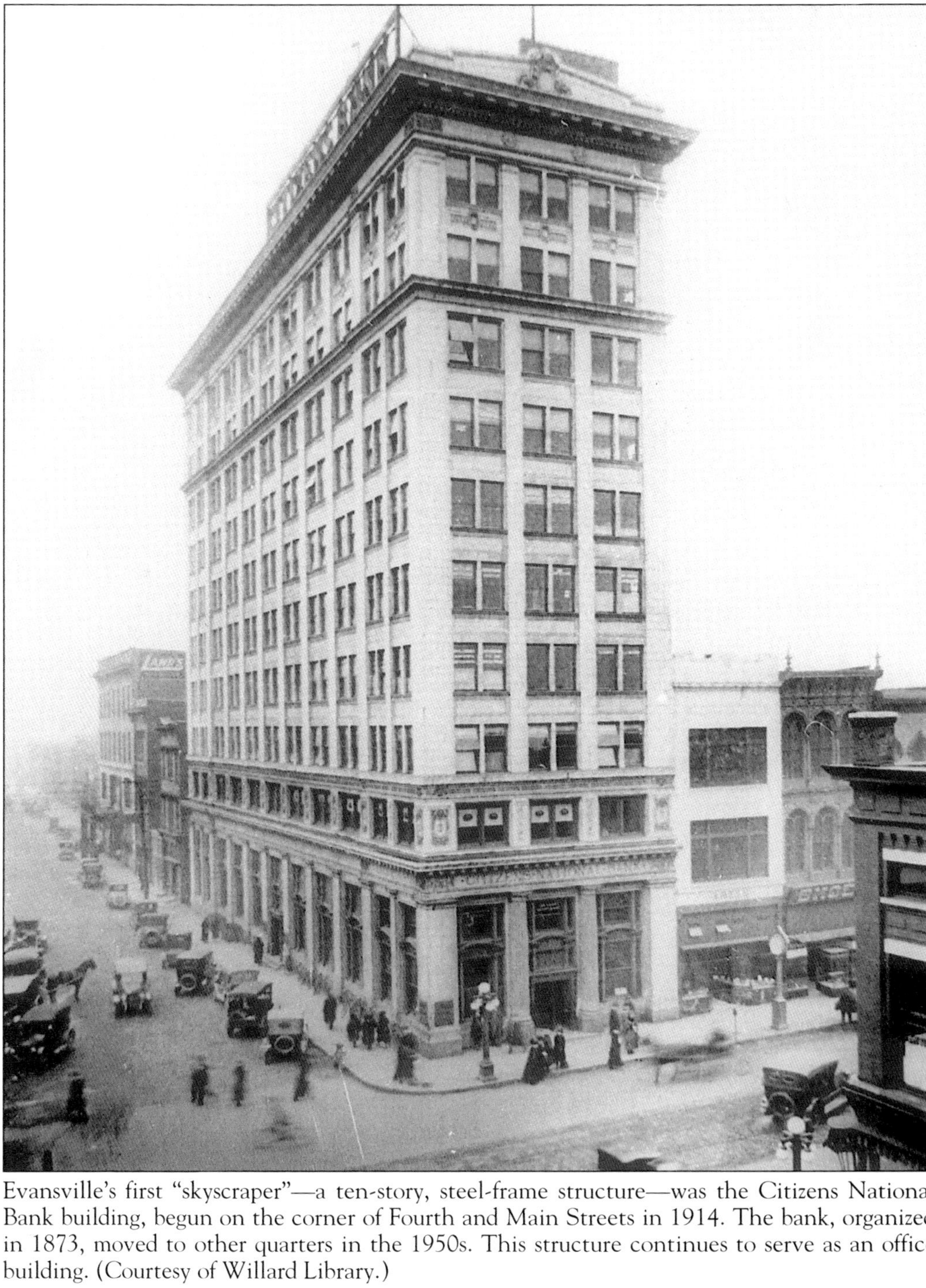

Evansville's first "skyscraper"—a ten-story, steel-frame structure—was the Citizens National Bank building, begun on the corner of Fourth and Main Streets in 1914. The bank, organized in 1873, moved to other quarters in the 1950s. This structure continues to serve as an office building. (Courtesy of Willard Library.)

This would become the second site of the Old State National Bank of Evansville, organized in 1834. This site on Main, near Fifth, was razed for the new building (1915). (Courtesy of Willard Library.)

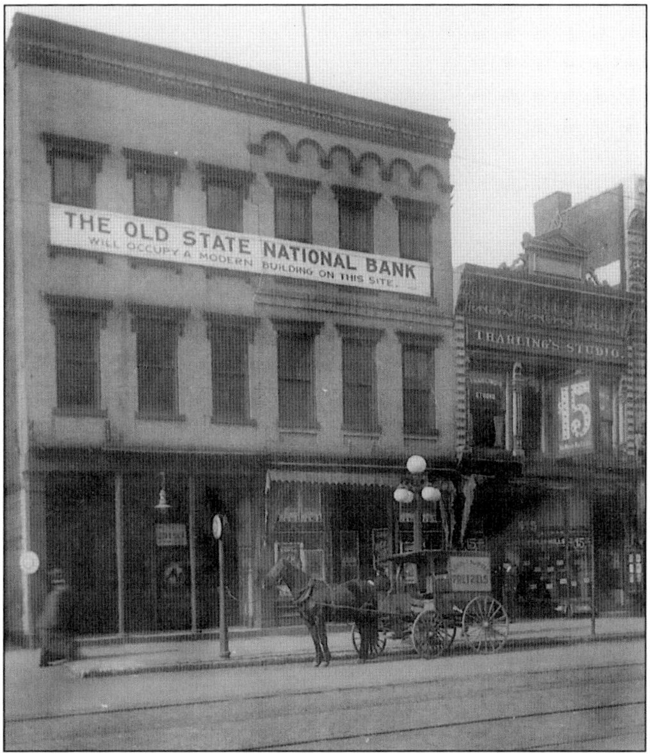

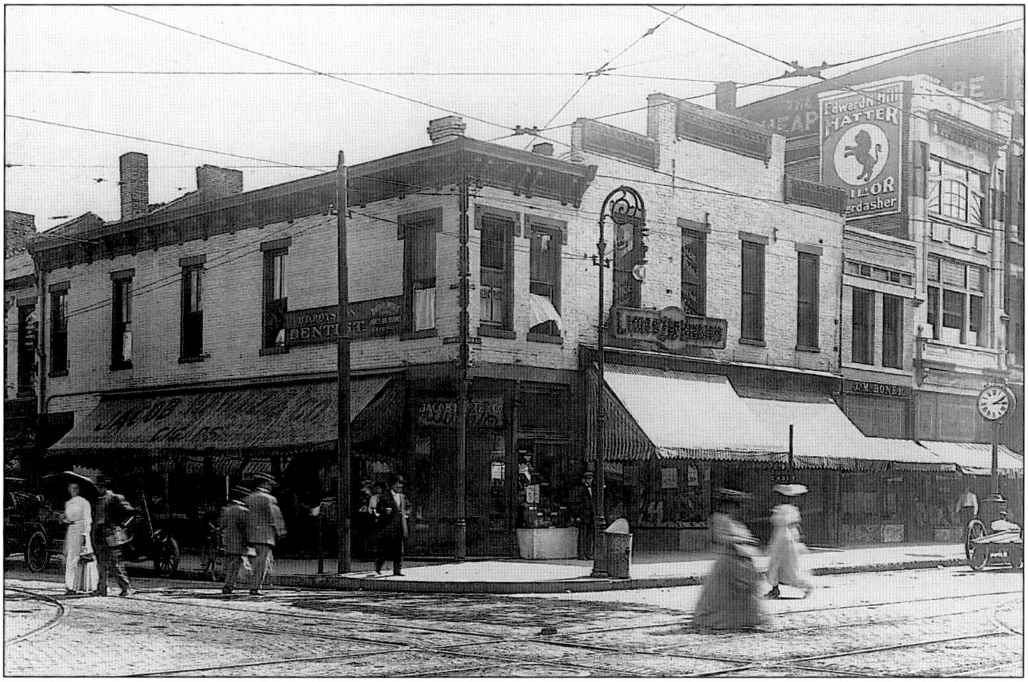

Main Street at Third in Evansville, c. 1914, illustrates the way in which main streets across America were uniform in pattern and style. Progress is evident in the presence of streetcar tracks, automobiles, and electric lighting and signs. (Courtesy of Willard Library.)

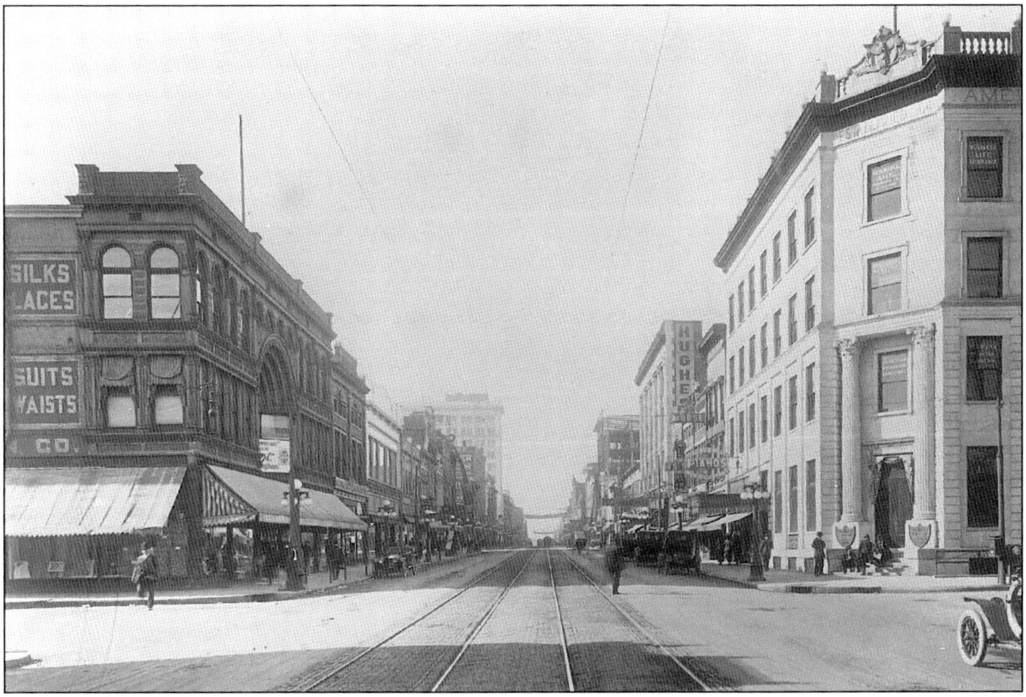

Looking down Main from Sixth to the Ohio in Evansville in 1915, one sees the new Citizens Bank building on the left (background) and the new Old National Bank building under construction on the right. Multiple forms of transportation are visible: double trolley tracks, horses and buggies, and automobiles. (Courtesy of USI.)

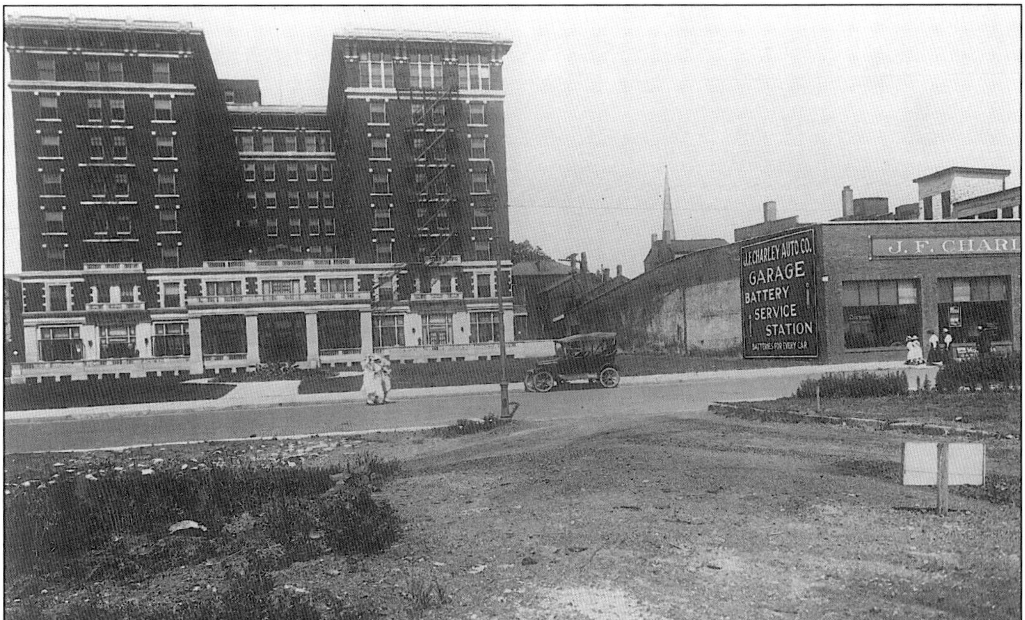

Named after prominent industrialist William McCurdy, this hotel opened on Evansville's Riverside Drive near the Ohio in 1917. It was the most elegant hotel on either side of the river below Louisville. (Courtesy of USI.)

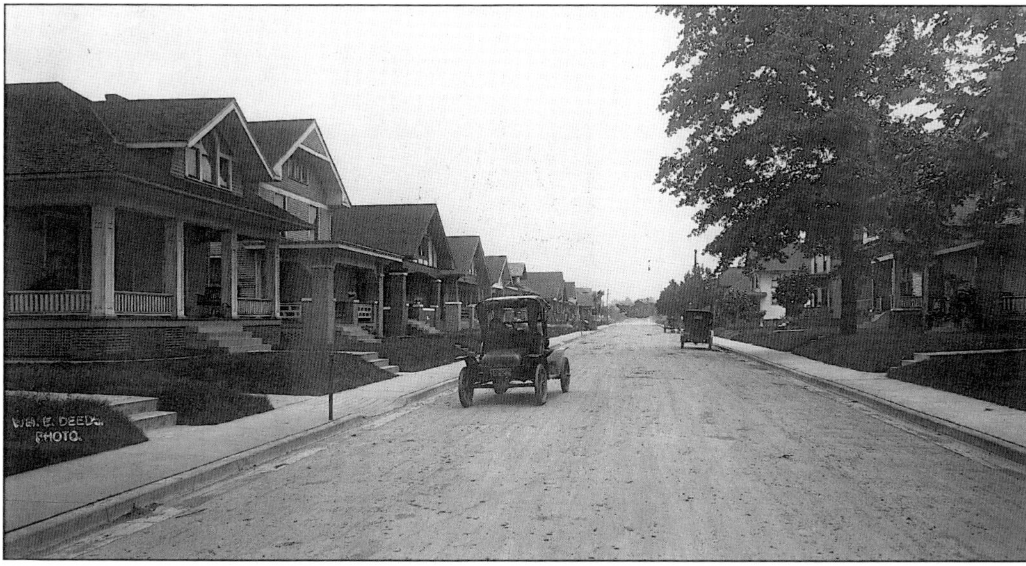

Streetcar service and then automobiles were responsible for the development of residential districts on the outskirts of cities. This is Gum Street, from Evans to Kentucky, in the Bayard Park neighborhood of Evansville in 1915. Residents for the most part belonged to the emerging white-collar class, working downtown but living far from the central city. (Courtesy of USI.)

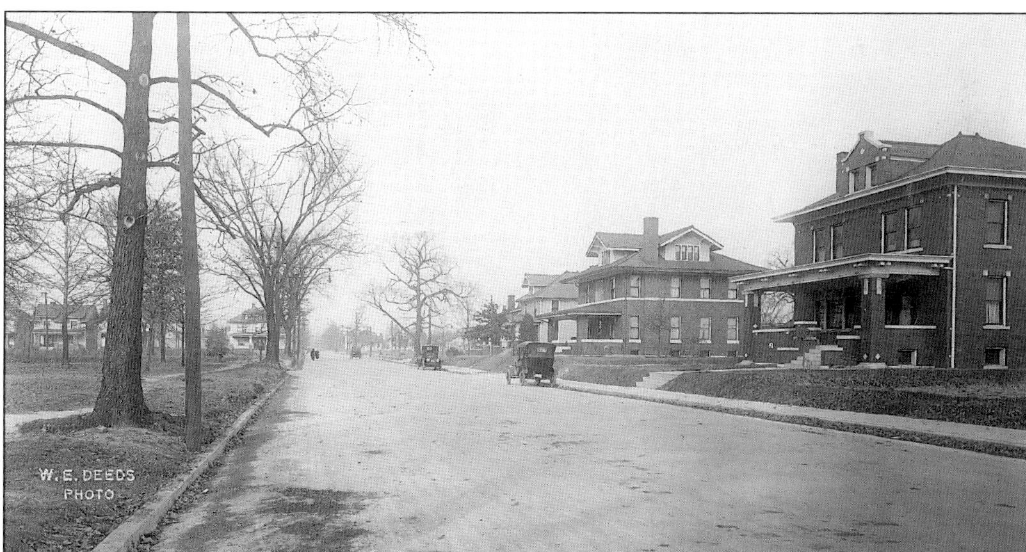

This photograph of Kentucky Avenue in Evansville demonstrates the consequence of the automobile in accelerating residential construction at the city's eastern fringe. (Courtesy of Willard Library.)

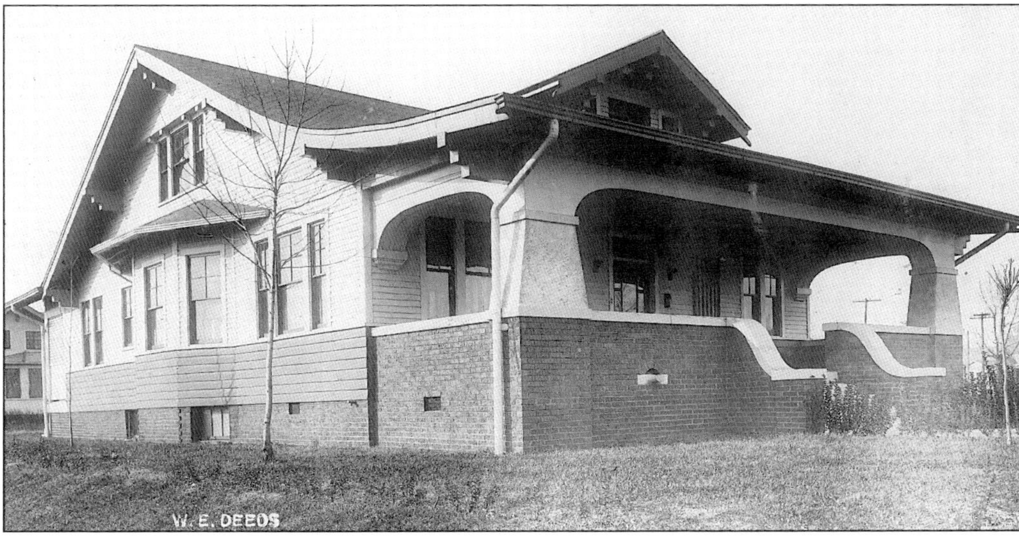

The prairie-style bungalow at Kentucky and Ravenswood on Evansville's east side, *c.* 1920, was typical of home construction in the teens. (Courtesy of Willard Library.)

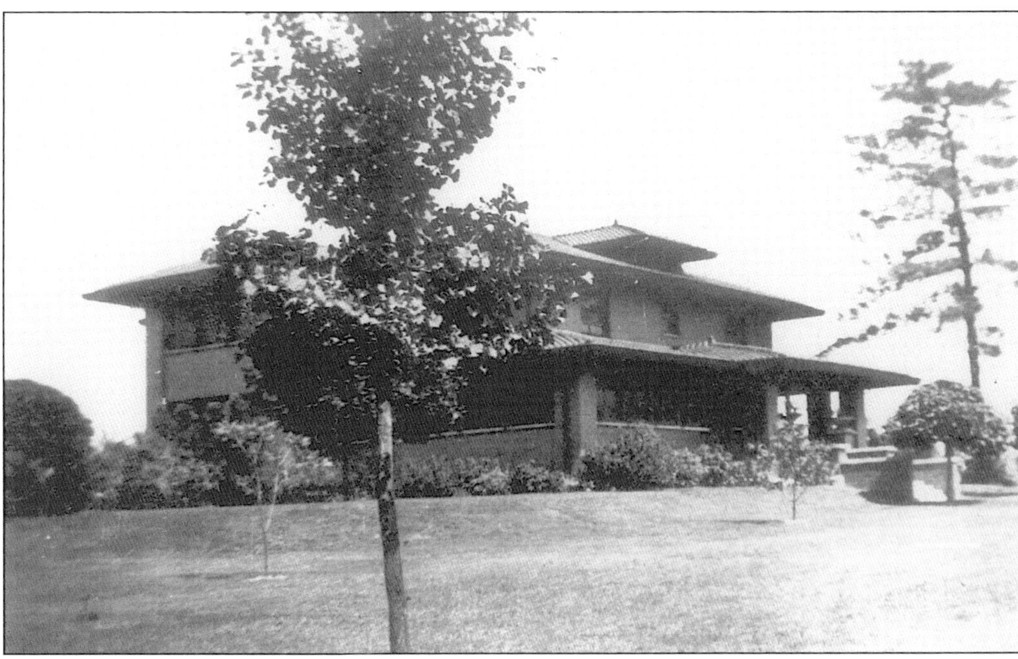
The elegant, prairie-style home of prominent businessman and industrialist Robert Graham in Washington, completed on the eve of World War I, symbolized not only his achievements but also the progress of his community. Residents looked upon such edifices with great pride. (Courtesy of Willard Library.)

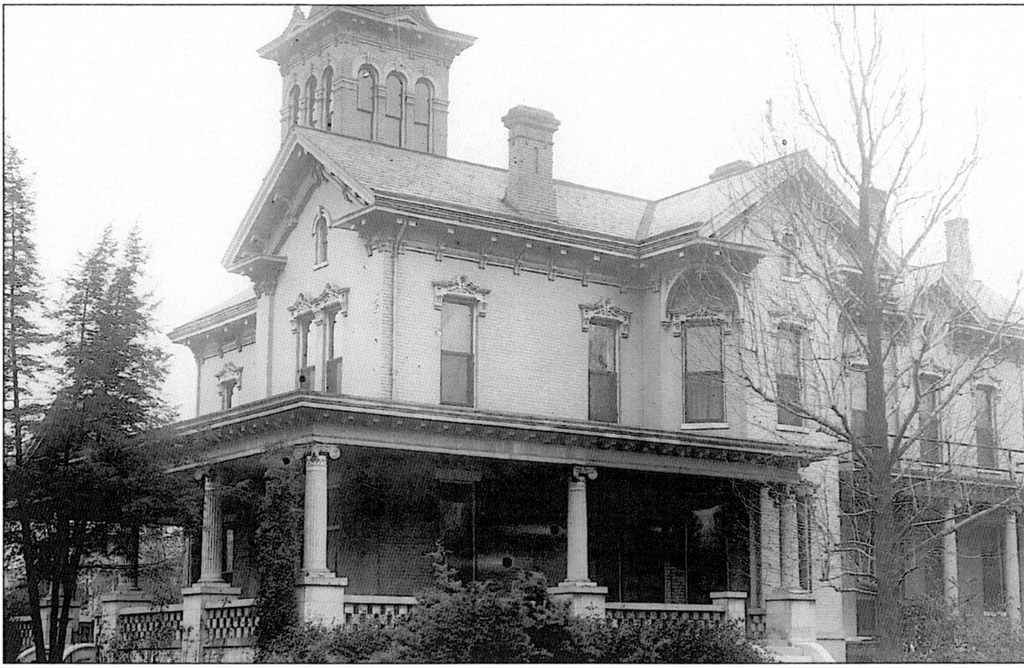

The comfortable home of German-American businessman William Scherffius Sr. was located on Wabash Avenue in Evansville. Most German Americans like him resided on First, Fulton, or Wabash Avenues, not in the Anglo-American residential section upriver of downtown. (Courtesy of Willard Library.)

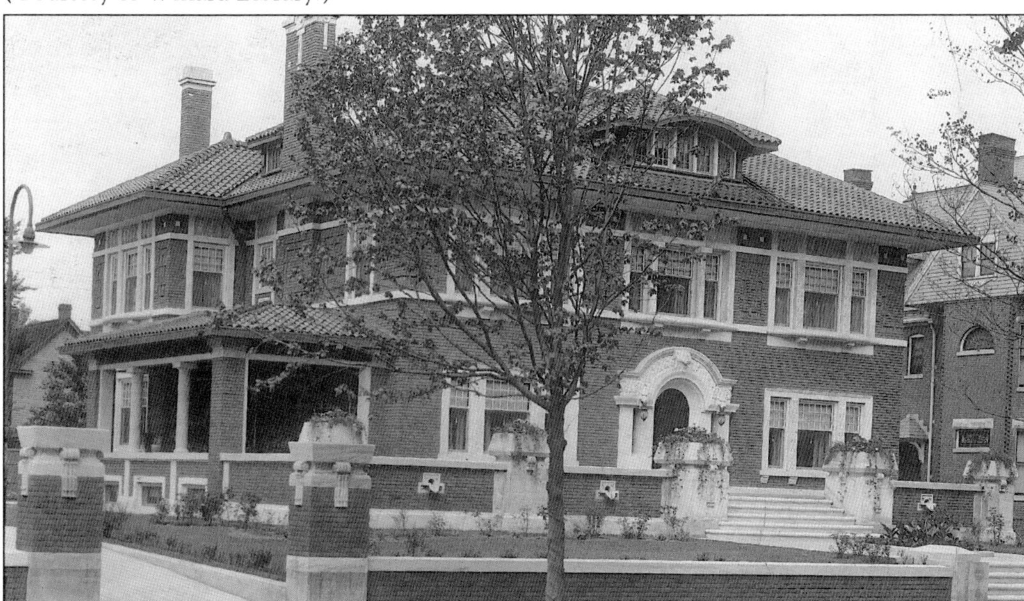

The home of cigar manufacturer John Fendrich on First Street was completed in 1917. One of the largest and most luxurious in Evansville, it helped to signify the entrance of German-American leaders into Evansville's elite. W.L. Klewer was the architect. Nearby and at the same time, furniture maker and mayor Benjamin Bosse also built a fancy new home. (Courtesy of Willard Library.)

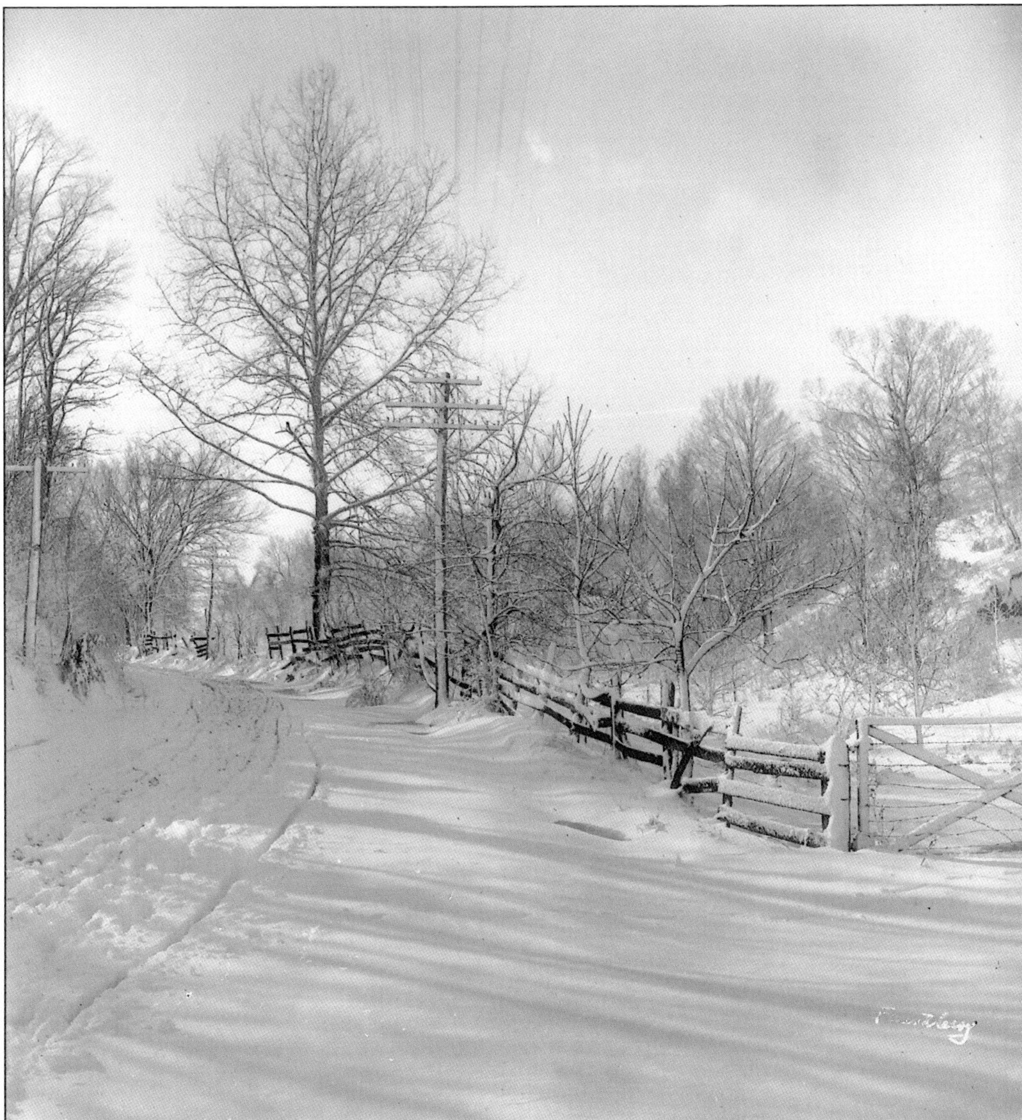

This rural Posey County road was blanketed with a heavy coat of snow. Like innumerable roads like it in southern Indiana, it would have been virtually impassable, reinforcing the isolation and self-sufficiency of farm families at the time. (Courtesy of USI.)

Three

Getting Around

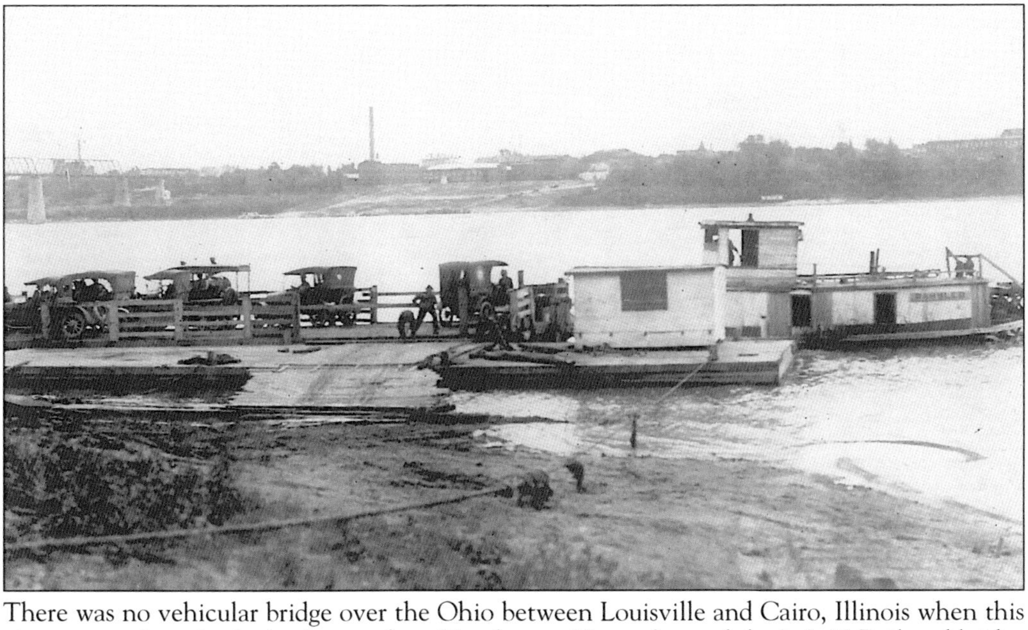

There was no vehicular bridge over the Ohio between Louisville and Cairo, Illinois when this photo was taken. In the background are Henderson, Kentucky, and the L & N Railroad bridge (1885). In the foreground, at the southern tip of Vanderburgh County, Indiana, is the Henderson ferry. A vehicular bridge was opened in 1932. (Courtesy of Willard Library.)

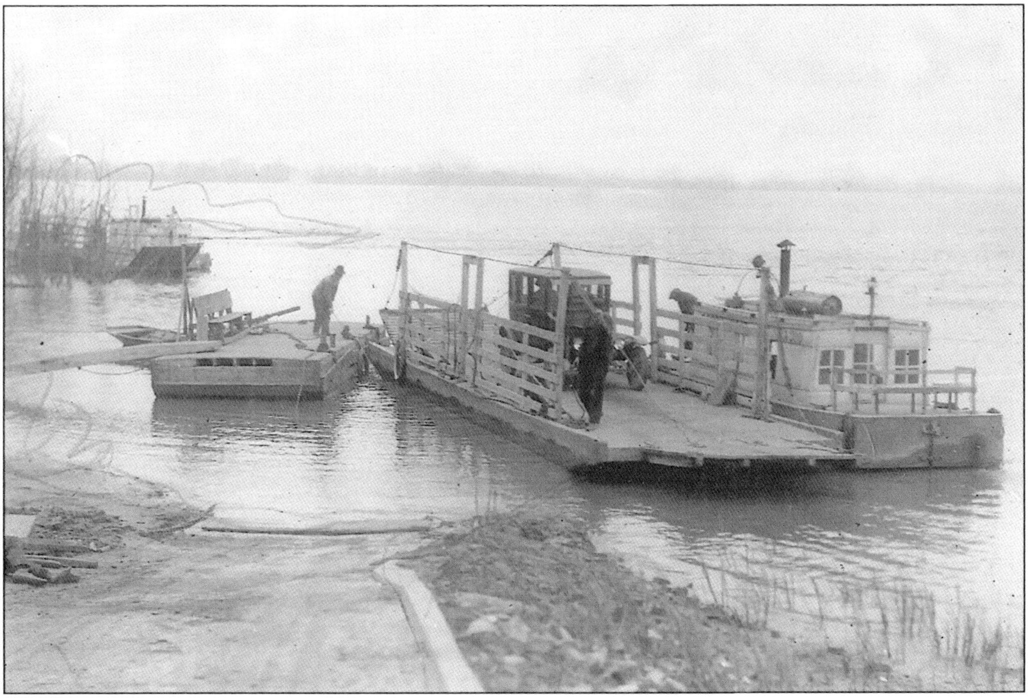

The Ohio River ferry at Rockport was a mainstay of travel across to Owensboro until after World War II. (Courtesy of Willard Library.)

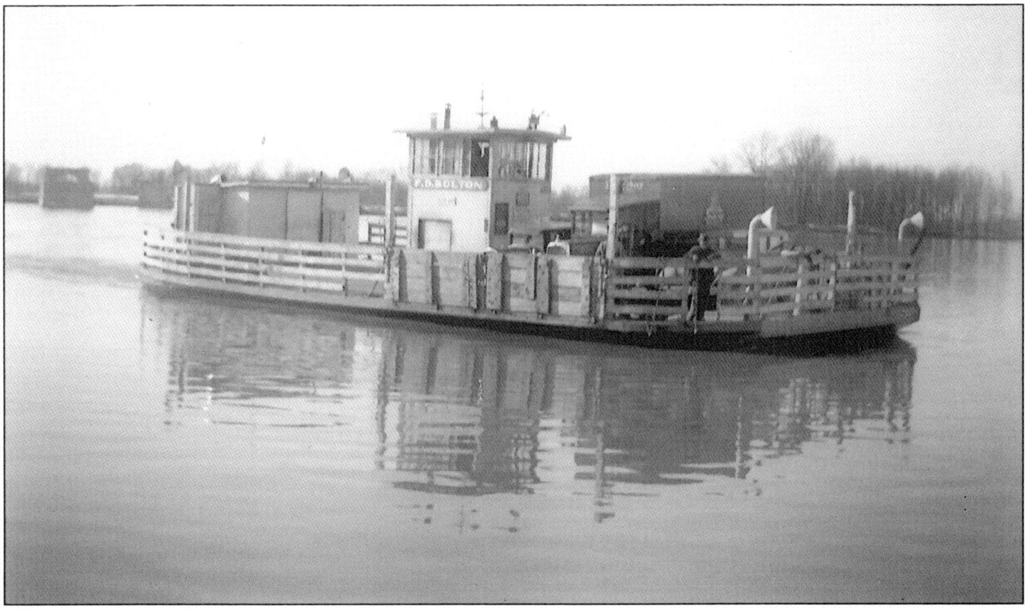

This is the Wabash River ferry at New Harmony. A bridge near this site was opened in the early 1930s. (Courtesy of USI.)

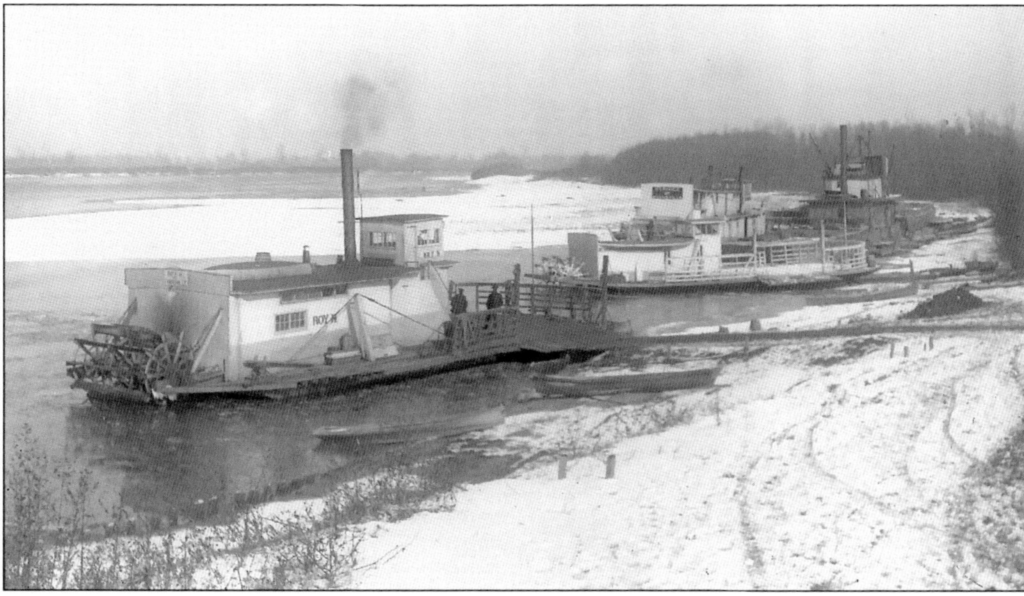

Three steamboats are tied up at the New Harmony landing in winter. (Courtesy of USI.)

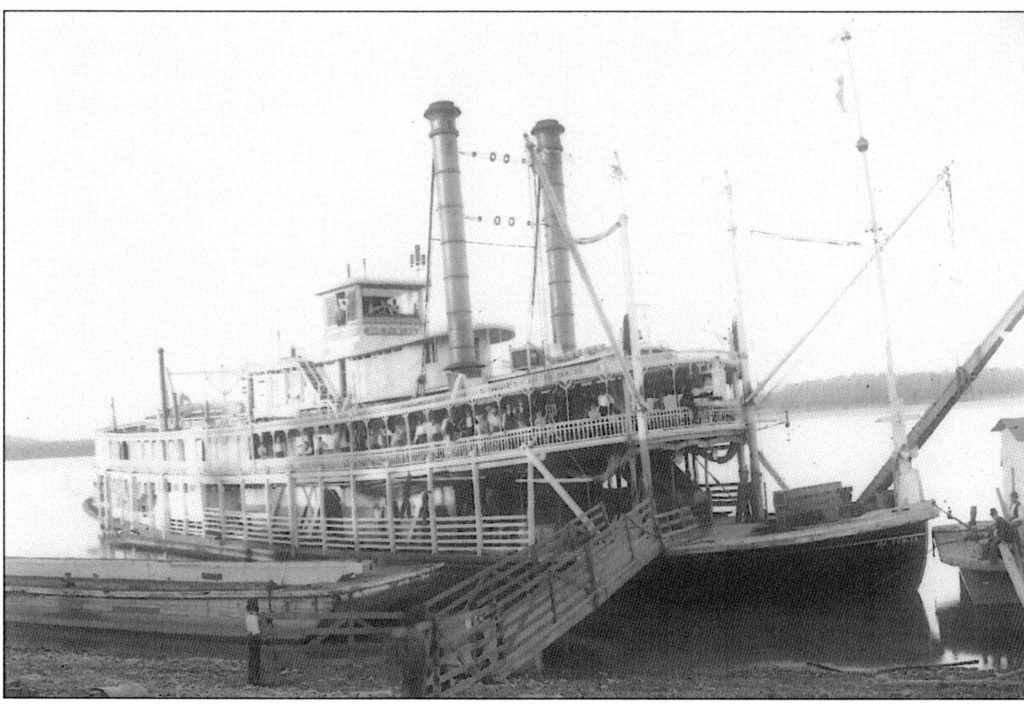

This is the steamer *Joe Fowler* on the Wabash at New Harmony. The boat carried people, farm products, and livestock. (Courtesy of USI.)

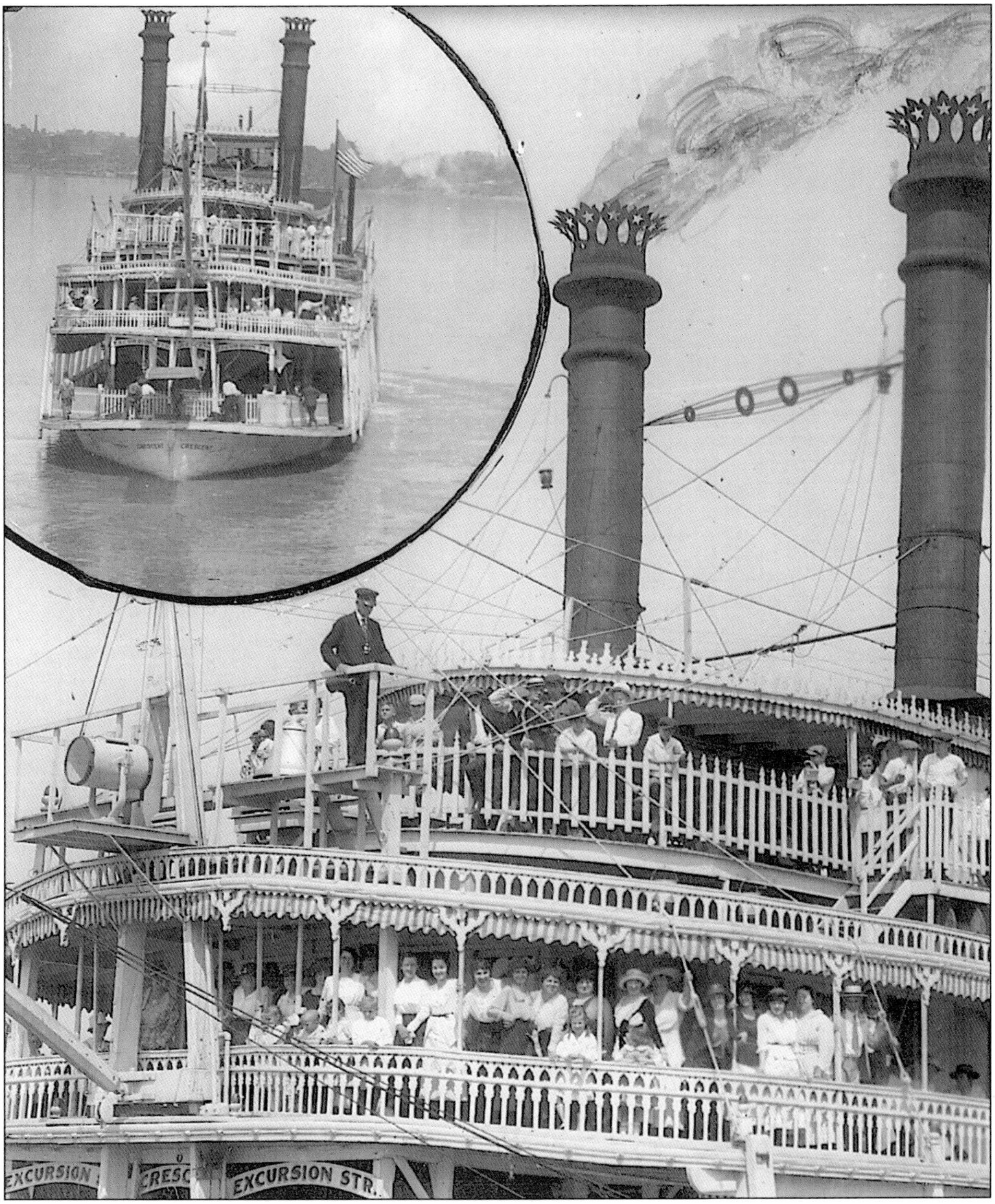

Steamboat excursions—in this case, on the *Crescent* at Evansville—were quite popular in the teens. This is one of many collages produced by *Evansville Courier* photographer Karl Kae Knecht. (Courtesy of Willard Library.)

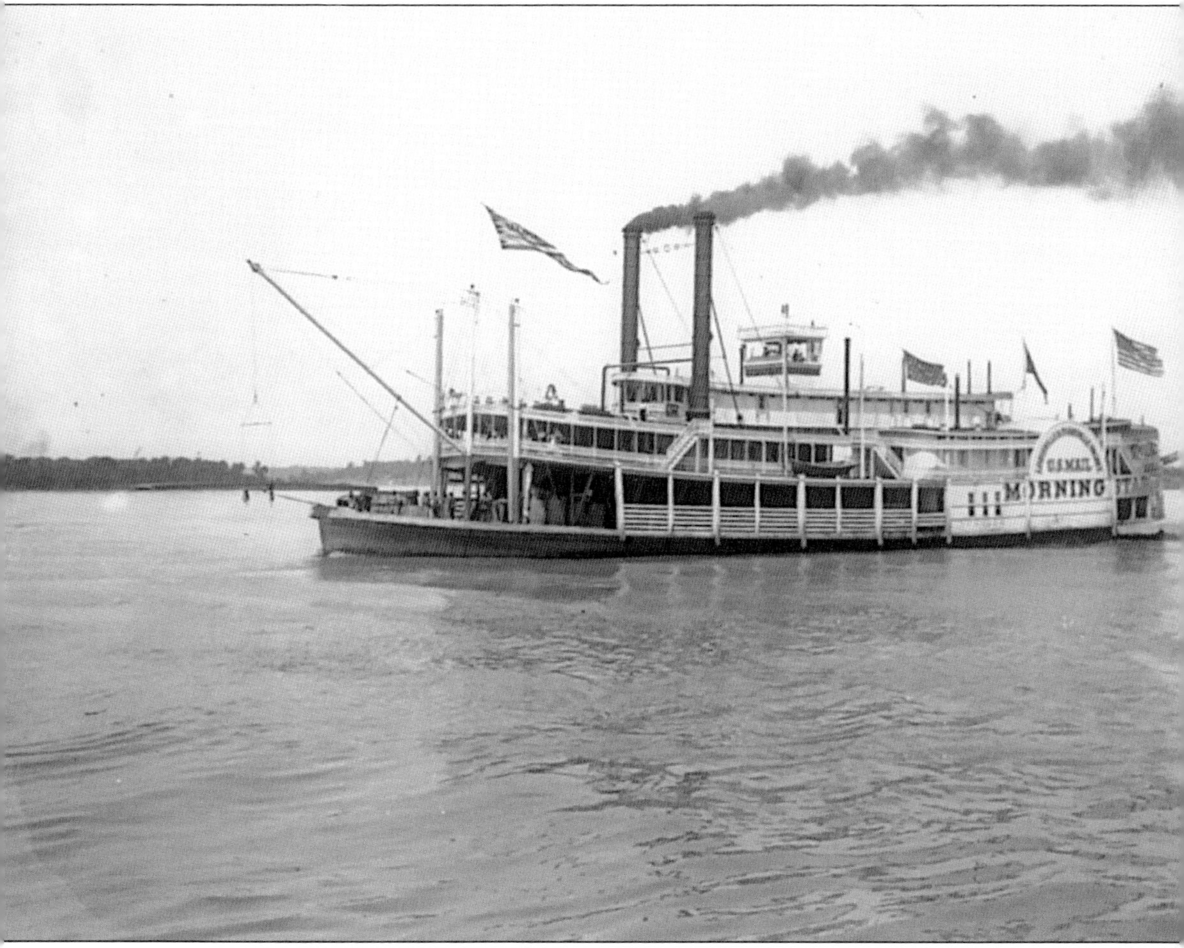

The *Morning Star* was one of the last packet boats to ply the waters of the lower Ohio. It is seen here near Evansville. (Courtesy of USI.)

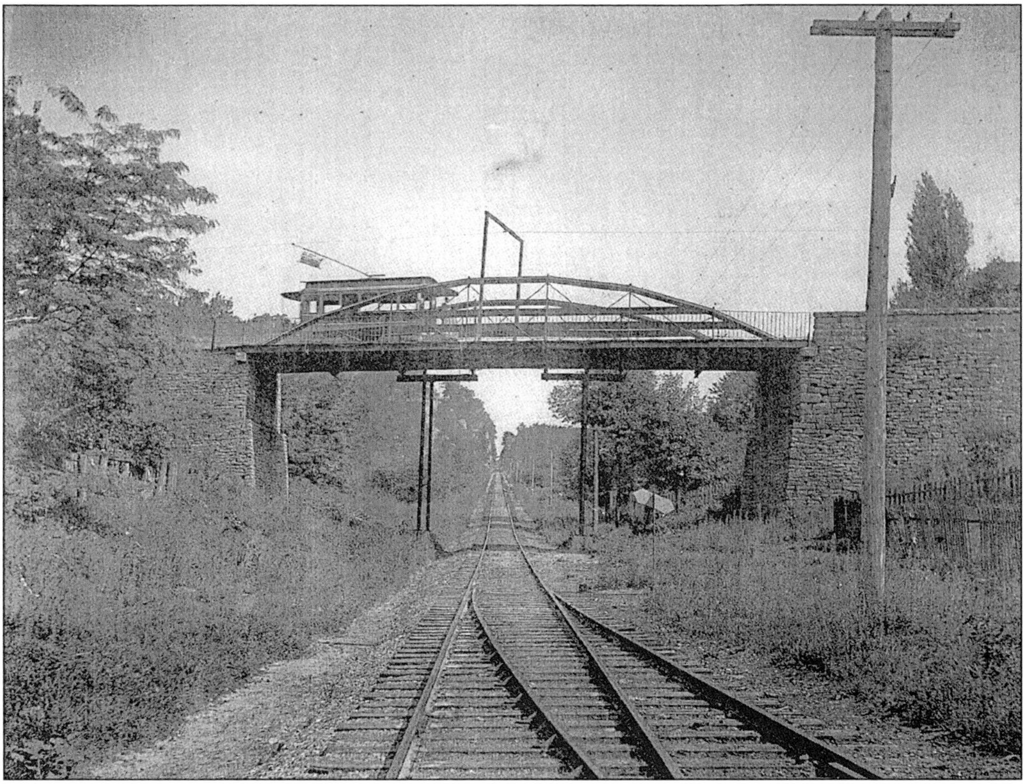

An open trolley car is crossing the Main Street bridge over the Madison Railroad incline c. 1910. Buses replaced trolleys in Madison after World War I. (Courtesy of Jefferson County Historical Society.)

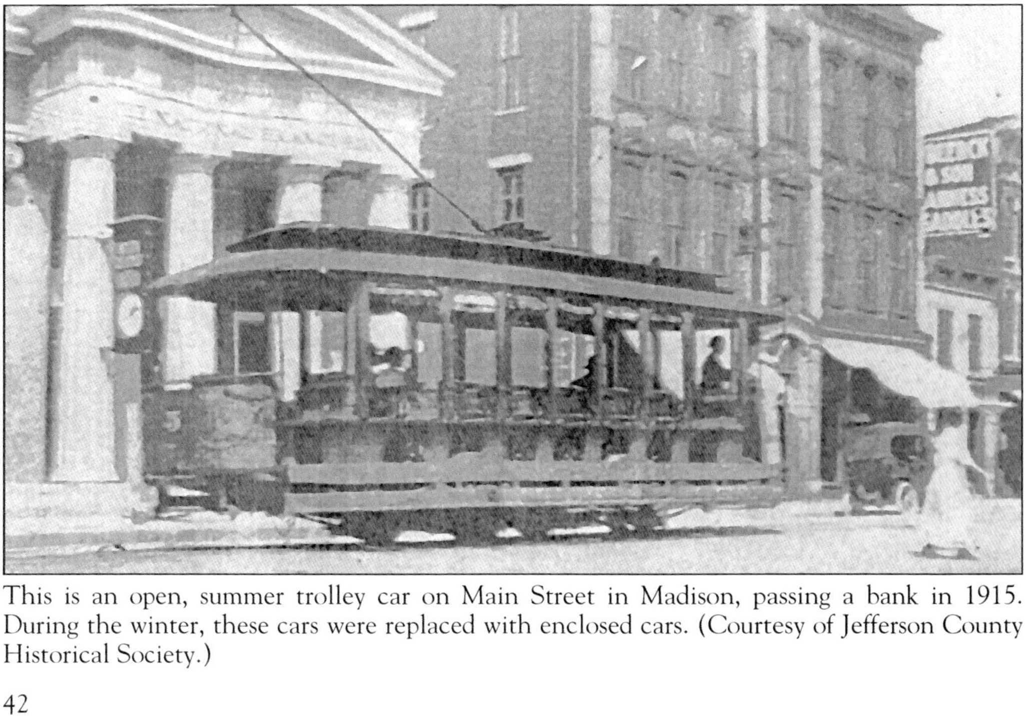

This is an open, summer trolley car on Main Street in Madison, passing a bank in 1915. During the winter, these cars were replaced with enclosed cars. (Courtesy of Jefferson County Historical Society.)

Vincennes had had street cars since 1893. Street car track was being re-laid on Second Street, near Main, in 1918. (Courtesy of Byron R. Lewis Historical Library, Vincennes University.)

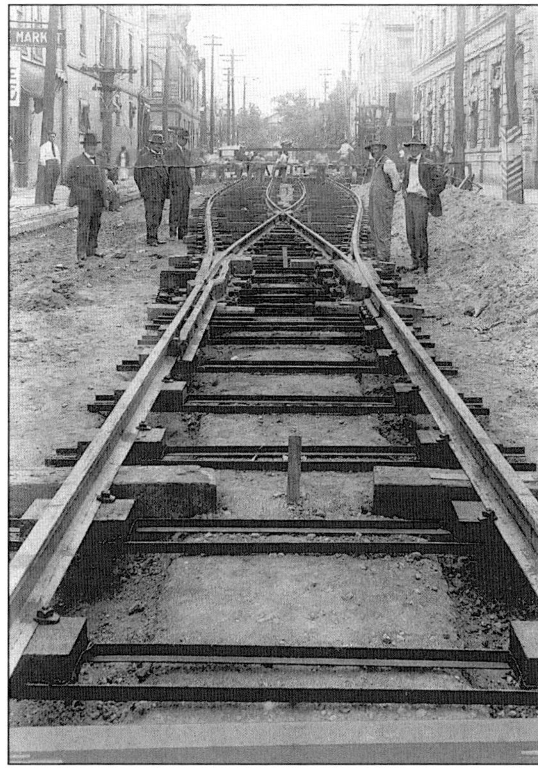

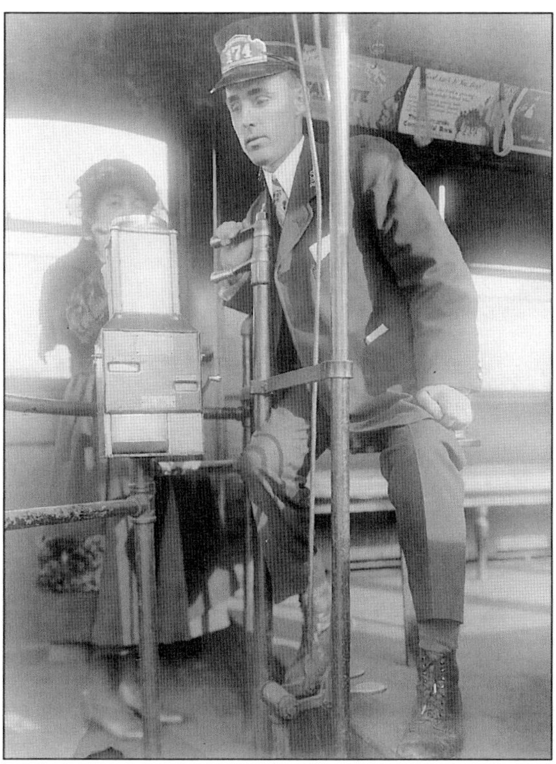

About 1920, coin-operated fare boxes were installed in Evansville streetcars. (Courtesy of Willard Library.)

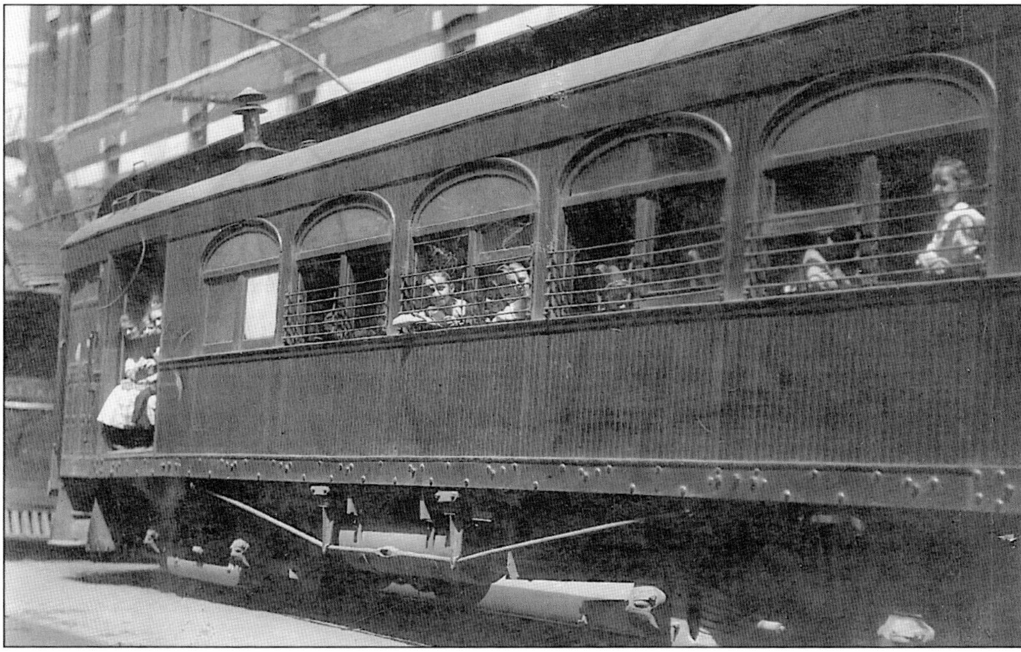

A "traction car" is parked at Second and Locust Streets in Evansville in 1918. Like several other southern Indiana cities, Evansville's interurban service commenced in the late 1880s, though both lines—the Evansville, Suburban, and Newburgh, and the Evansville and Ohio Valley—closed in the 1920s. As elsewhere, they were victims chiefly of automobiles and buses. Southern Indiana's most extensive line stretched from the Falls cities to Indianapolis. (Courtesy of Willard Library.)

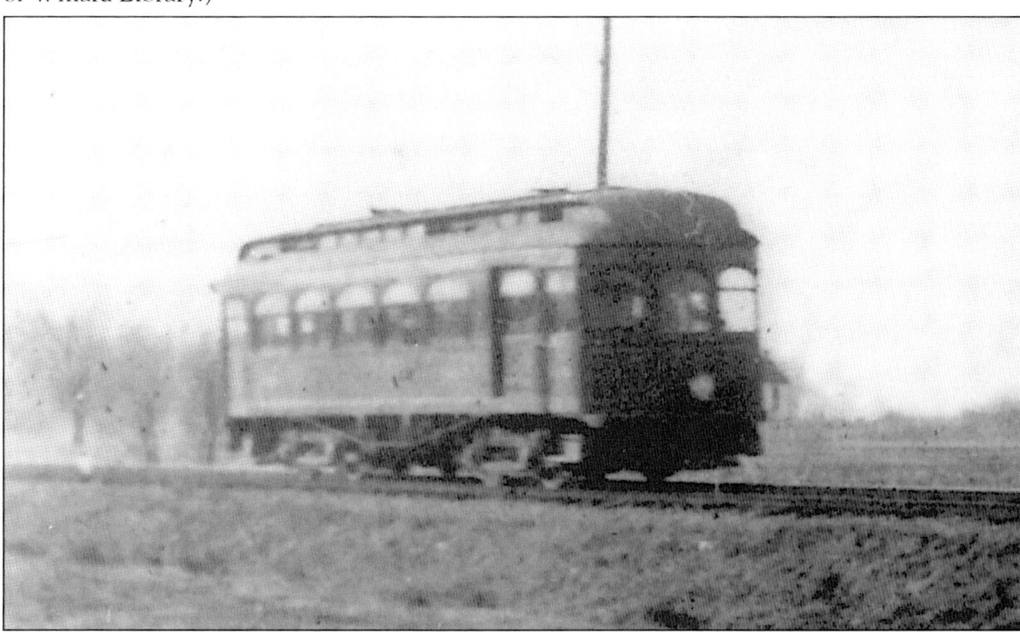

A traction car is shown on the Evansville and Ohio Valley Line near Mount Vernon in 1913. The line also served Princeton to the north, Rockport to the east, and Henderson to the south. (Courtesy of Willard Library.)

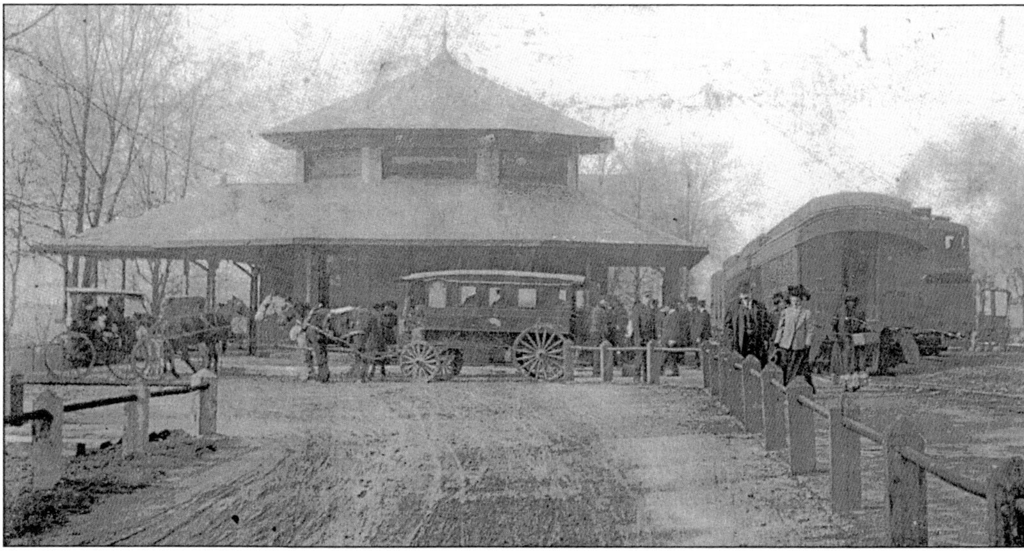

This is the Madison Railroad Station about 1910. The scene, from a postcard, shows the arrival of the morning Pennsylvania Railroad train from Indianapolis and the horse-drawn omnibuses waiting to take passengers to downtown Madison. The Madison and Indianapolis Railroad (1847) was the first in Indiana. The railroad station is today restored and part of the Jefferson County Historical Society Museum in Madison. (Courtesy of Jefferson County Historical Society.)

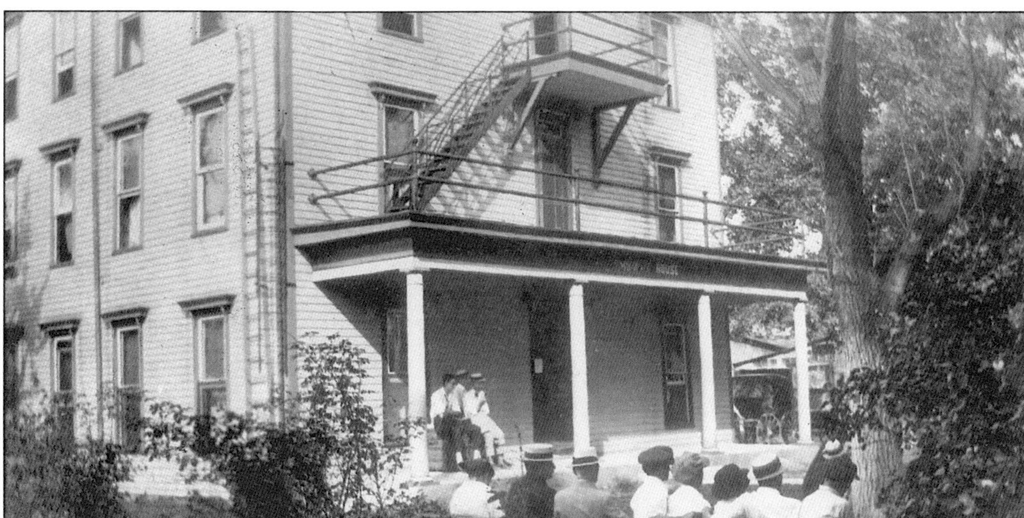

Murphy House (Marengo) served rail excursions to Marengo Cave, a half mile away. The station on the "Air Line" between Louisville and St. Louis was nearby, and guests usually had a chicken dinner there before returning home. The heyday of these excursions was 1900–1930. The railroad bisected the northern part of Crawford County in 1881, weakening the river towns of Alton and Leavenworth. The cave was discovered two years later. (Courtesy of Gary Roberson.)

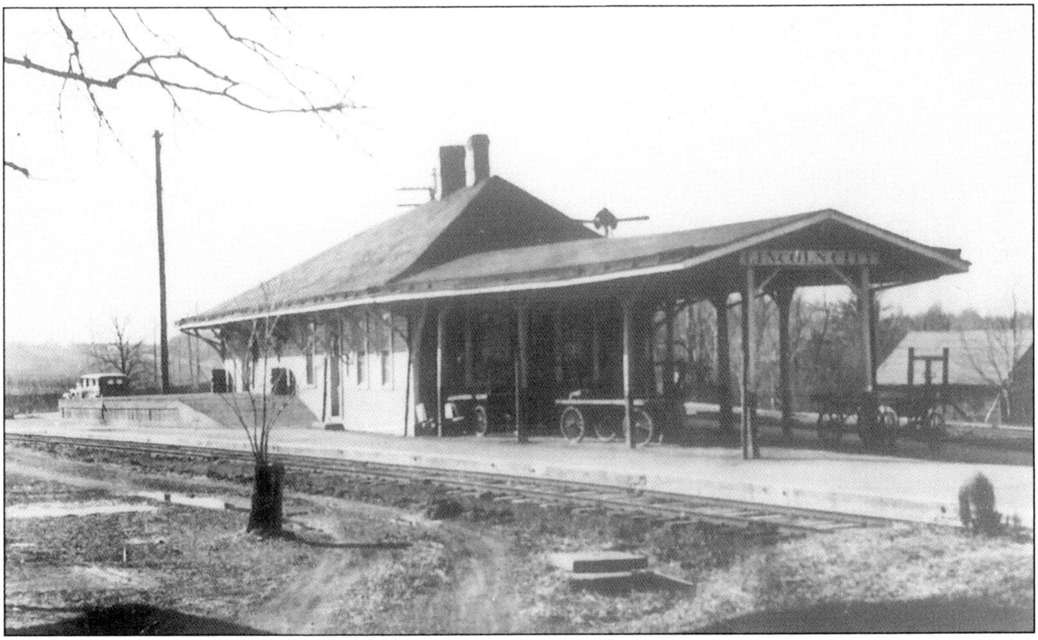

This is the railroad station in Lincoln City. (Courtesy of Lincoln Boyhood National Memorial.)

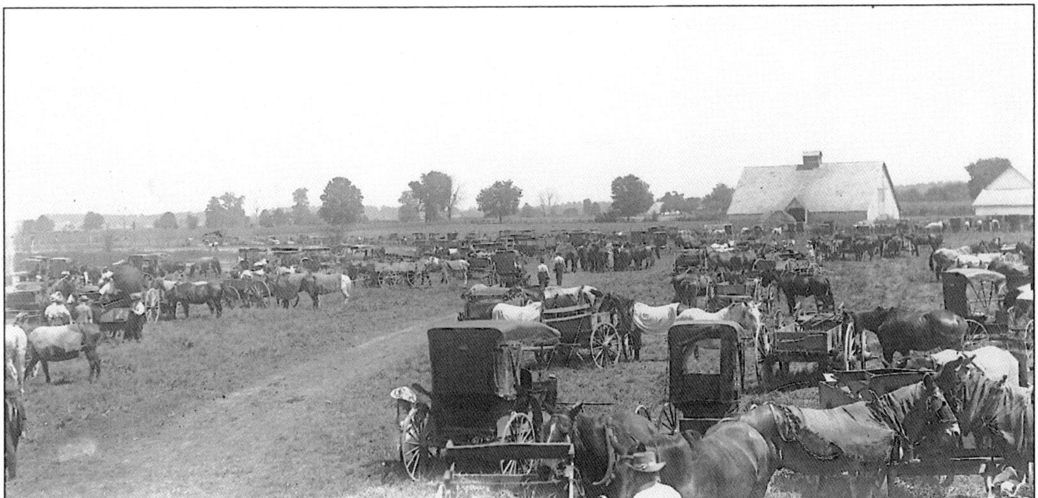

Despite the popularity of the automobile, horses and buggies dominated this scene of an unidentified social event in Posey County, possibly a fair. (Courtesy of USI.)

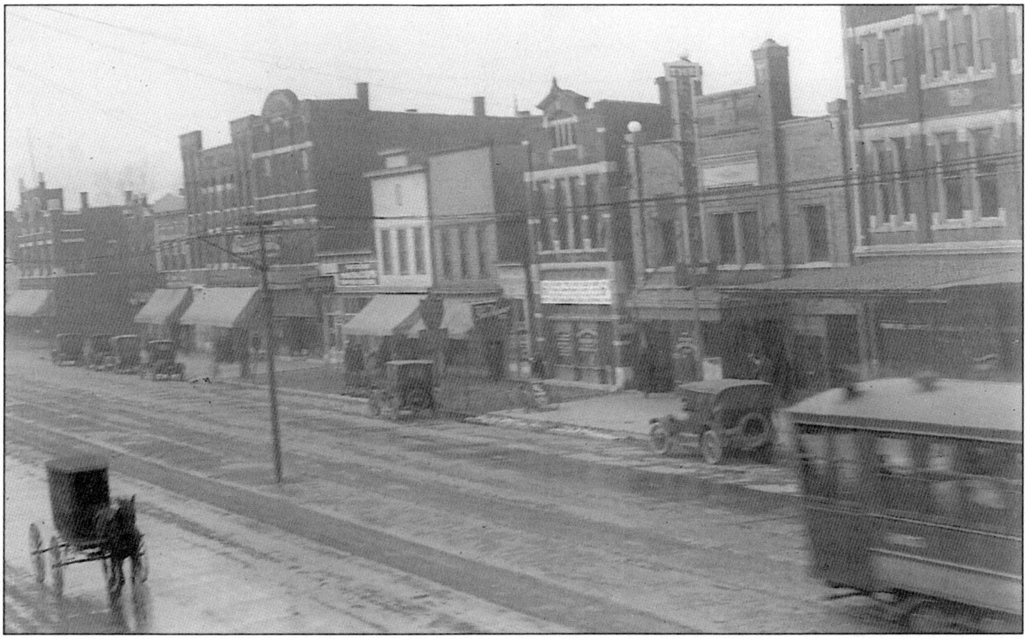

Showing the various modes of transport available to city dwellers by 1915, this photo of West Franklin Street in Evansville shows the horse and buggy, the streetcar, and the automobile. (Courtesy of Willard Library.)

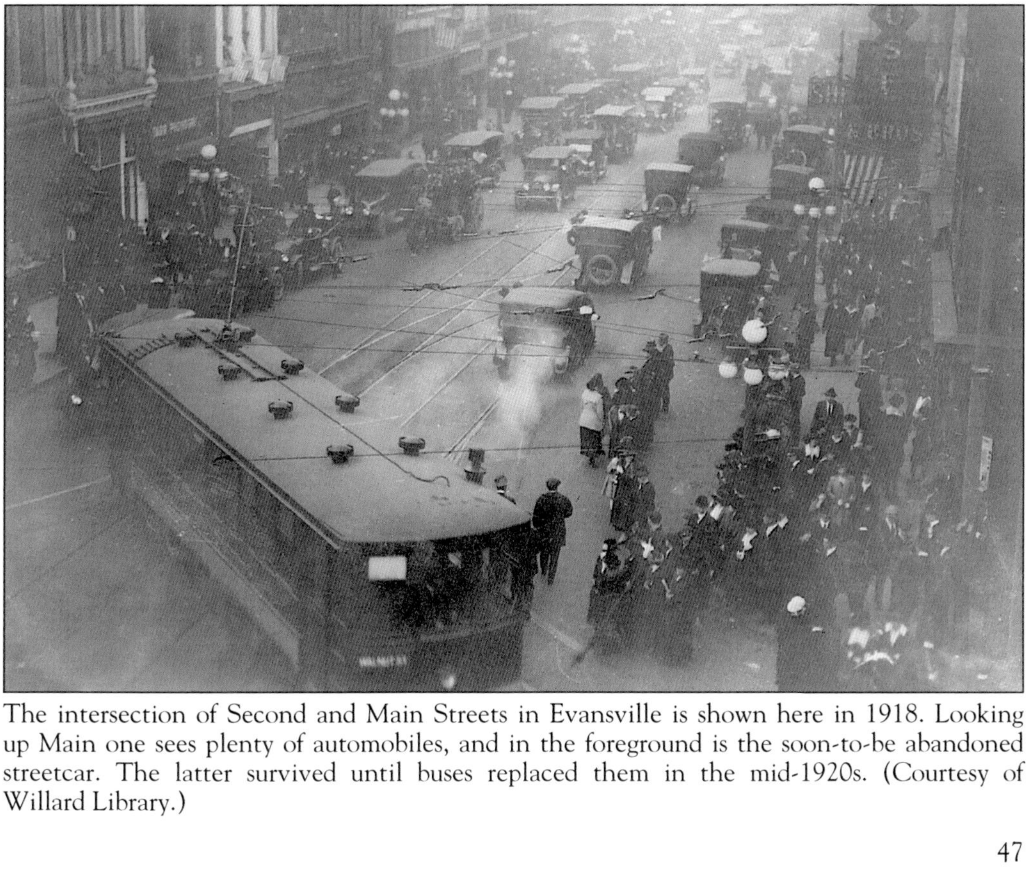

The intersection of Second and Main Streets in Evansville is shown here in 1918. Looking up Main one sees plenty of automobiles, and in the foreground is the soon-to-be abandoned streetcar. The latter survived until buses replaced them in the mid-1920s. (Courtesy of Willard Library.)

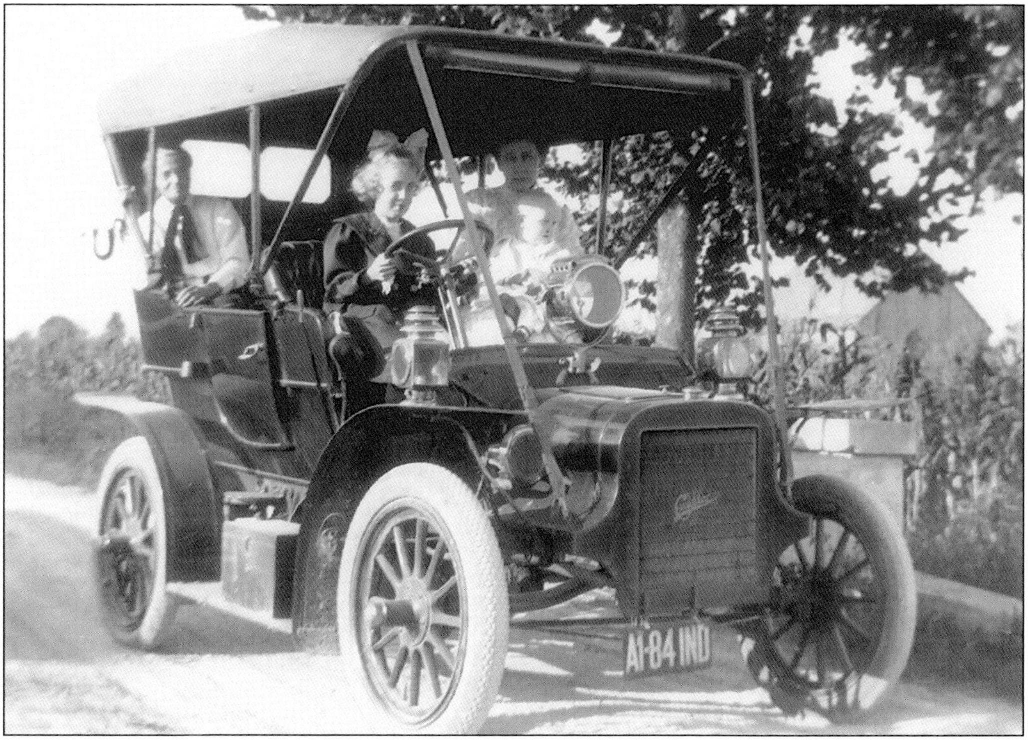

Photographer Thomas Mueller's family are shown in their proudest possession, a new 1914 Hupmobile, near Evansville. (Courtesy of USI.)

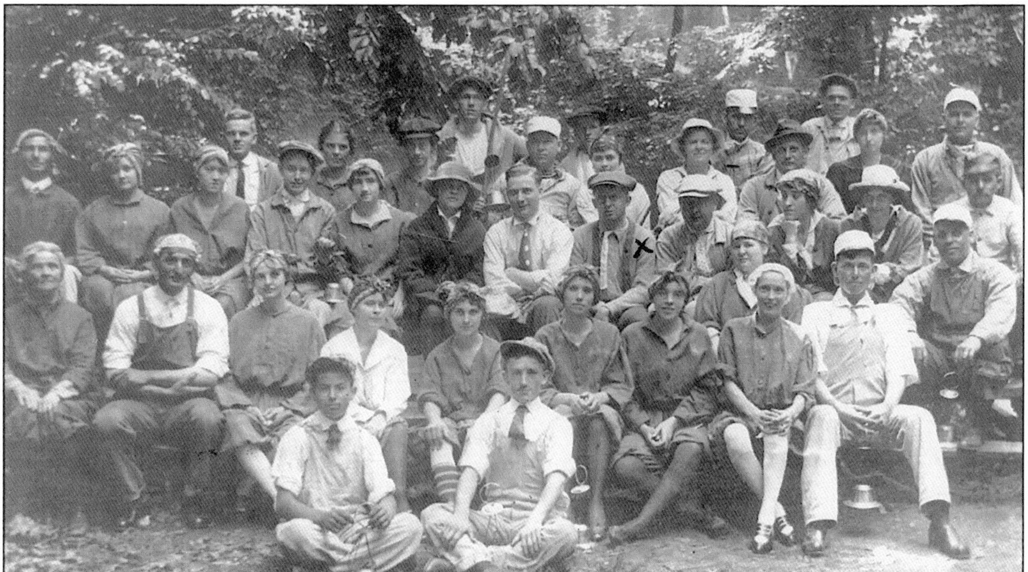

These are Evansville residents, including *Courier* photographer Karl Kae Knecht, at Mammoth Cave, Kentucky, in 1916. Touring by automobile was becoming an increasingly appealing and accessible form of recreation. It was one of the many ways that the impact of the auto was evident. (Courtesy of Willard Library.)

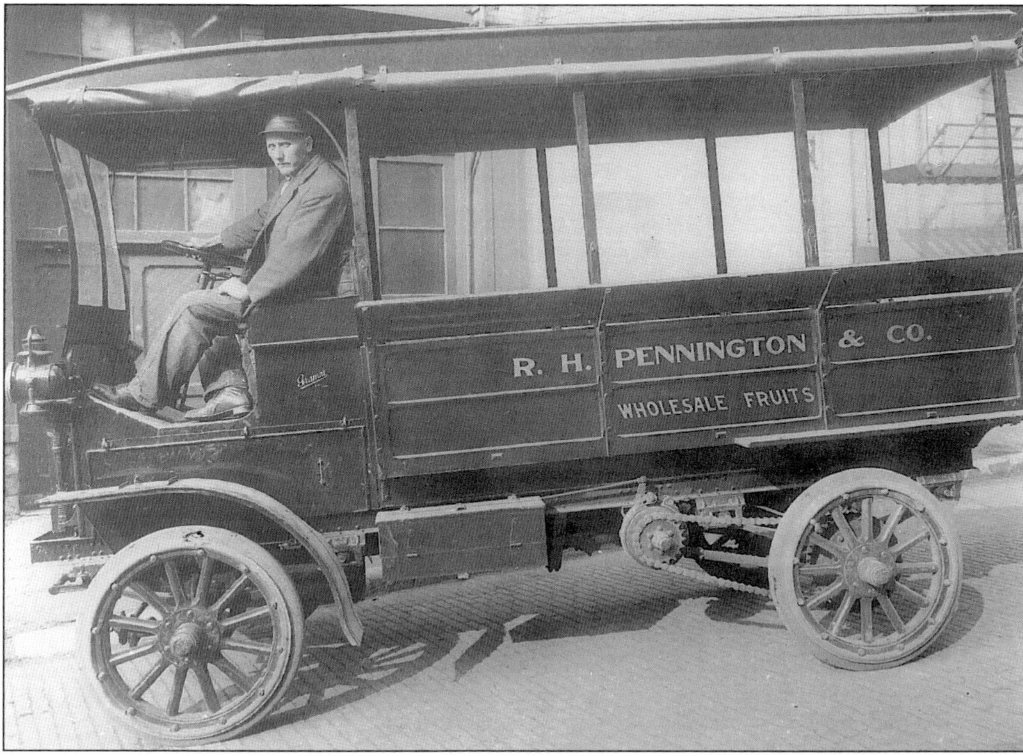

Motorized delivery trucks—in this case, the one employed by wholesale fruit dealer R.H. Pennington of Evansville—encouraged decentralization of cities because of their speed, durability, and load capacity. (Courtesy of USI.)

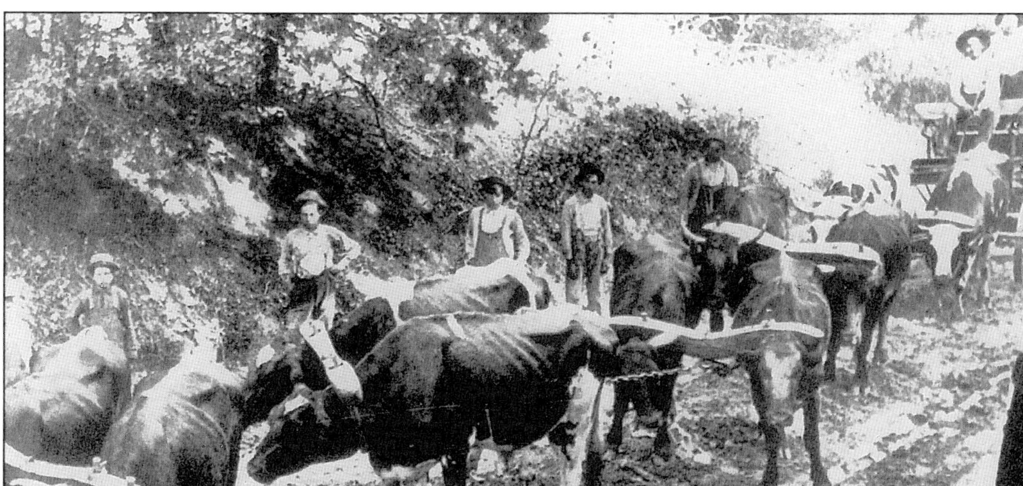

The Cole brothers from Alfordsville helped to build a road in Daviess County with teams of what appear to be somewhat emaciated oxen in 1911. (Courtesy of *Washington Times-Herald.*)

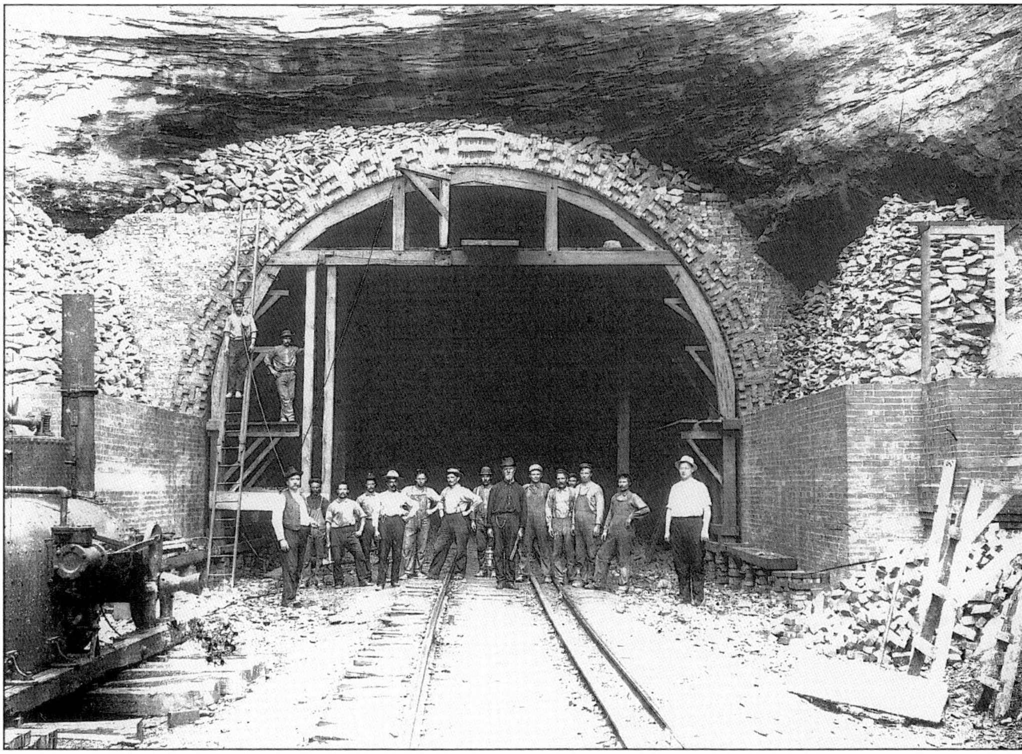

This is known as the Big Tunnel on the Baltimore and Ohio Railroad near Tunnelton. Workers are lining the tunnel with bricks *c.* 1910. The line, connecting Cincinnati and St. Louis, was opened in the mid-1850s and was the main east–west rail line across southern Indiana. Tunnelton, southeast of Bedford, gained its name by being located between the big and little tunnels to its east and west, respectively. (Courtesy of Maxine Kruse.)

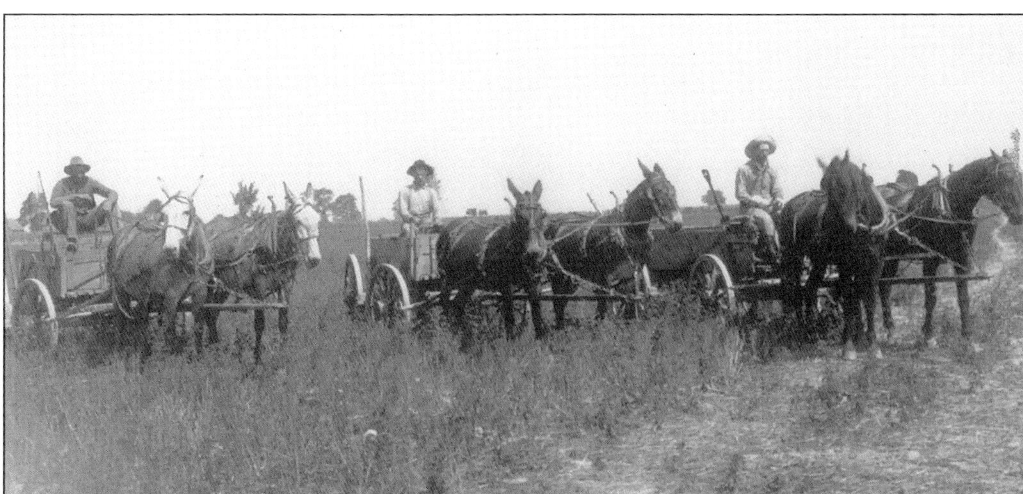

Highway construction (in this case, from Washington to Loogootee) was an increasingly common feature of southern Indiana life by World War I. Leonidas S. Horrall was contractor for this highway, which was paved with gravel. (Courtesy of *Washington Times-Herald*.)

Four

Making a Living

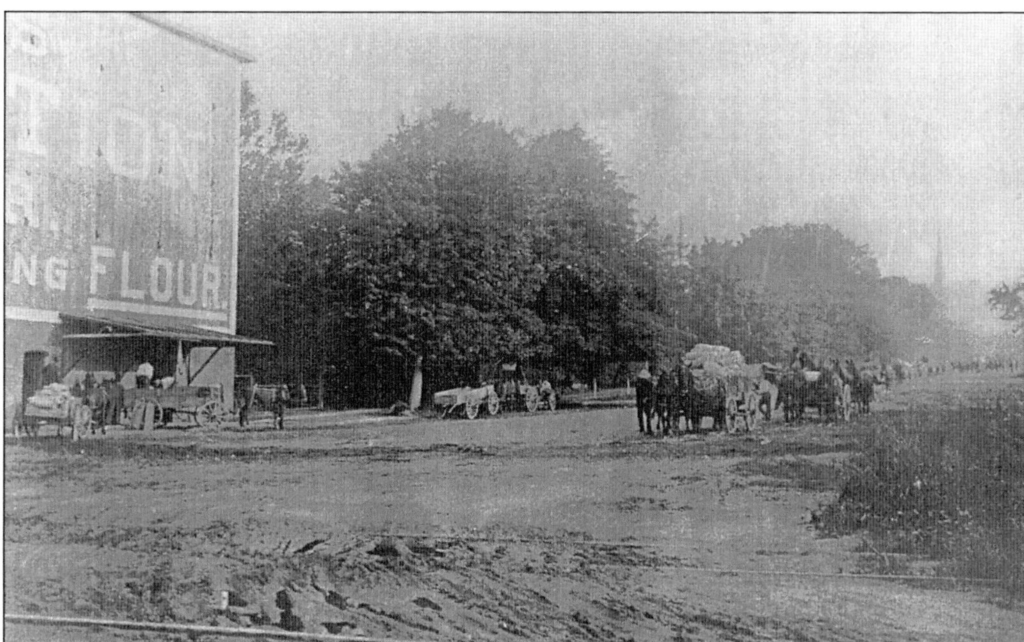

This is Trow's Flour Mill, located on Madison's riverfront, in late summer 1918. The mill was a busy place at that time, as farmers lined up with their wagons of wheat to be milled. Here, Broadway Street has a block-long line of wagons waiting their turn to unload at the mill. The mill was destroyed in the 1937 Ohio River flood and is now the site of a municipal swimming pool. (Courtesy of Jefferson County Historical Society.)

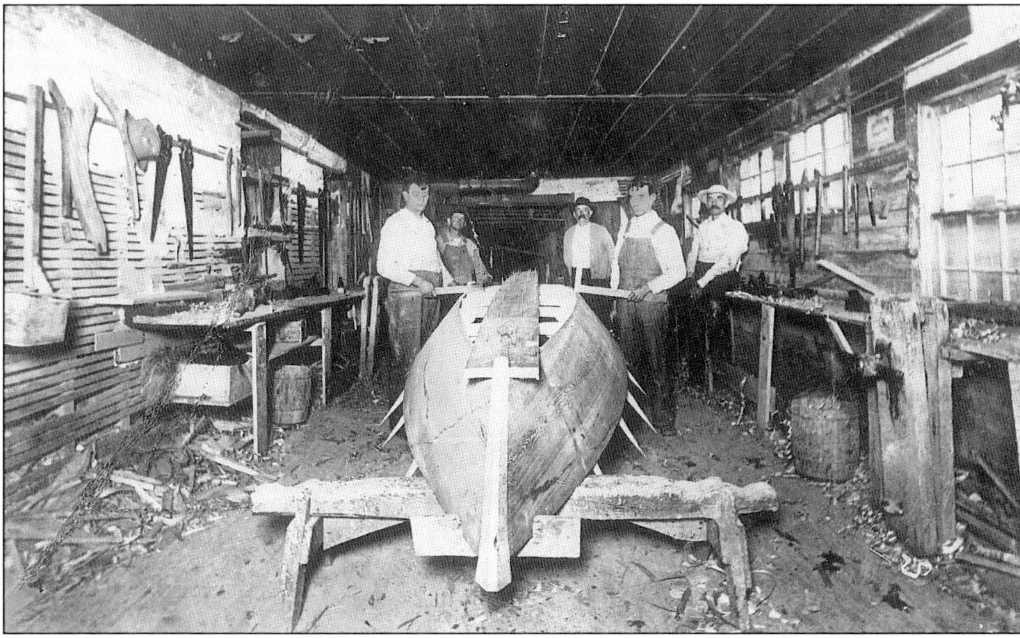

The Lyon Skiff Company in Leavenworth, begun *c.* 1830, manufactured skiffs that were shipped all over the country. The founder initially sold wood to steamboats and gradually moved into the skiff business. Skiffs ferried passengers and freight from riverboats to and from landings like Leavenworth's. The company was a victim of the 1937 flood. Shown, from left to right, are as follows: Nort[on?] Whitcomb, Ray Lyon, Wal[ter?] Lyon, Fos[ter?] Carver, and George Pearson. (Courtesy of Elaine Stephenson.)

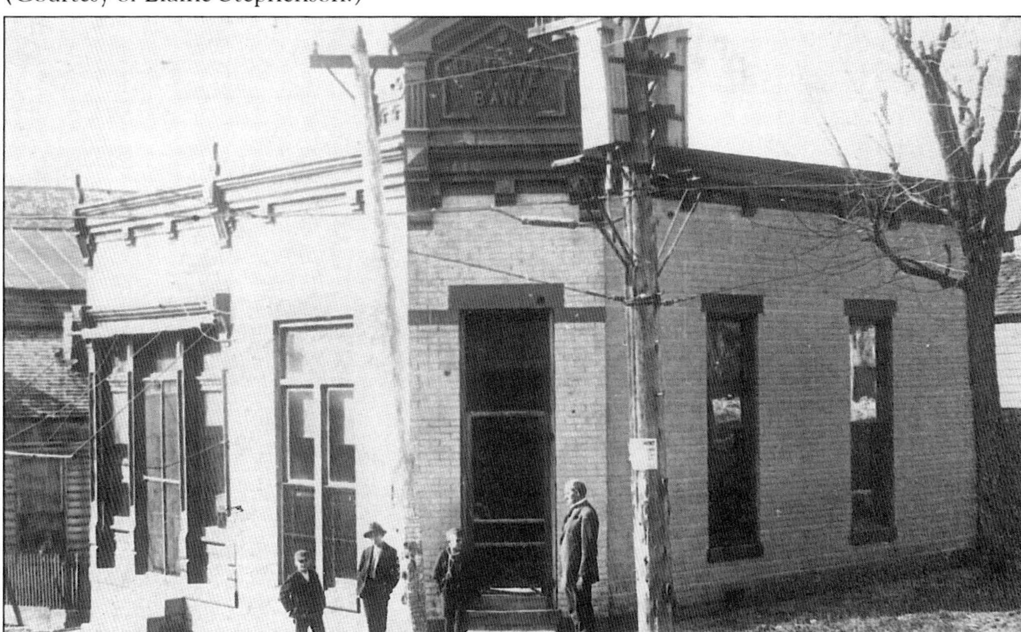

The Leavenworth State Bank, shown here *c.* 1920, was a mainstay of the local economy. It was one of many local business victims of the 1937 flood. (Courtesy of Elaine Stephenson.)

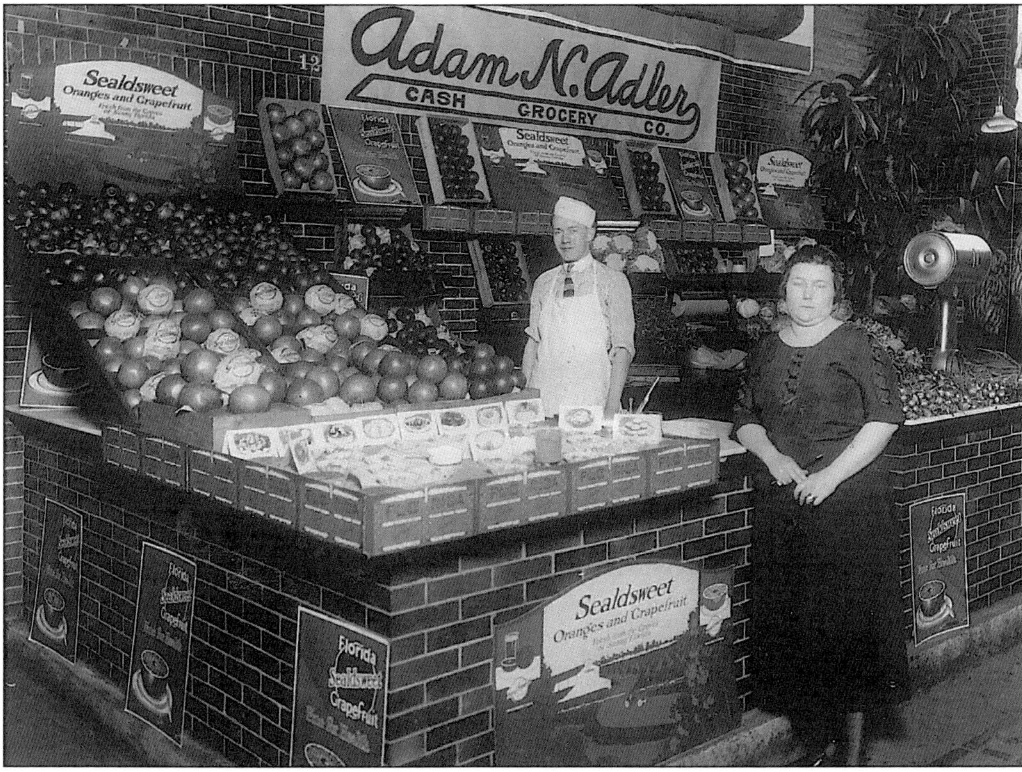

The Adam Adler Grocery had a stall at the Evansville Municipal Market, established on First Avenue in 1917 during the administration of Benjamin Bosse. (Courtesy of Willard Library.)

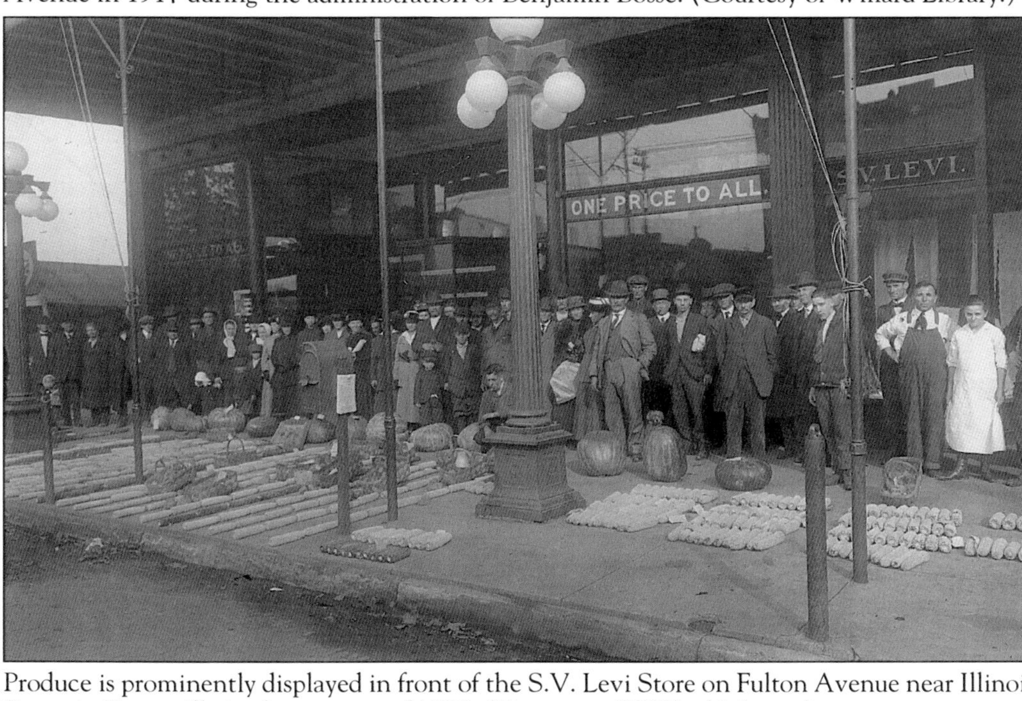

Produce is prominently displayed in front of the S.V. Levi Store on Fulton Avenue near Illinois Street in Evansville in the summer of 1912. (Courtesy of Willard Library.)

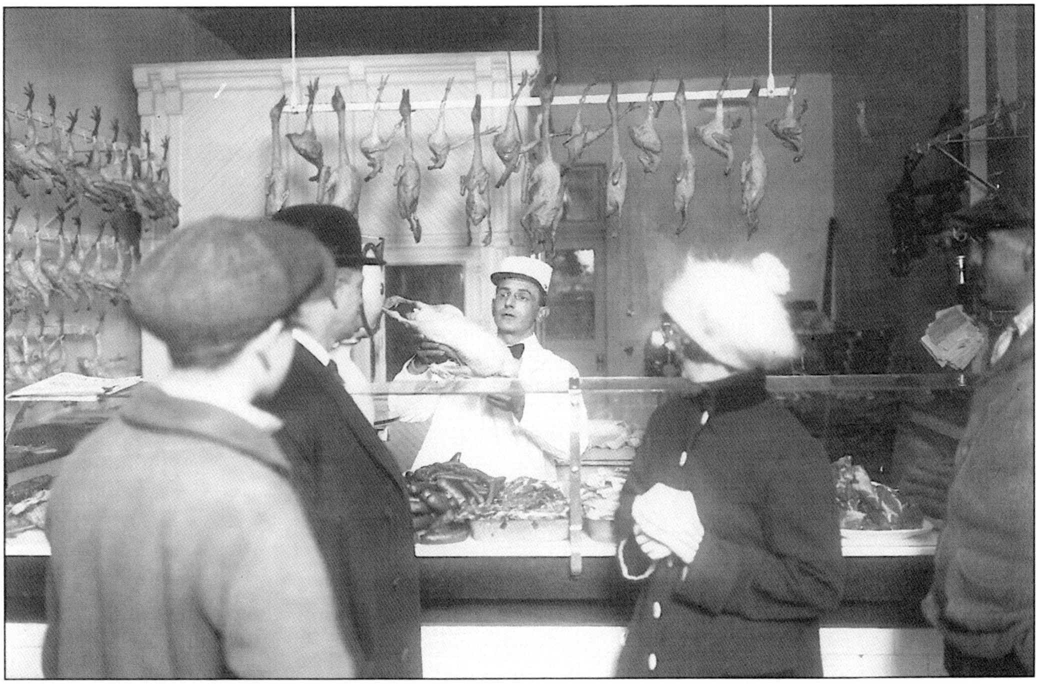

Photographed here is an unidentified Evansville butcher, about 1914, probably at Thanksgiving or Christmas. (Courtesy of USI.)

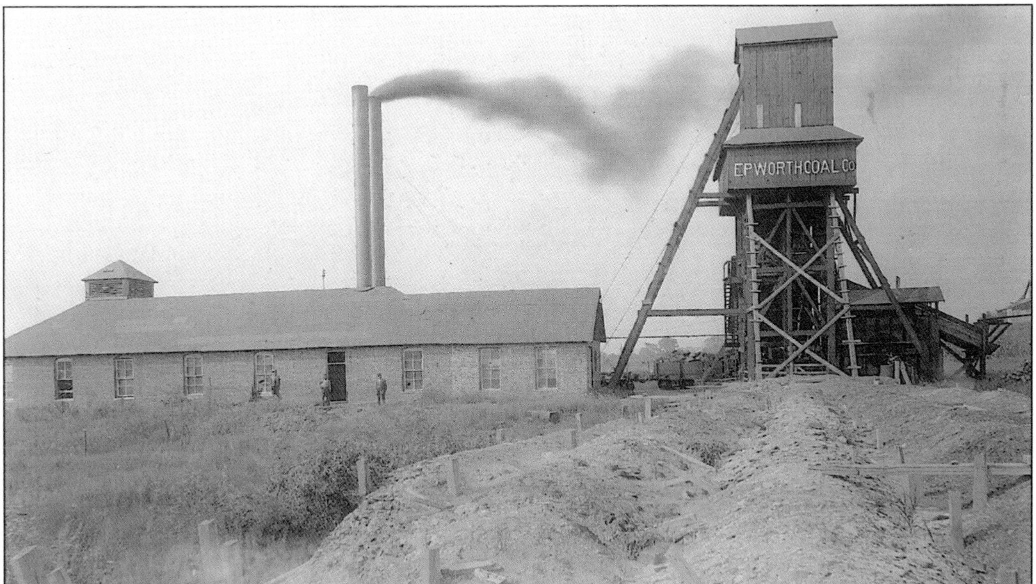

The Epworth Coal Company in Warrick County was one of many deep-shaft mines in southwest Indiana. Commercial mining in the region began nearby in the 1830s. Soft coal maintained regional industry and residential heating. In the 1920s, surface mining was implemented to save money for overcapitalized mine operators. Growing use of fuel oil for home heating was another challenge. Concerns about the effects of coal smoke on public health also grew. (Courtesy of Willard Library.)

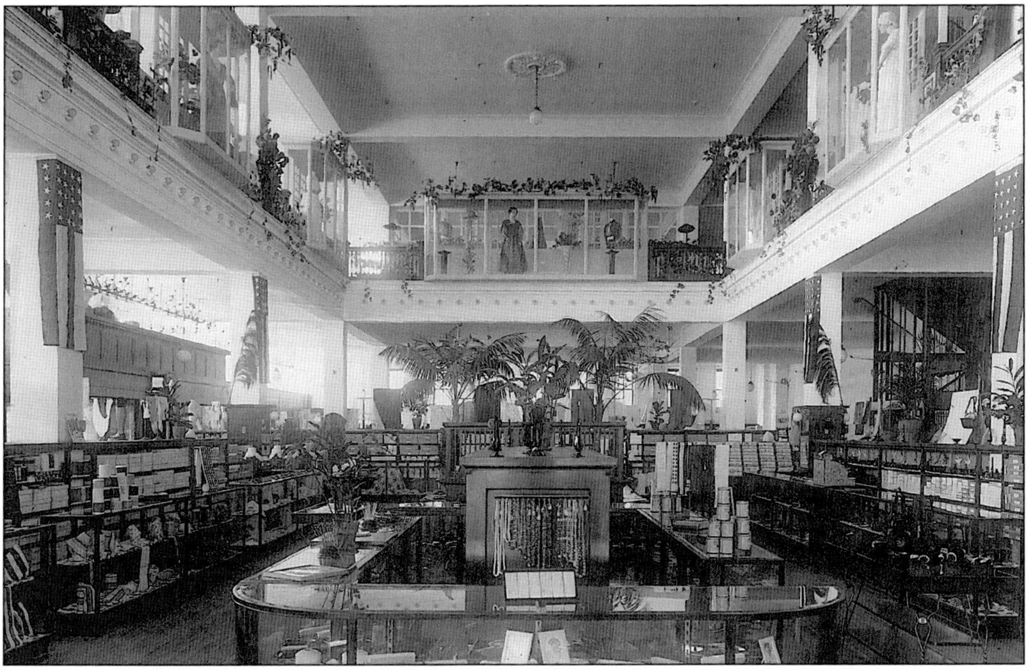

The interior of Lahr's Department Store on Main Street in Evansville in 1912 evokes the elegance and the appeal of this relatively new form of retail activity in southern Indiana cities. The store was later known as Shears. (Courtesy of Willard Library.)

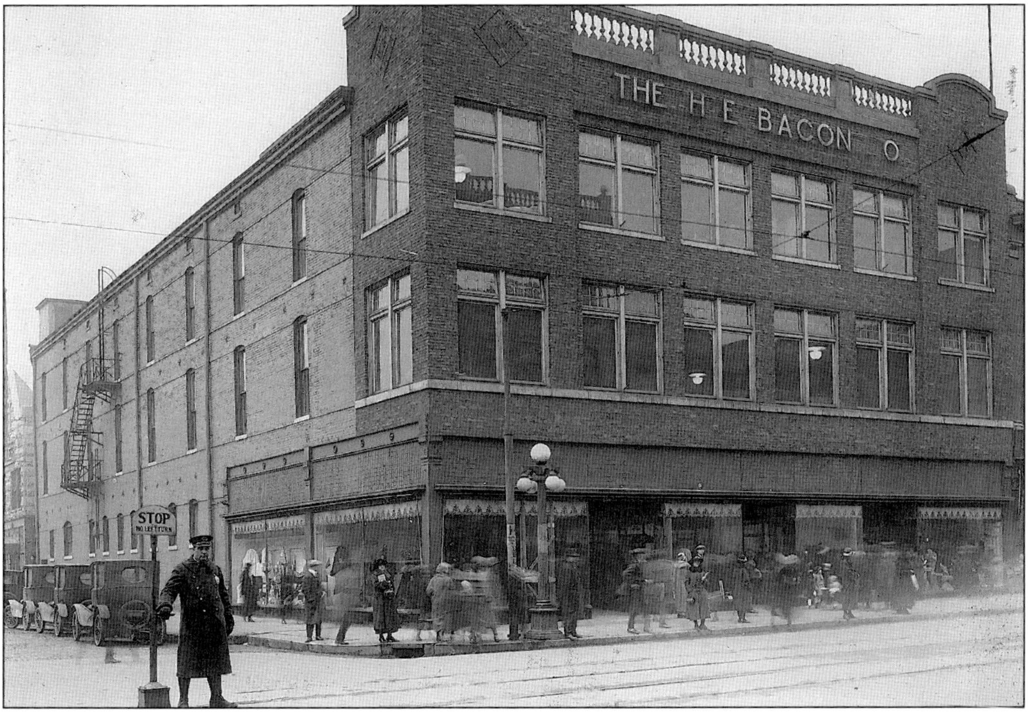

This is the exterior of the H.E. Bacon Department Store, by 1920 one of the mainstays of Main Street in Evansville. (Courtesy of Willard Library.)

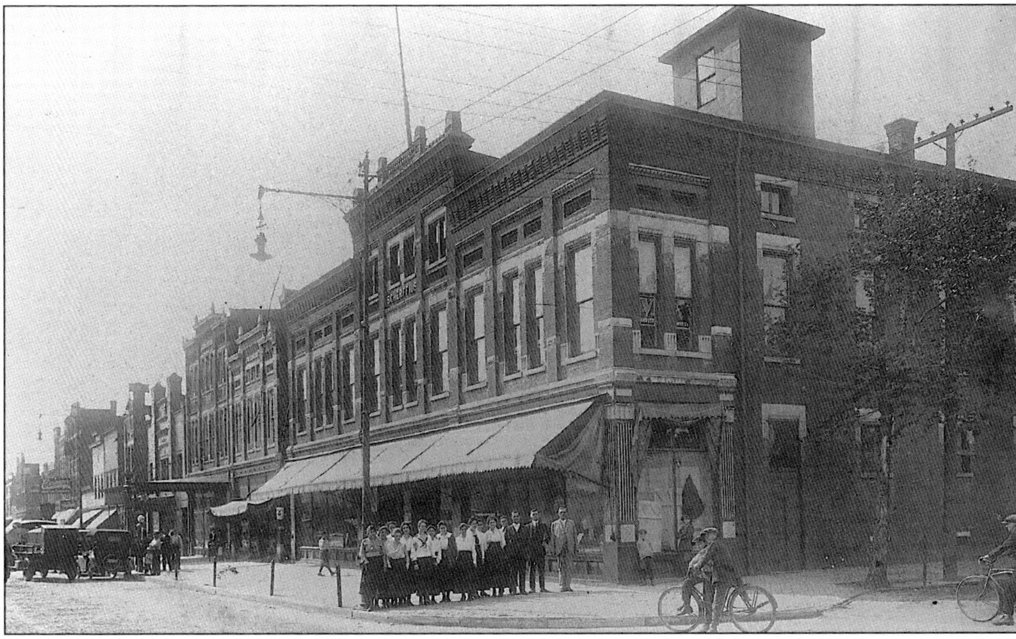

Managers and workers are shown in front of the Scherffius Department Store on West Franklin Street in Evansville, heart of the Lamasco section. German-born William Scherffius Sr. arrived in Evansville at age 17 in 1873 and eventually opened his own dry goods store. This building was erected in 1893. His son, William Jr., ran the store. (Courtesy of Willard Library.)

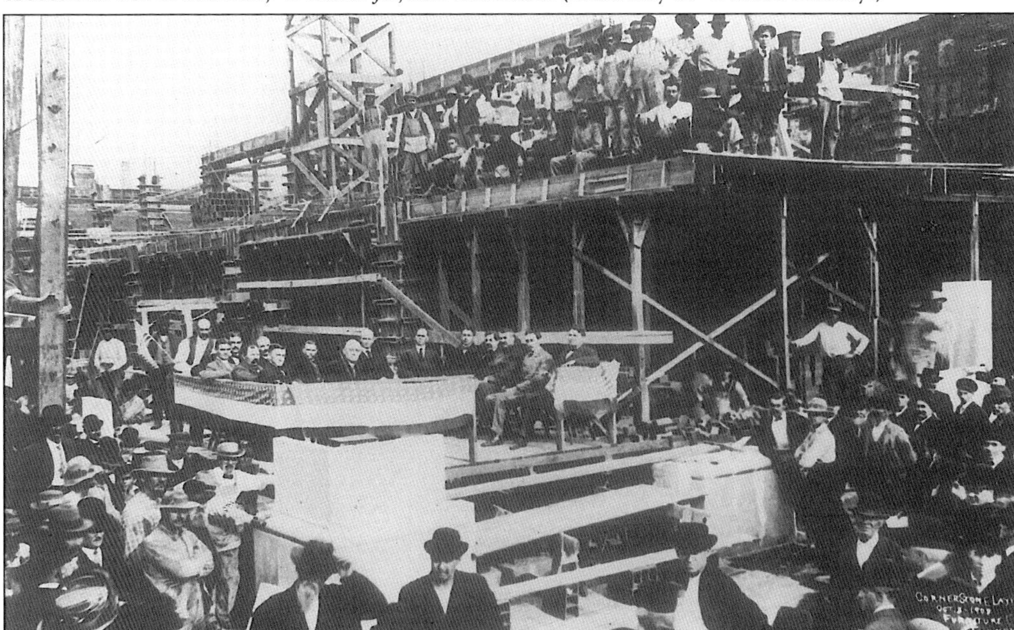

The cornerstone laying of the Furniture Exchange at Fourth and Vine in Evansville signified the importance of furniture factories and of their efforts at collaborative marketing. On the right is Benjamin Bosse, head of Globe–Bosse–World, touted as the world's largest furniture factory. He would be elected mayor in 1913. Furniture was, between the 1870s and the late 1920s, one of the two most valuable products in Evansville manufacturing. (Courtesy of USI.)

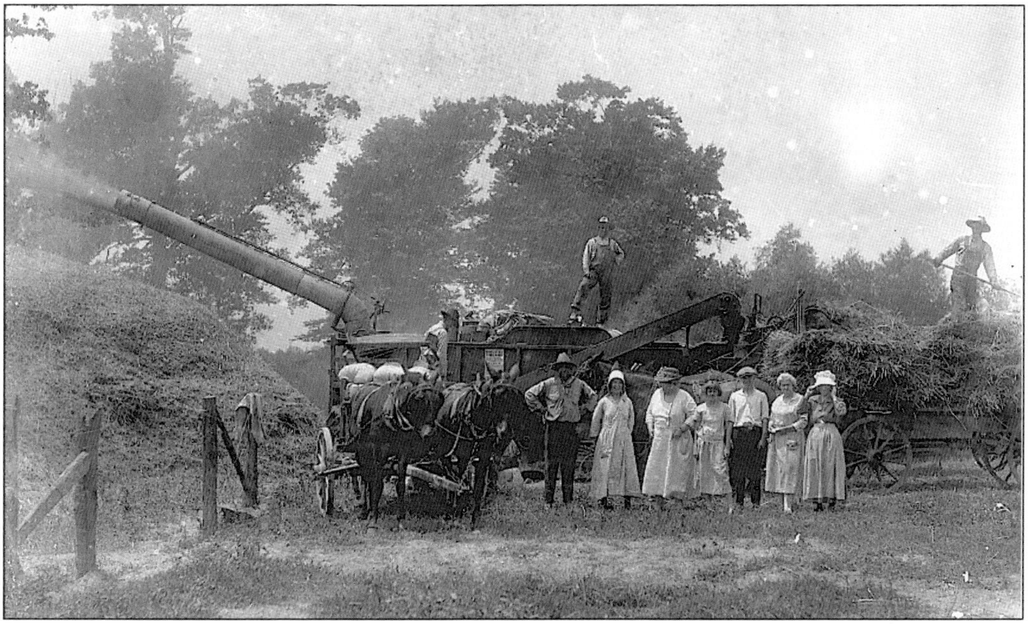

A wheat separator, probably a Keck–Gonnerman made in Mount Vernon, is being used to process a Posey County wheat harvest. Power was probably provided by a steam engine. The separator shook the kernels free from the stalks, which were blown into a huge pile. Men and boys tended the steam engine, lifted the wheat into the separator, shoveled grain into adjacent wagons, and attended to the mounting heap of straw, which was in turn taken to barns for storage. (Courtesy of USI.)

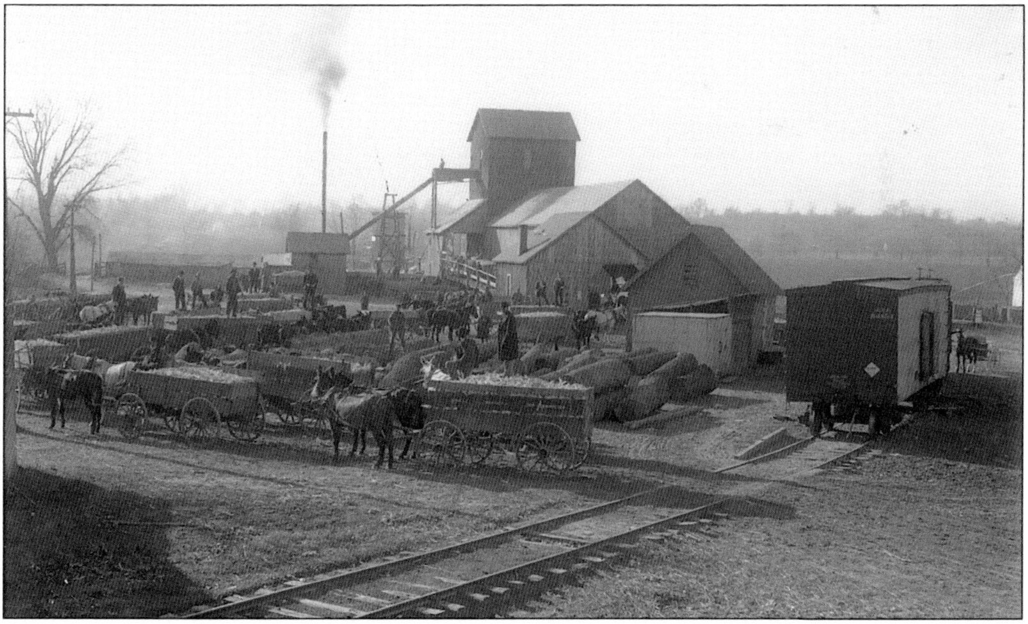

Wagons loaded with corn are lined up at a Posey County elevator, probably in New Harmony, just after harvest. The Illinois Central railroad siding would provide access to national markets. That would also make southern Indiana farmers, like their counterparts across the nation, increasingly dependent on market forces beyond their control. (Courtesy of USI.)

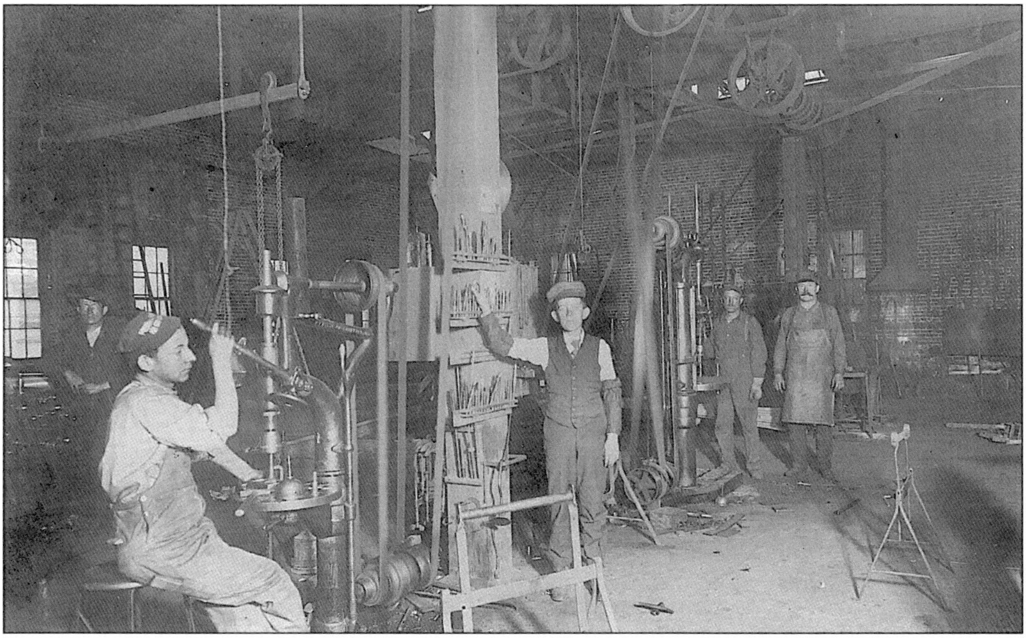

These are workers at Evansville's Lindenschmidt Foundry, one of a number of similar facilities in Evansville. Its work force was more skilled than most, and it attracted many German Americans. Located at 411 Ingle Street, it manufactured fire escapes and ornamental iron work for buildings, among other things. Foundry workers earned nearly 50 percent more than average wage earners. Many, though, were only boys. (Courtesy of John Payne.)

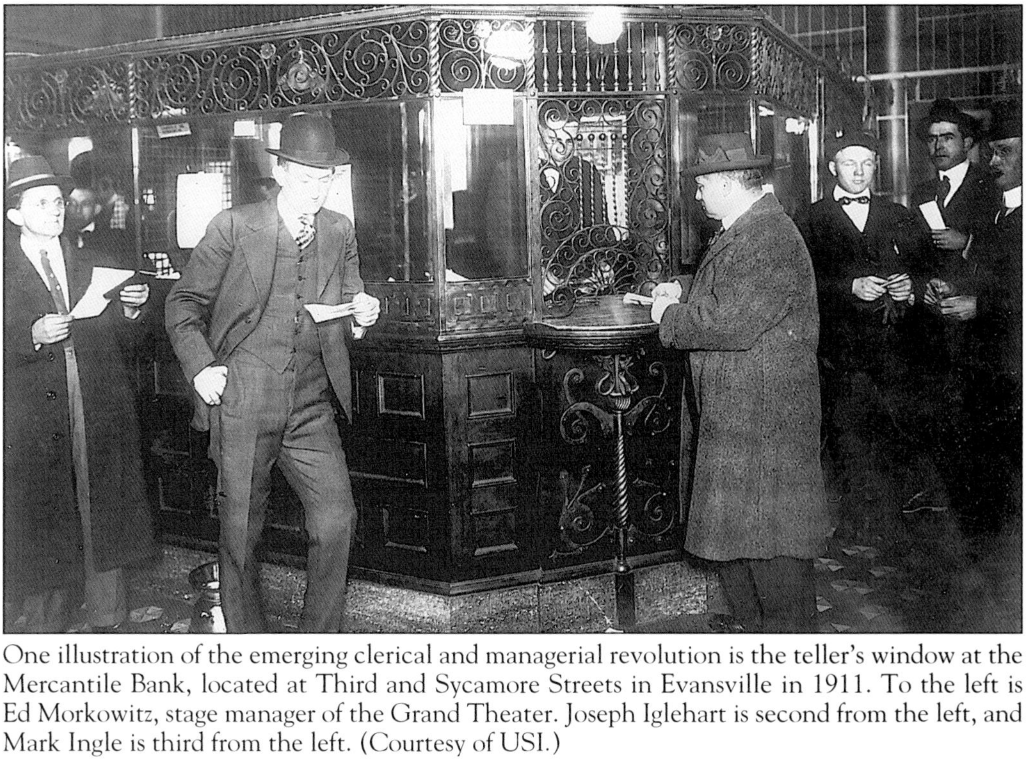

One illustration of the emerging clerical and managerial revolution is the teller's window at the Mercantile Bank, located at Third and Sycamore Streets in Evansville in 1911. To the left is Ed Morkowitz, stage manager of the Grand Theater. Joseph Iglehart is second from the left, and Mark Ingle is third from the left. (Courtesy of USI.)

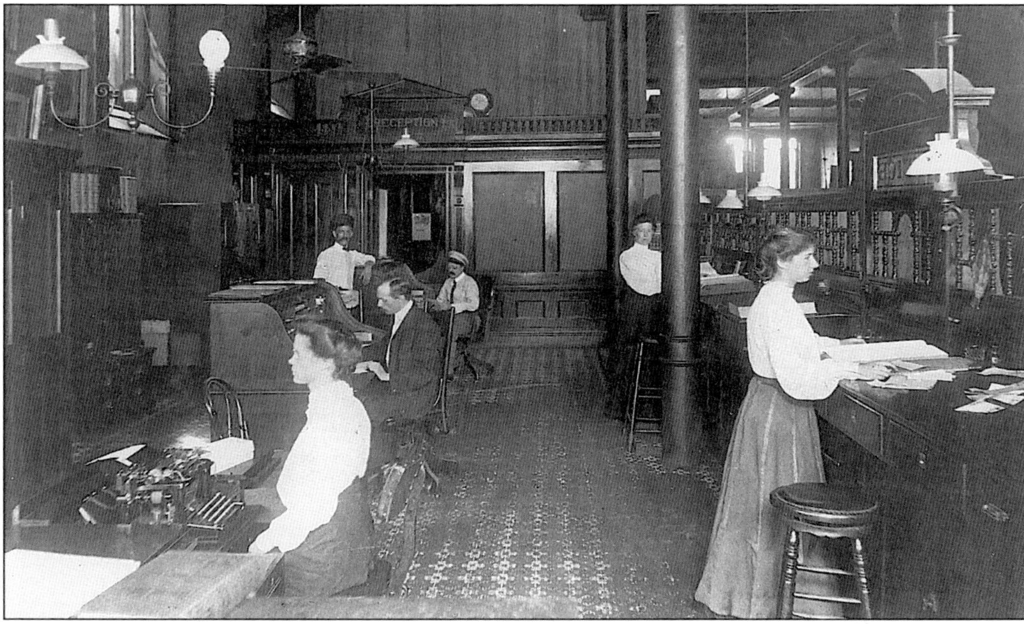

White-collar workers were increasingly a part of the age of the industrial city. These are office workers at the Evansville Gas Company, a predecessor of Southern Indiana Gas and Electric. (Courtesy of USI.)

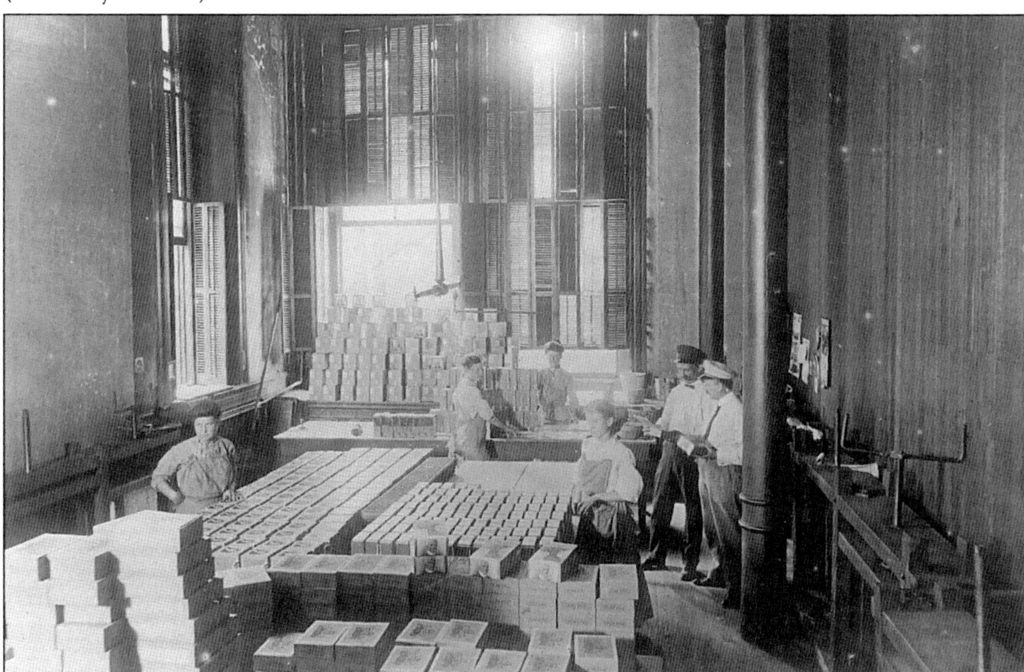

Most workers in the packing room at H. Fendrich and Company in Evansville are women, except for the supervisors. Fendrich moved to a new facility adjacent to Willard Library in 1912. About nine thousand women were employed in Evansville in 1915; two out of five made cigars. Most worked at Fendrich. The boxes bear the resemblance of Charles Denby, Evansville diplomat. Cigar makers developed diverse labels to appeal to varied tastes. (Courtesy of USI.)

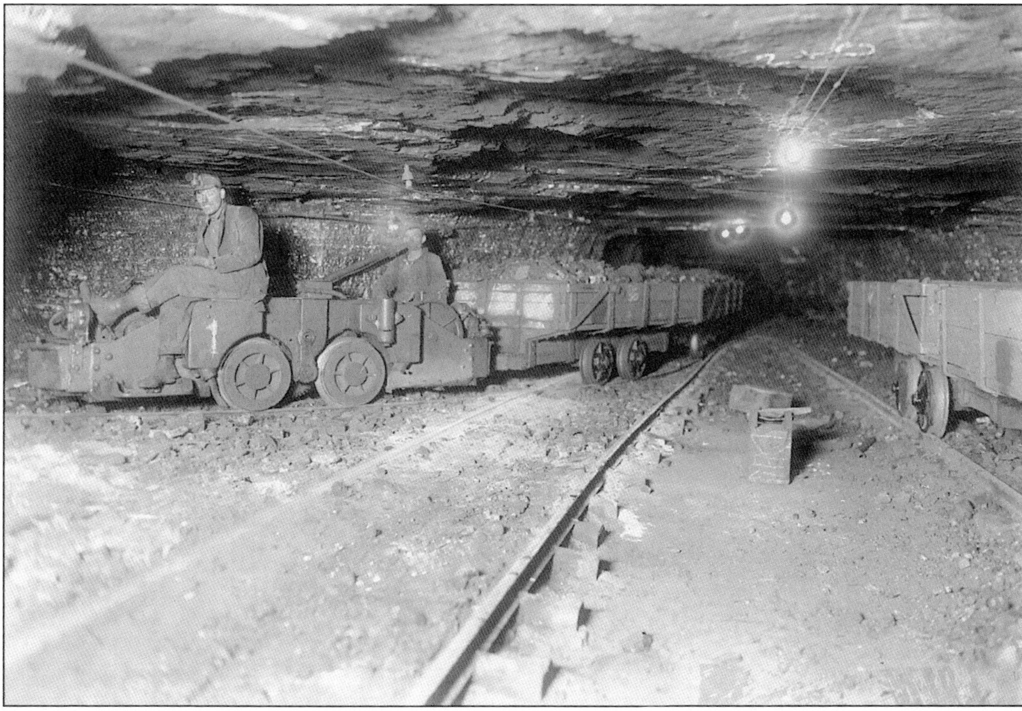

A rare scene, these coal miners were photographed deep below the surface in a bituminous (high sulphur) coal mine outside Bicknell, near Vincennes, in 1916. Coal mining closer to Vincennes had played out by 1900. After World War I, surface or strip mining would become a commonplace feature of Indiana coal production. (Courtesy of Lewis Library.)

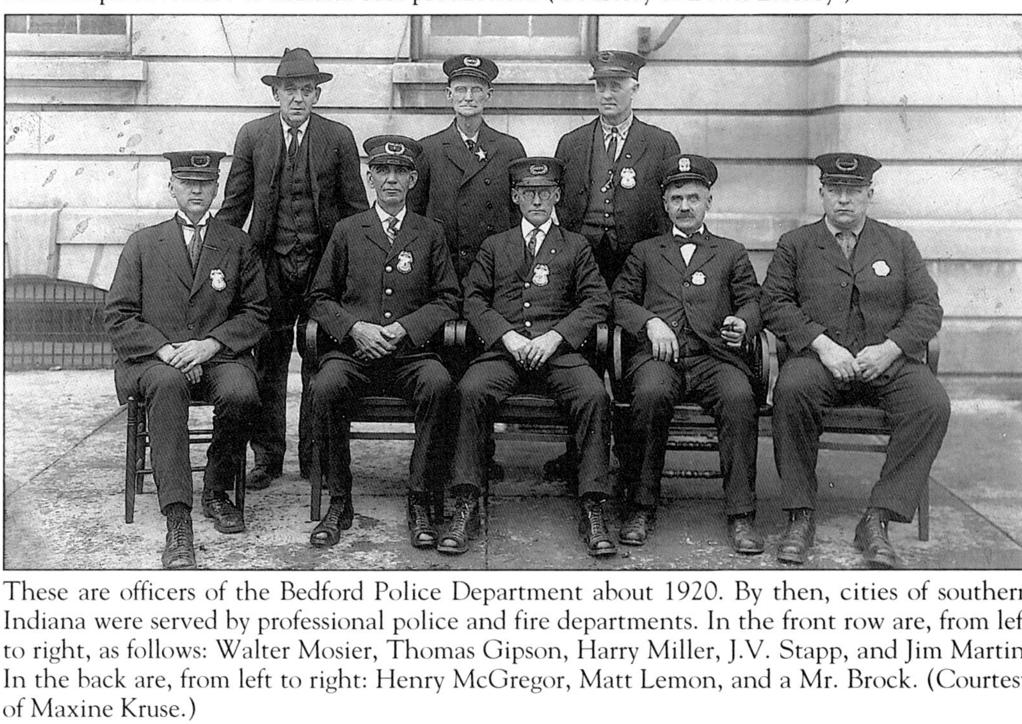

These are officers of the Bedford Police Department about 1920. By then, cities of southern Indiana were served by professional police and fire departments. In the front row are, from left to right, as follows: Walter Mosier, Thomas Gipson, Harry Miller, J.V. Stapp, and Jim Martin. In the back are, from left to right: Henry McGregor, Matt Lemon, and a Mr. Brock. (Courtesy of Maxine Kruse.)

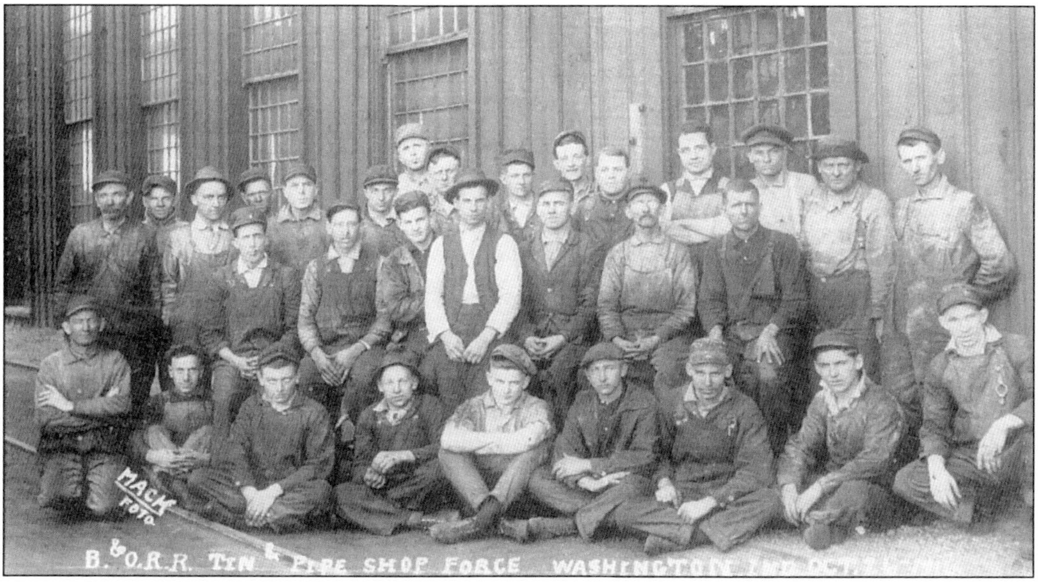

Shown here is the Baltimore and Ohio Tin and Pipe Shop force in Washington on October 26, 1916. The B and O repair shops in Washington were for years the chief employer in the city. Apprentices in this particular shop earned 7¢ an hour, working ten-hour days, six days a week. Journeymen earned twice that amount per hour. There was no provision for overtime pay. (Courtesy of *Washington Times-Herald.*)

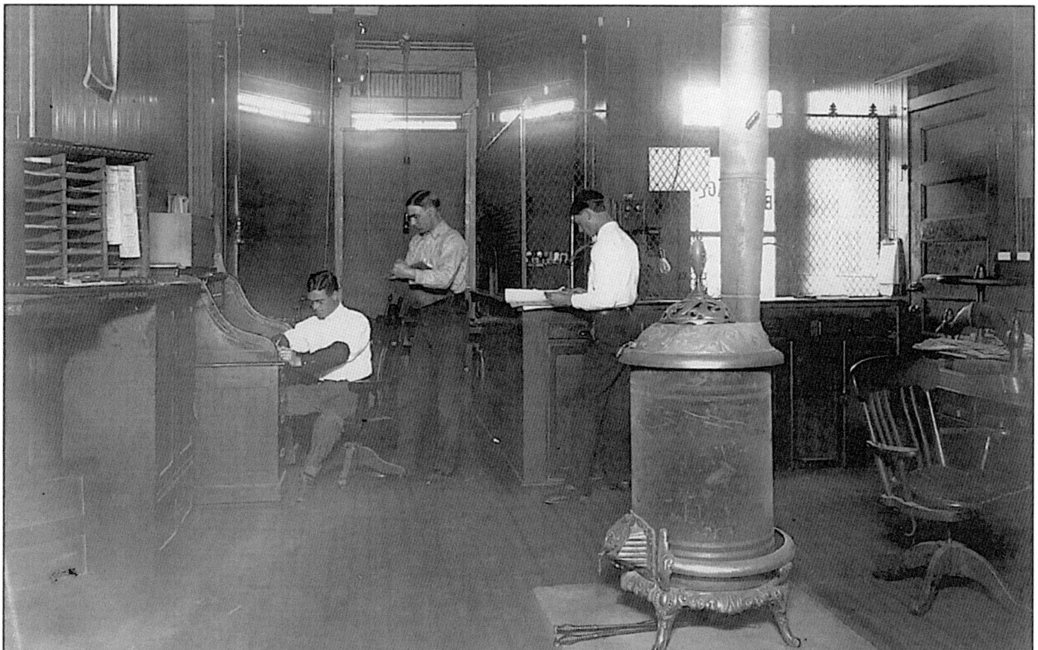

Employees of the Southern Railroad in Jasper were photographed in the railroad station about 1910. They are, from left to right, Lloyd Claycomb, Romis Chambers, and Claude Line. (Courtesy of John Fierst.)

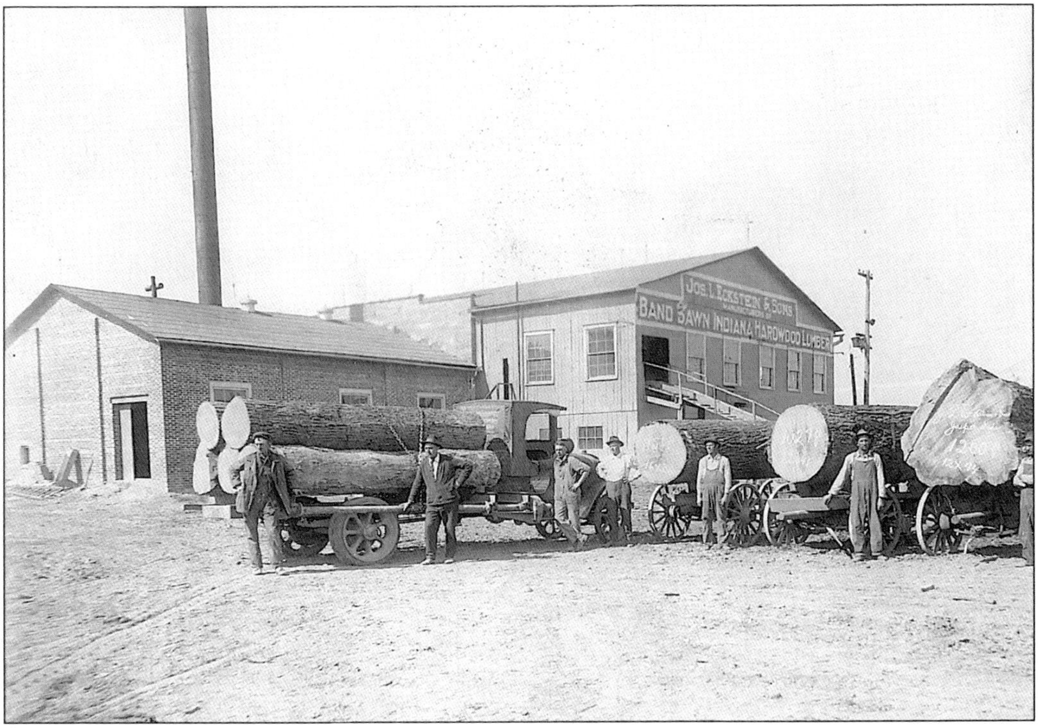

These are workers of Joseph L. Eckstein and Sons in Jasper about 1920. Wood products were then and remain the core of the city's economy. (Courtesy of John Fierst.)

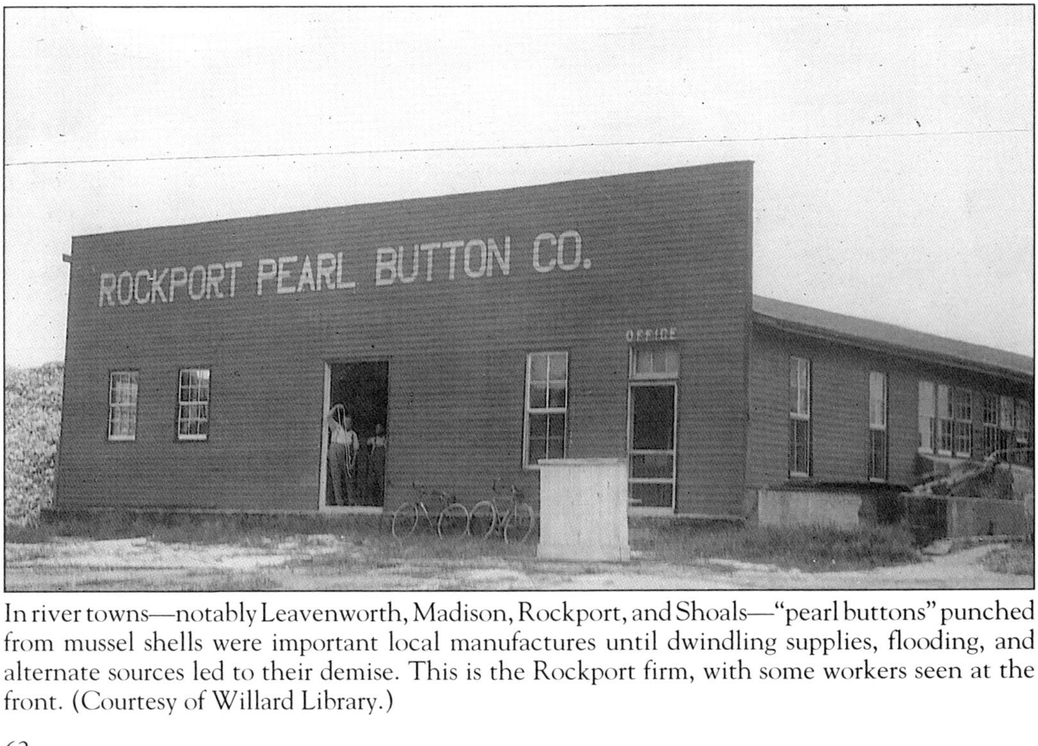

In river towns—notably Leavenworth, Madison, Rockport, and Shoals—"pearl buttons" punched from mussel shells were important local manufactures until dwindling supplies, flooding, and alternate sources led to their demise. This is the Rockport firm, with some workers seen at the front. (Courtesy of Willard Library.)

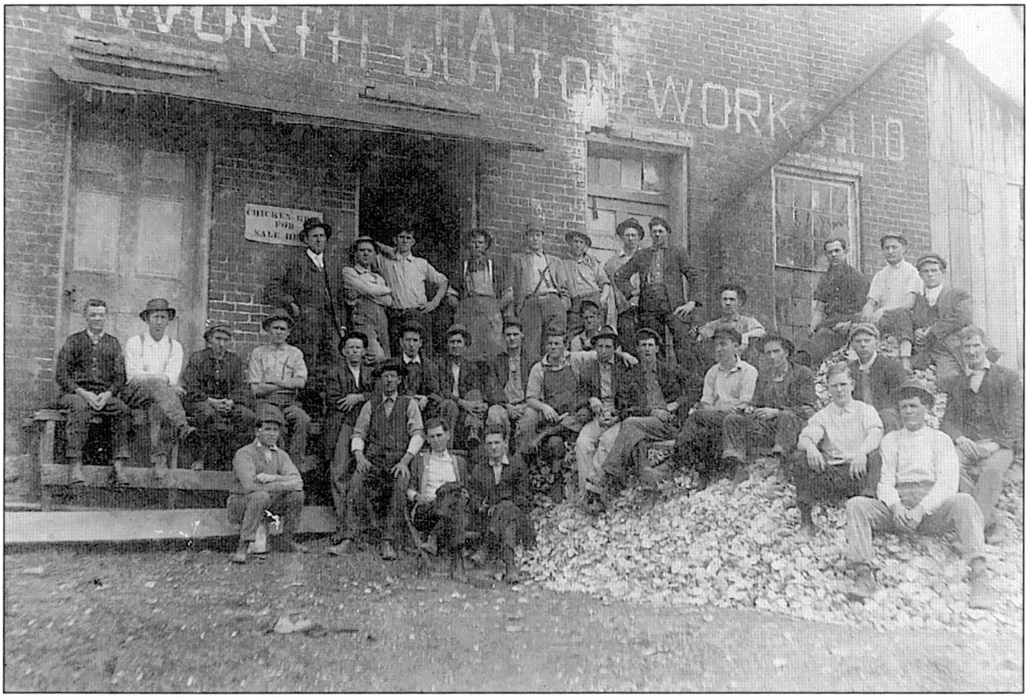

These are workers for the Leavenworth Button Company, established in 1902 in the old town hall on Court Street. Discarded shells are prominent. This company went out of business after the 1937 flood. (Courtesy of Marcella Beals.)

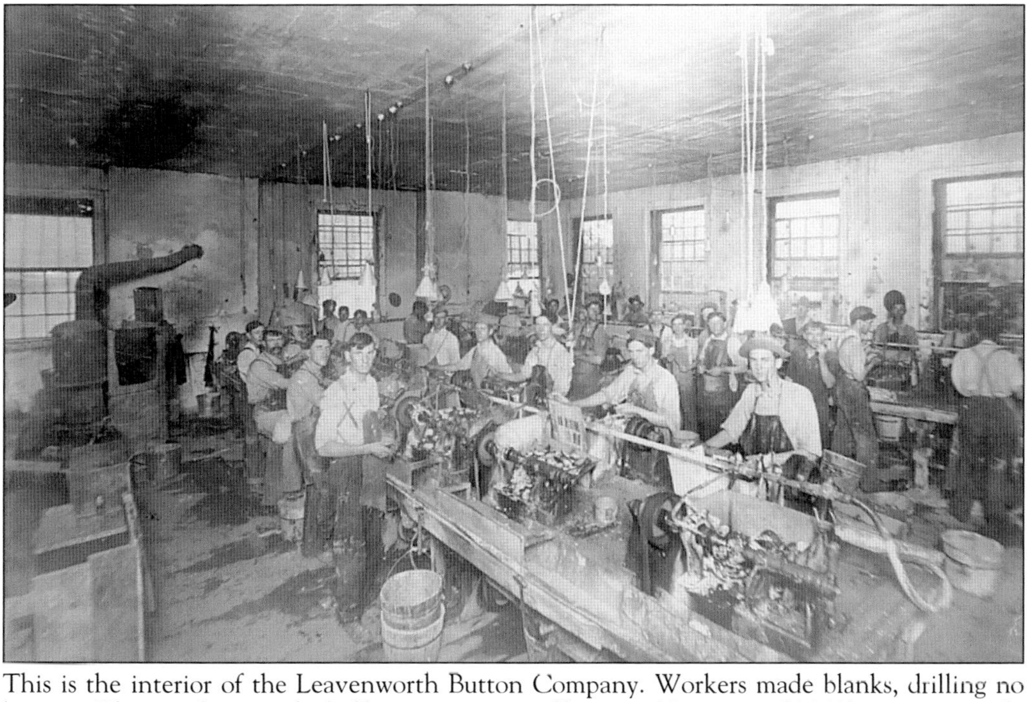

This is the interior of the Leavenworth Button Company. Workers made blanks, drilling no buttons. They made six and a half cents per gross of buttons (Courtesy of 1868), approximately $7 a week. Work was seasonal. (Courtesy of Marcella Beals.)

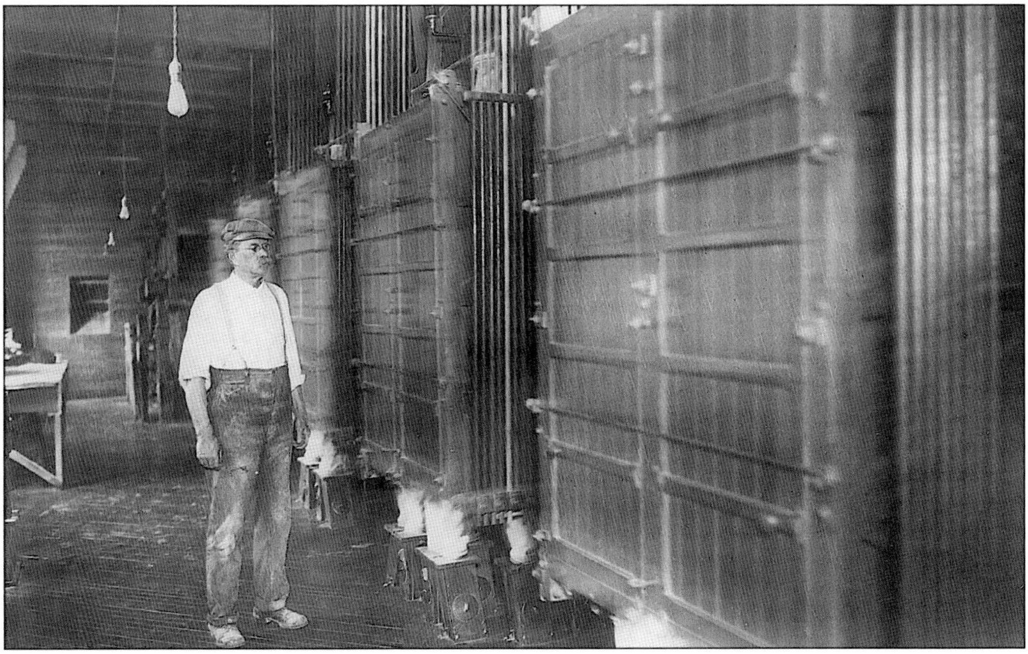

This is a miller at the newly opened Igleheart Brothers Mill on Outer First Avenue in Evansville in 1910. The mill produced the city's first brand name (and one of Indiana's first) product: "Swans Down Cake Flour." Flour mills in the city, as elsewhere, employed relatively few men but accounted for a significant part of the value of its manufactured goods. (Courtesy of Willard Library.)

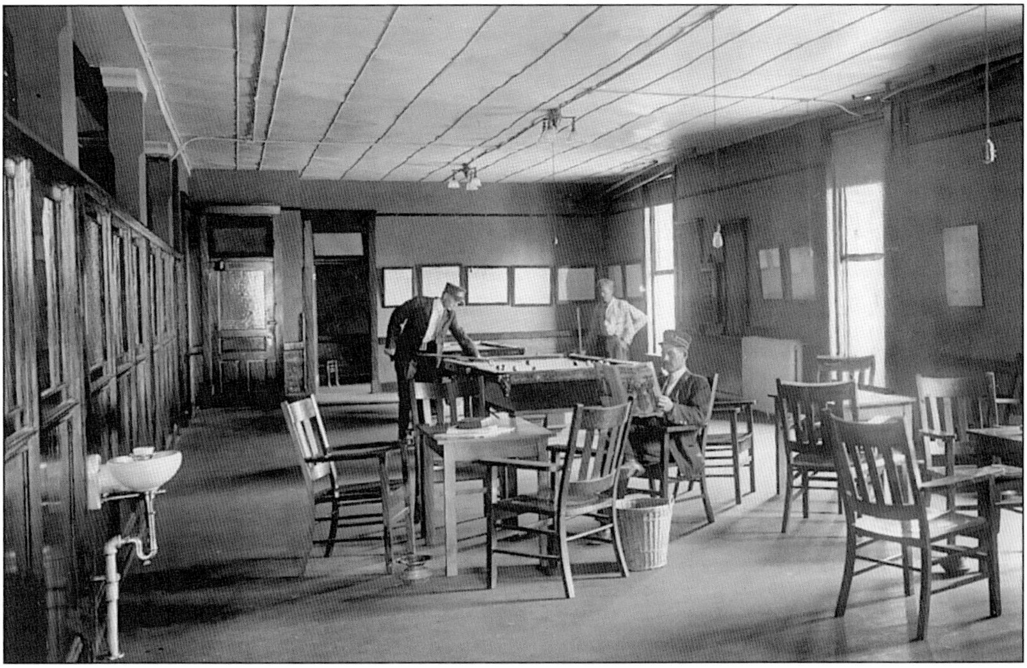

Street railway workers in Evansville are photographed in their lounge at Second and Locust Streets. (Courtesy of Willard Library.)

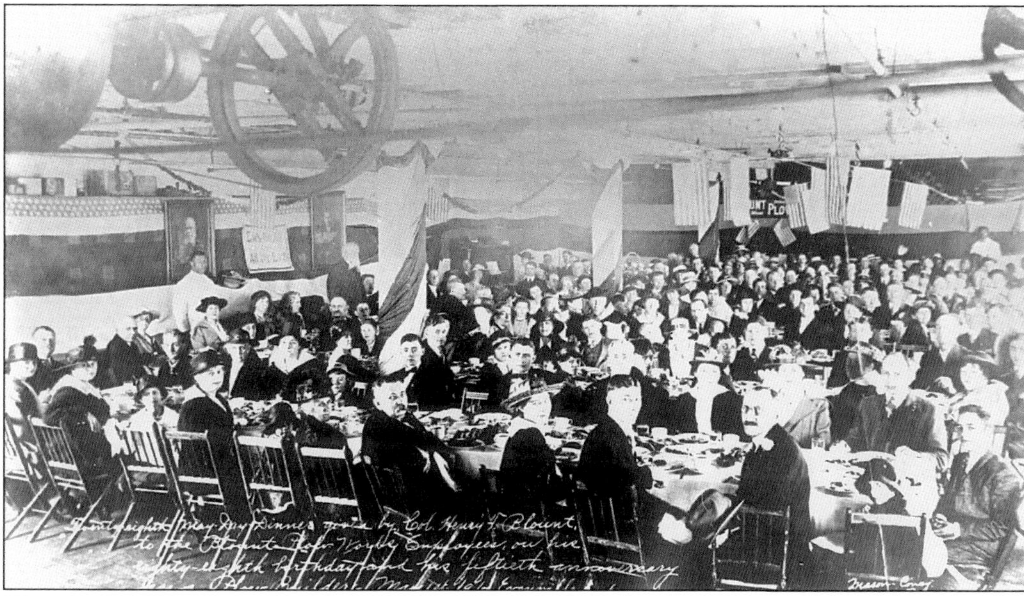

This is a banquet in 1917 for employees of Henry F. Blount's Plow Works in Evansville. They are celebrating the 50th anniversary of the company and the founder's 85th birthday. Blount, who made a fortune selling plows mostly in the South, left the city in the late 1880s to live on an estate in the Georgetown section of the nation's capital. He returned annually to visit on his birthday. (Courtesy of USI.)

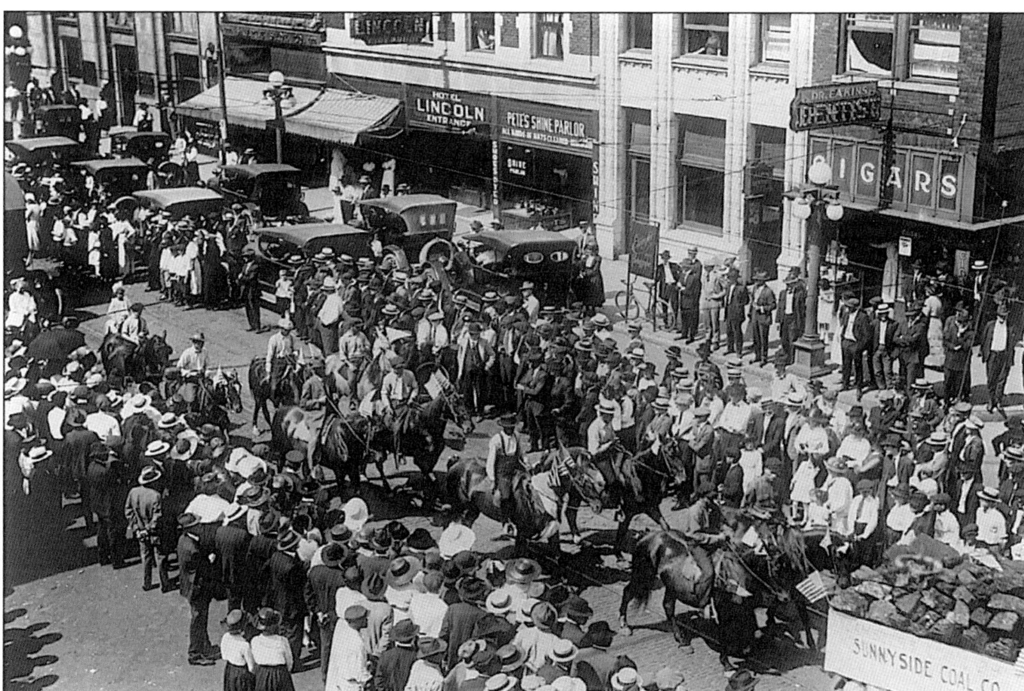

Labor Day 1920 on Evansville's Main Street, near Fifth, included a group of workers from Sunnyside Mines. (Courtesy of USI.)

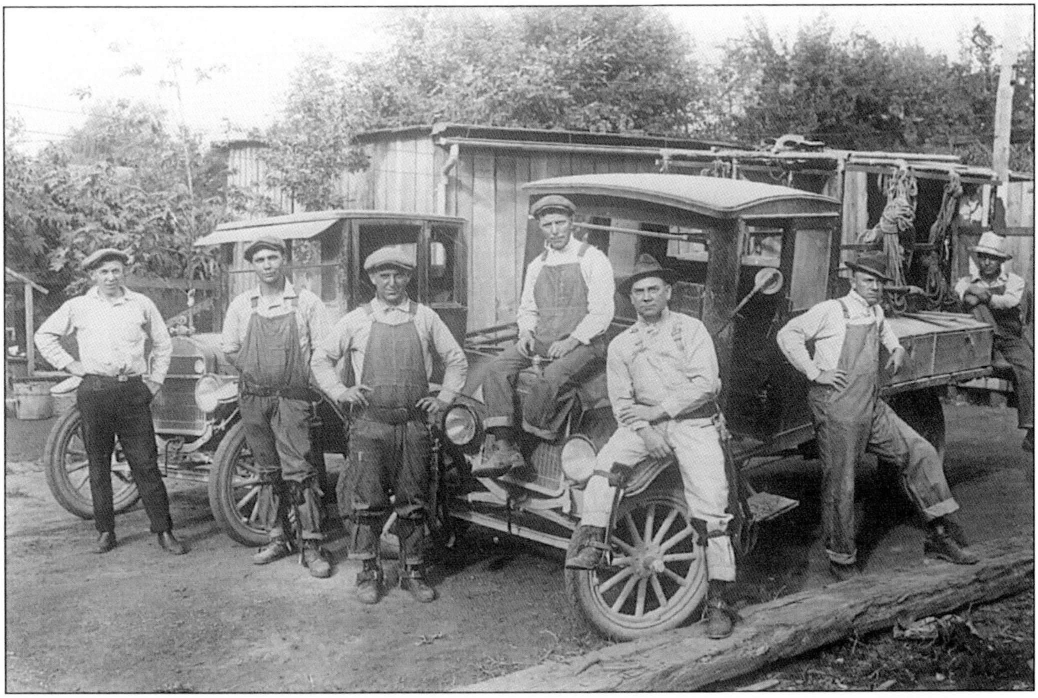

Southern Indiana Gas and Electric workers are shown here in 1920. (Courtesy of USI.)

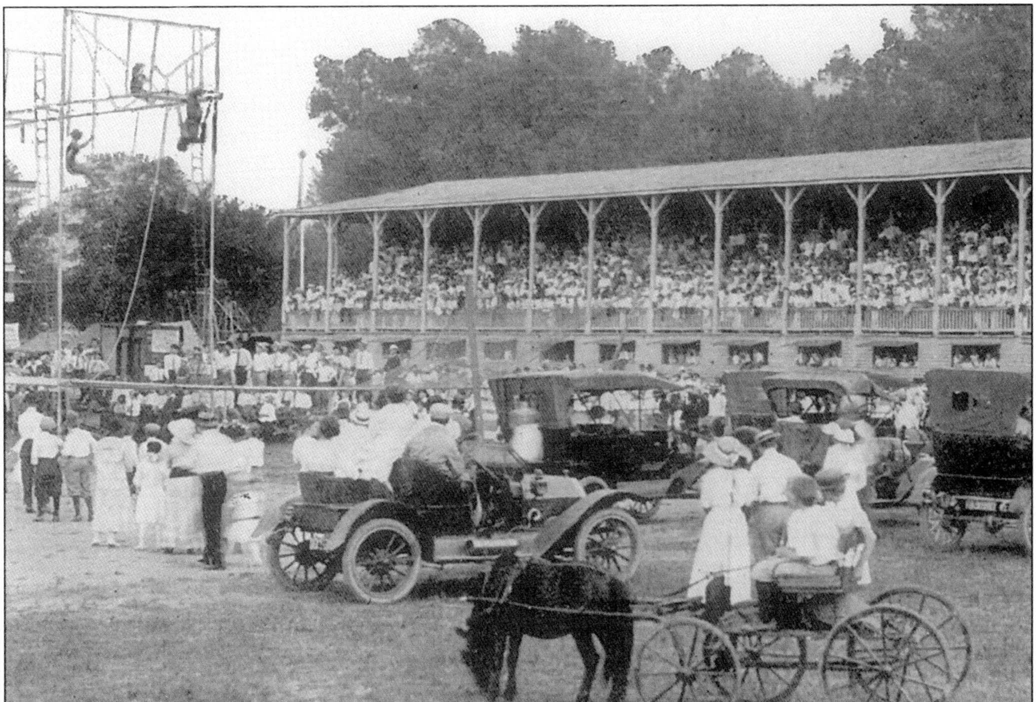

This is the Rockport County Fair about 1920. Horse and buggy transport remains predominant, but the growing impact of the automobile age is clear. A group of acrobats is performing in front of the stands. (Courtesy of Willard Library.)

Five

JOINING TOGETHER

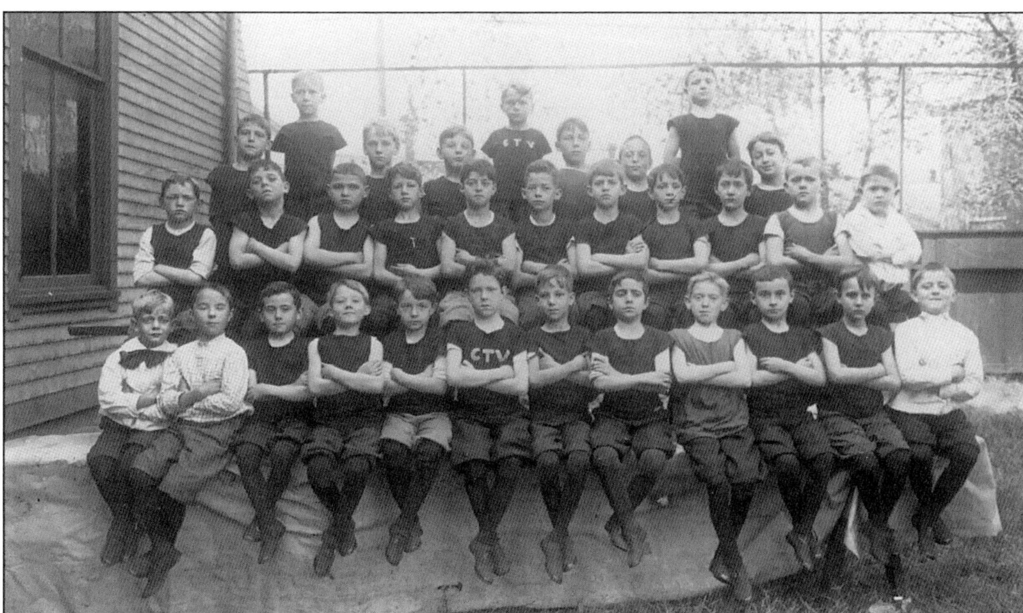

These are members of the Central Turnverein Youth Organization in Evansville *c.* 1915. The Turnverein, formed in the 1850s in several Indiana cities, promoted physical fitness and cultural development—two aims of the "Forty-Eighters" who migrated from Germany to America in the 1850s. A number of programs—as this photo reveals—were designed for youth. During World War I the organization changed its name to "Central Turners." (Courtesy of USI.)

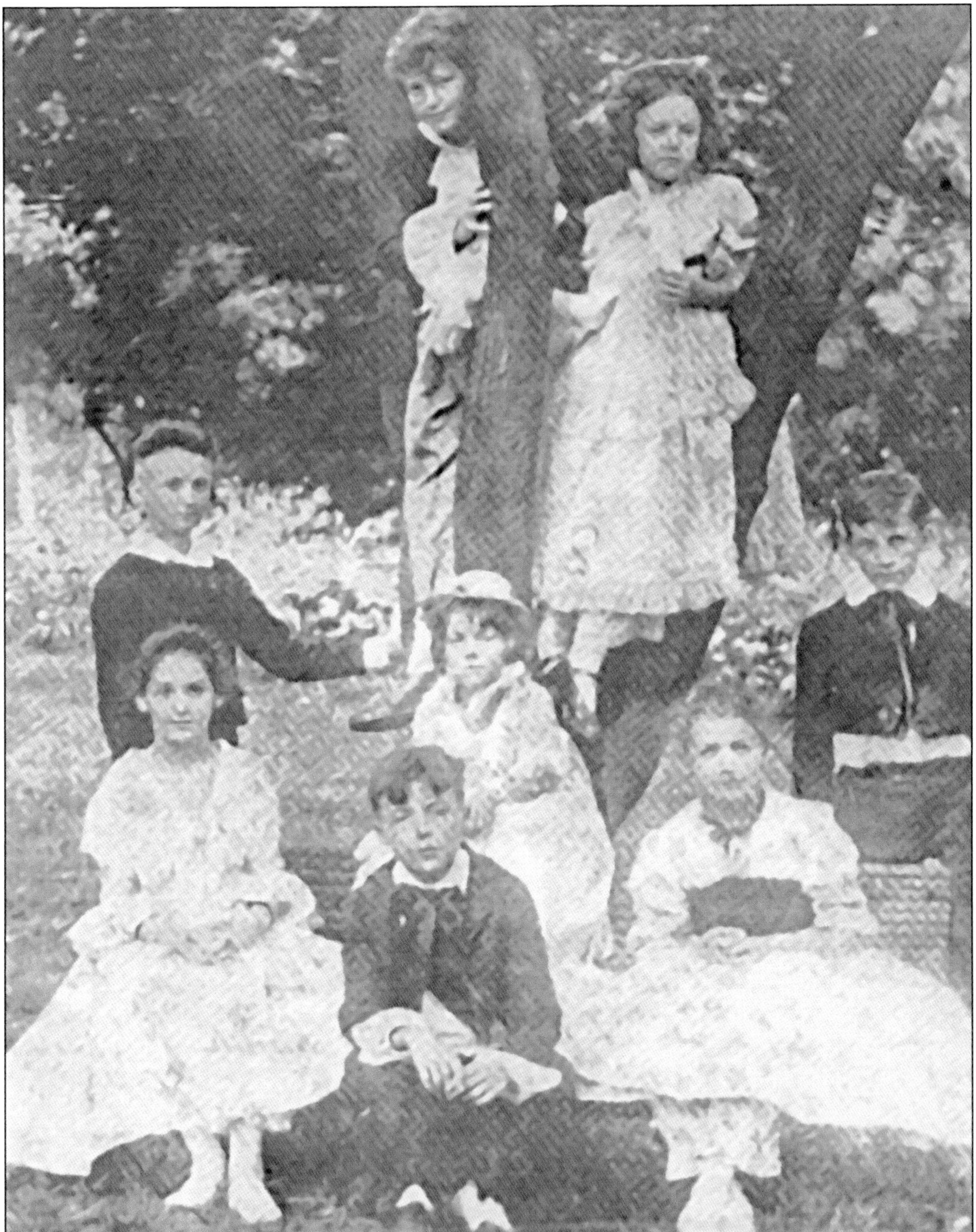

These children were dressed for a state centennial historical pageant at the Lanier Mansion in 1916. Lanier at that time was owned by the Jefferson County Historical Society and operated as their museum until 1925, when it became a state-owned property. (Courtesy of Jefferson County Historical Society.)

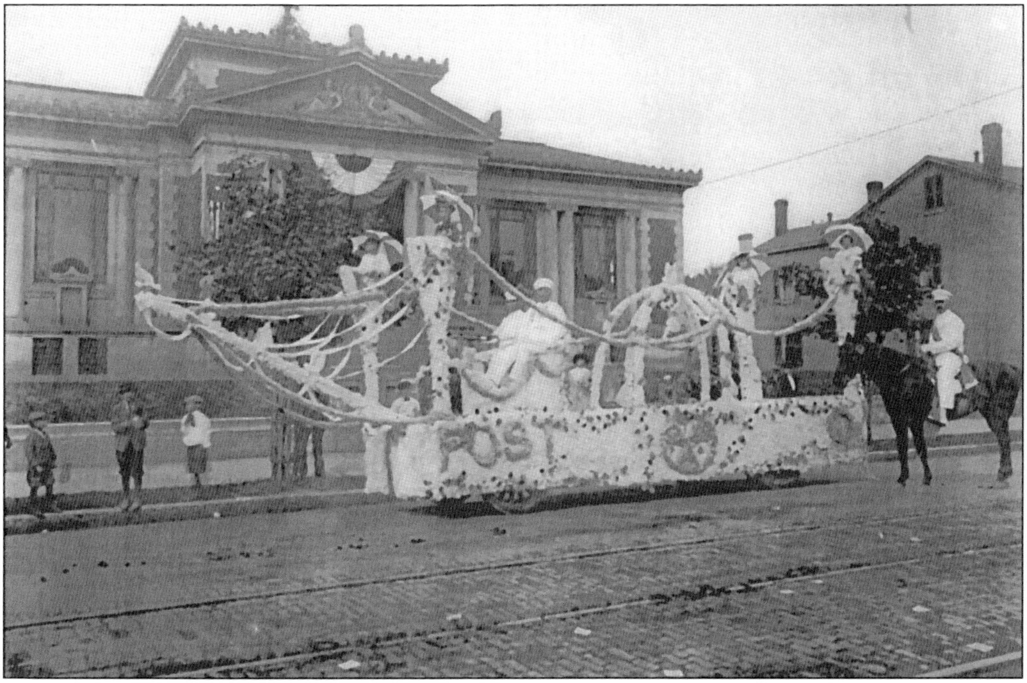

This float participated in New Albany's centennial parade in 1913. In the background is the Carnegie Library, opened in 1902 at a cost of $50,000. The building now houses the Carnegie Center for Art and History. (Courtesy of New Albany–Floyd County Public Library.)

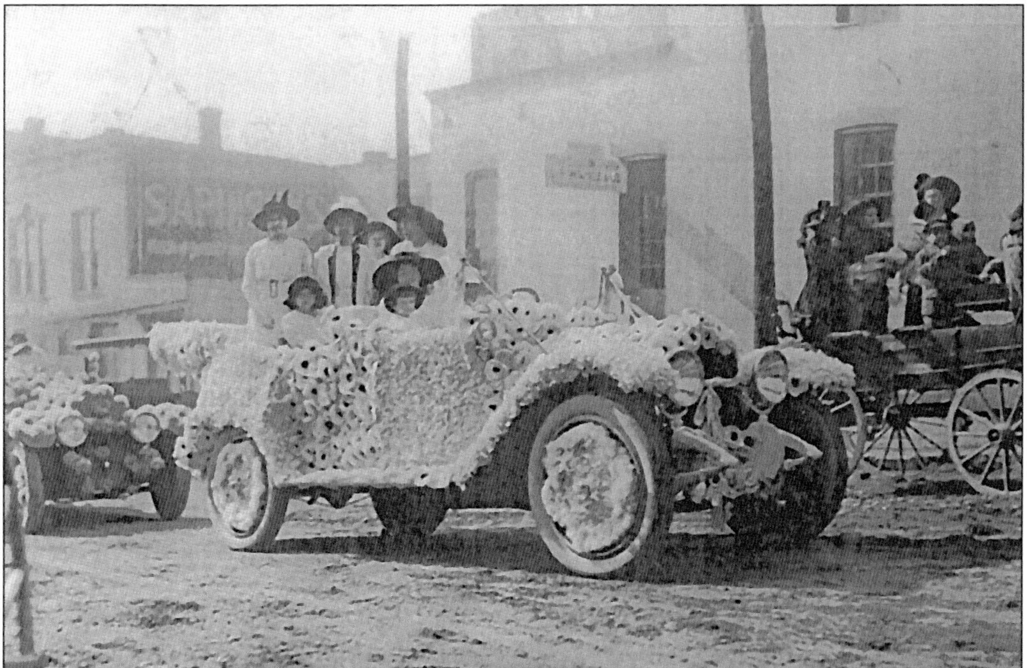

A decorated car in the 1913 New Albany Centennial Parade passes by commercial buildings at the corner of High and State Streets. (Courtesy of New Albany-Floyd County Public Library.)

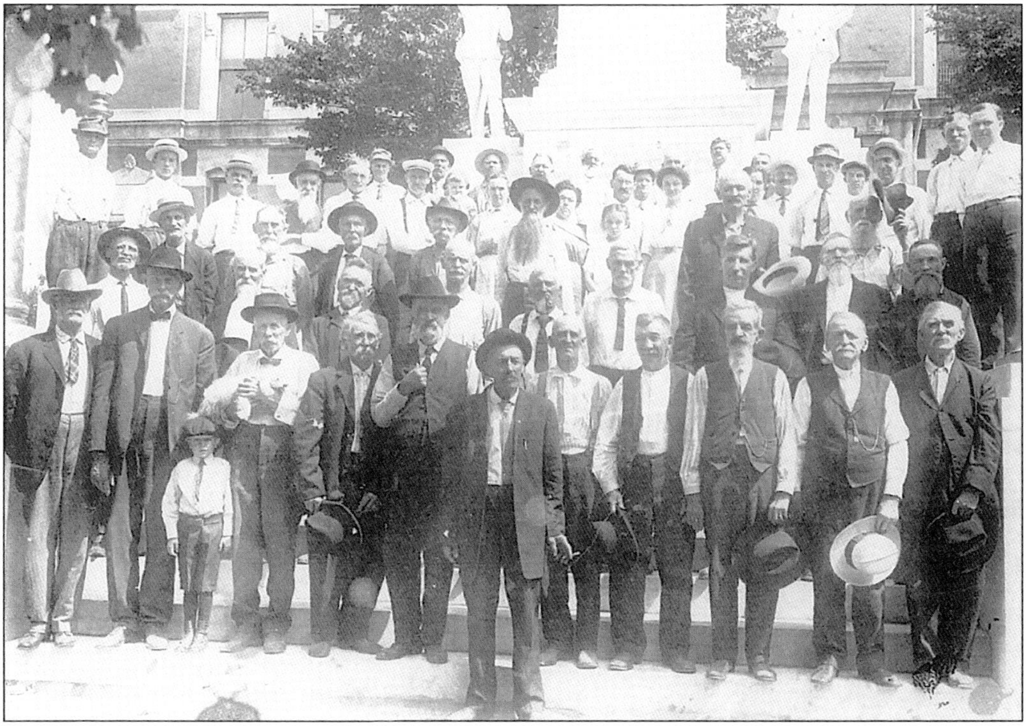

A group of what appears to be mostly Civil War veterans gathered on the steps of the Daviess County Courthouse in Washington in 1913 for the dedication of the Soldiers and Sailors Monument. (Courtesy of *Washington Times-Herald.*)

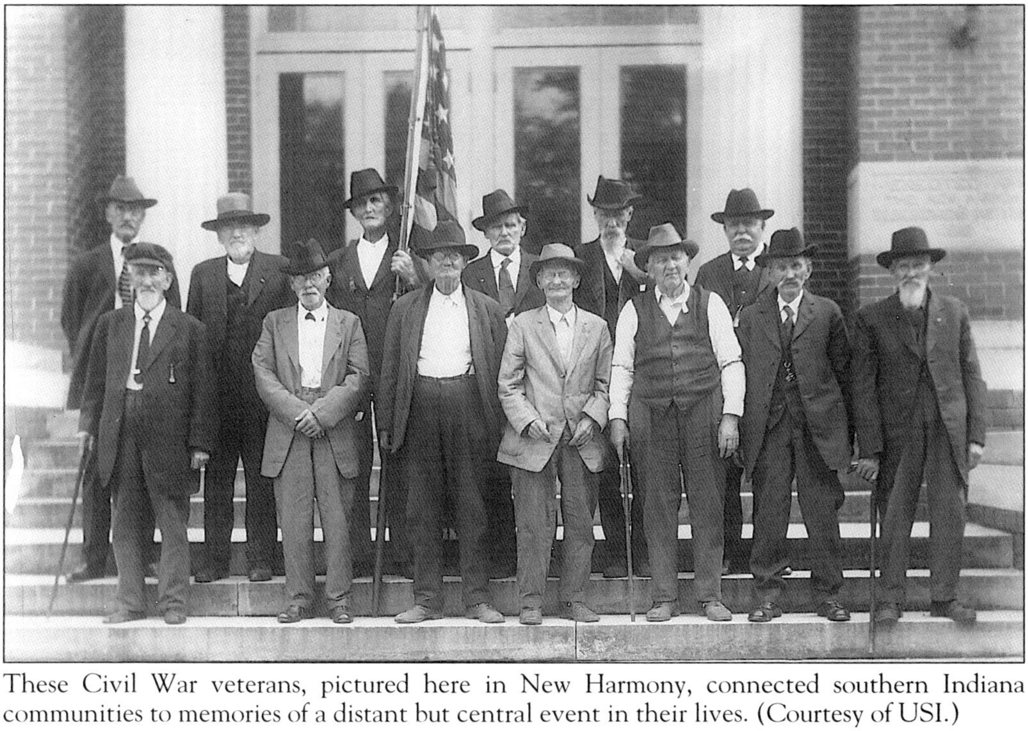

These Civil War veterans, pictured here in New Harmony, connected southern Indiana communities to memories of a distant but central event in their lives. (Courtesy of USI.)

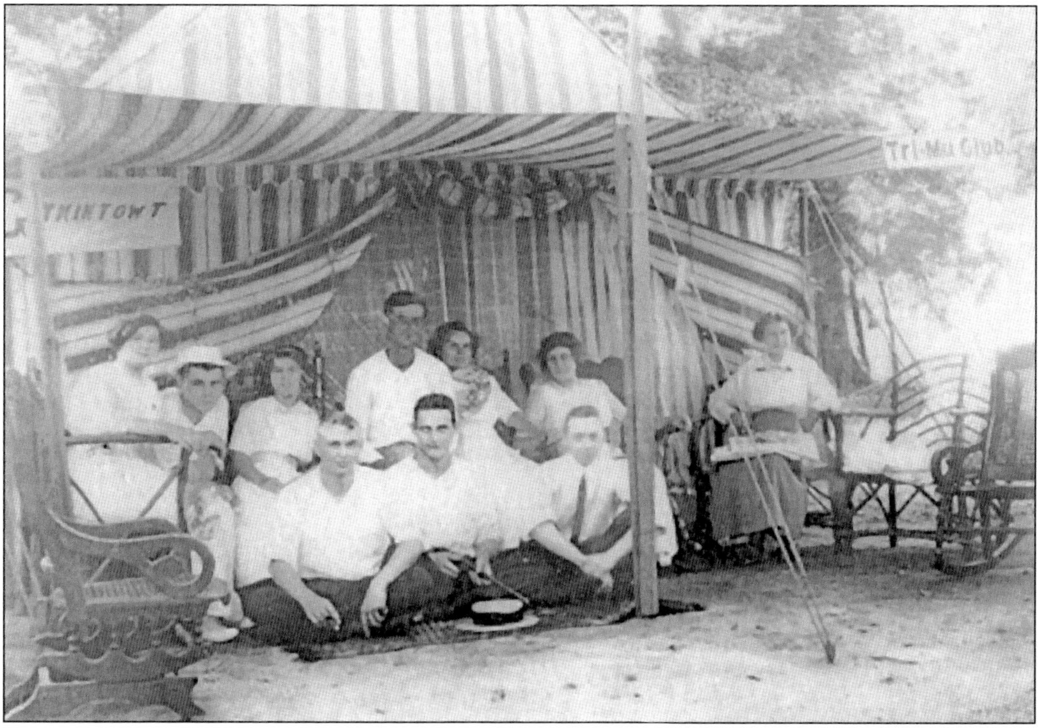

Chautauqua gatherings were commonplace in southern Indiana and the region in the teens. This is the Tri-Mu Club's tent at Glenwood Park in New Albany in 1913. Approximately ten members are in the photograph. (New Albany-Floyd County Public Library.)

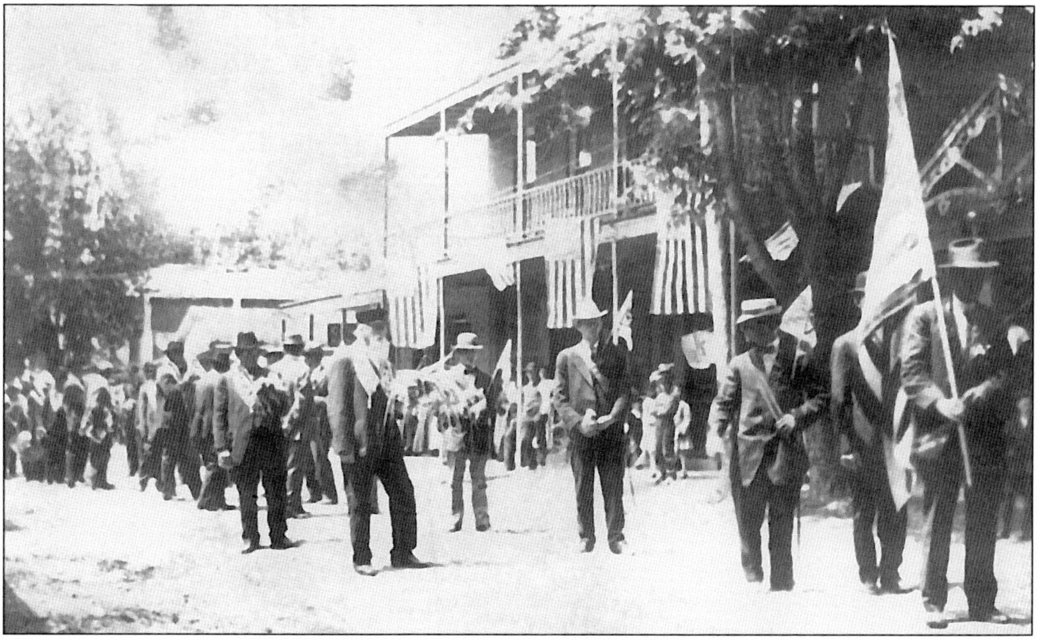

The Memorial Day parade in Leavenworth *c.* 1920 ended at Cedar Hill Cemetery. Lee Wiser, a Civil War veteran from nearby Dry Run, is the bearded man participating in the procession. (Courtesy of Elaine Stephenson.)

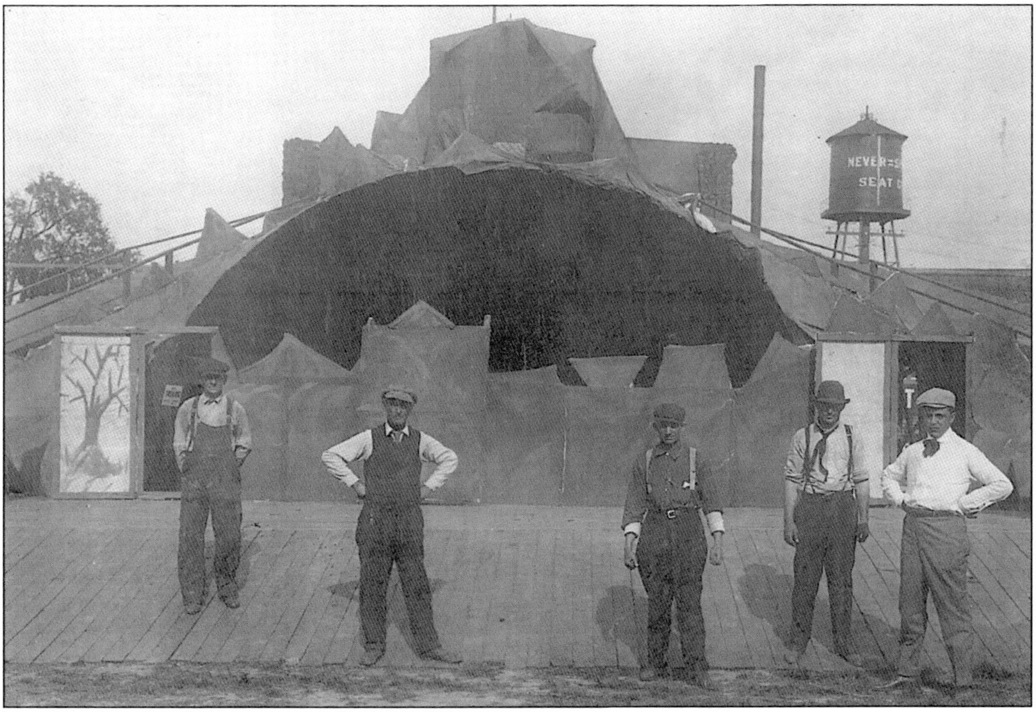

This was a set designed for use at Evansville's Bosse Field during the state centennial celebration of 1916. The mayor's secretary, Carl Dreisch, coordinated the event. On the back of the photo, the photographer, Karl Kae Knecht, labeled this a "terrible" amateur effort. (Courtesy of Willard Library.)

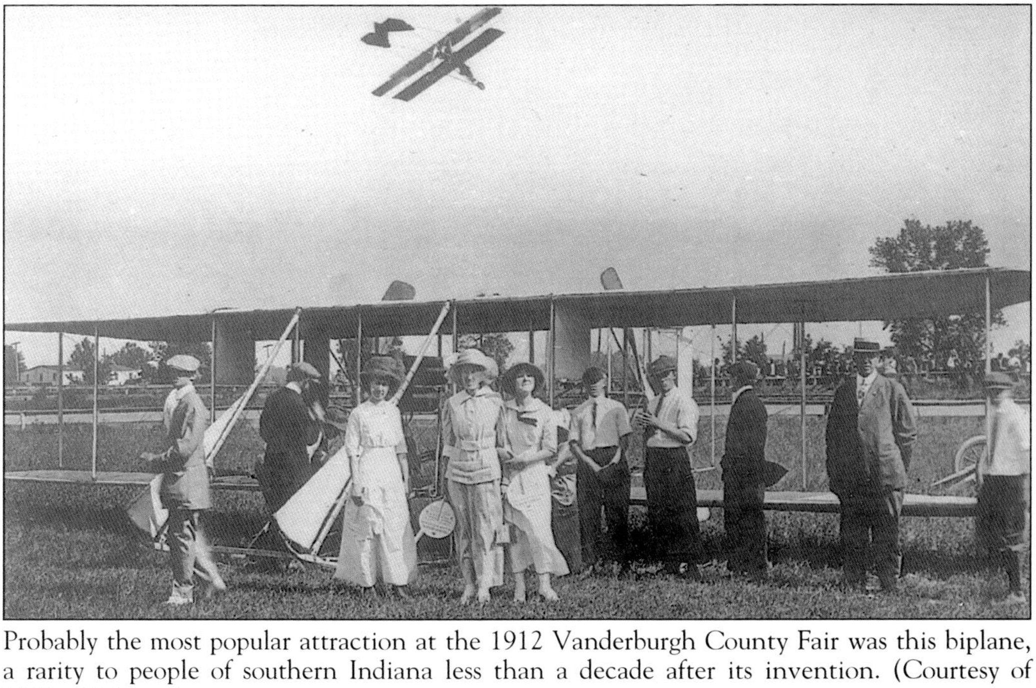

Probably the most popular attraction at the 1912 Vanderburgh County Fair was this biplane, a rarity to people of southern Indiana less than a decade after its invention. (Courtesy of Willard Library.)

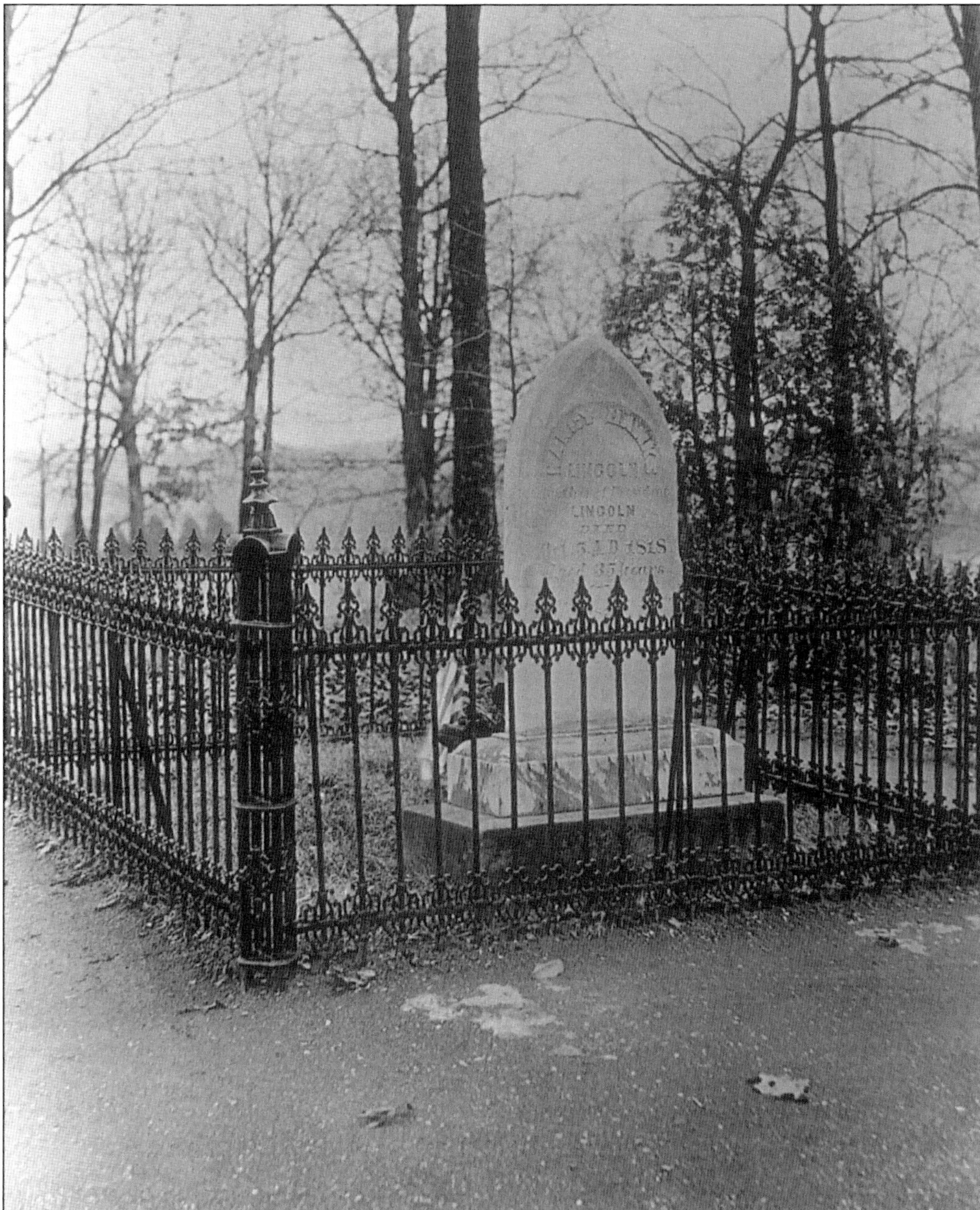

Shrines and memorials were essential elements in the civic culture of this time. This is the gravestone erected in honor of Nancy Hanks Lincoln, mother of the martyred president, that was preserved and protected by citizens of Spencer County and its environs. (Courtesy of Willard Library.)

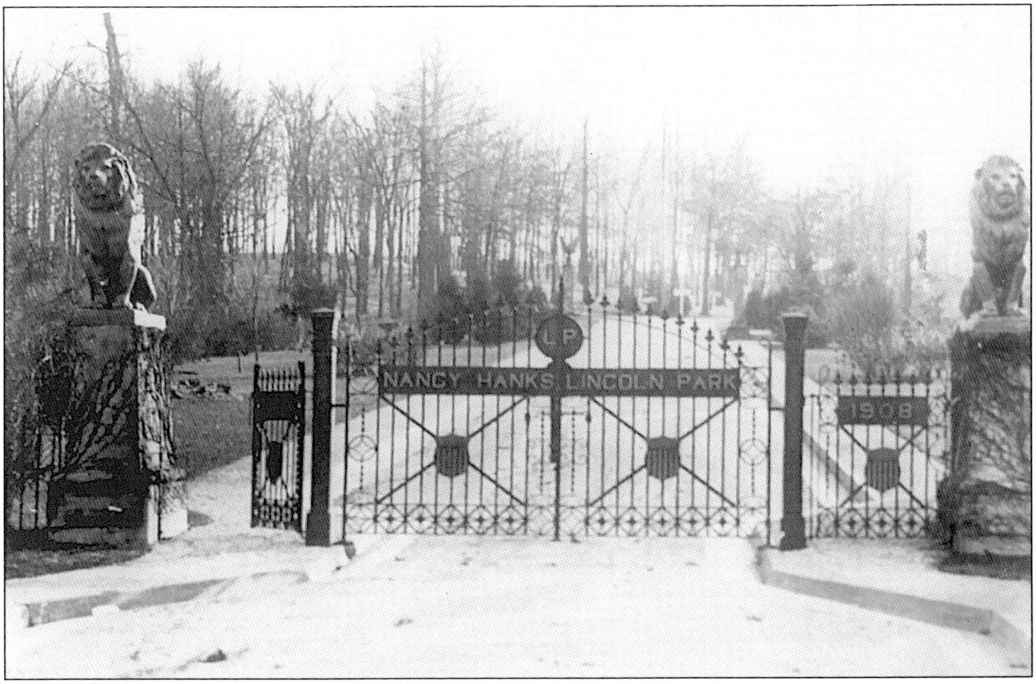

In 1908 citizens erected entry gates to the park near Gentryville and Lincoln City that memorialized the grave of Nancy Hanks Lincoln, the mother of the great Civil War president, who had died of the milk sickness a few years after coming to Indiana in the fall of 1816. The site later became a state memorial and, in 1962, a property of the National Park Service. (Courtesy of Lincoln Boyhood National Memorial.)

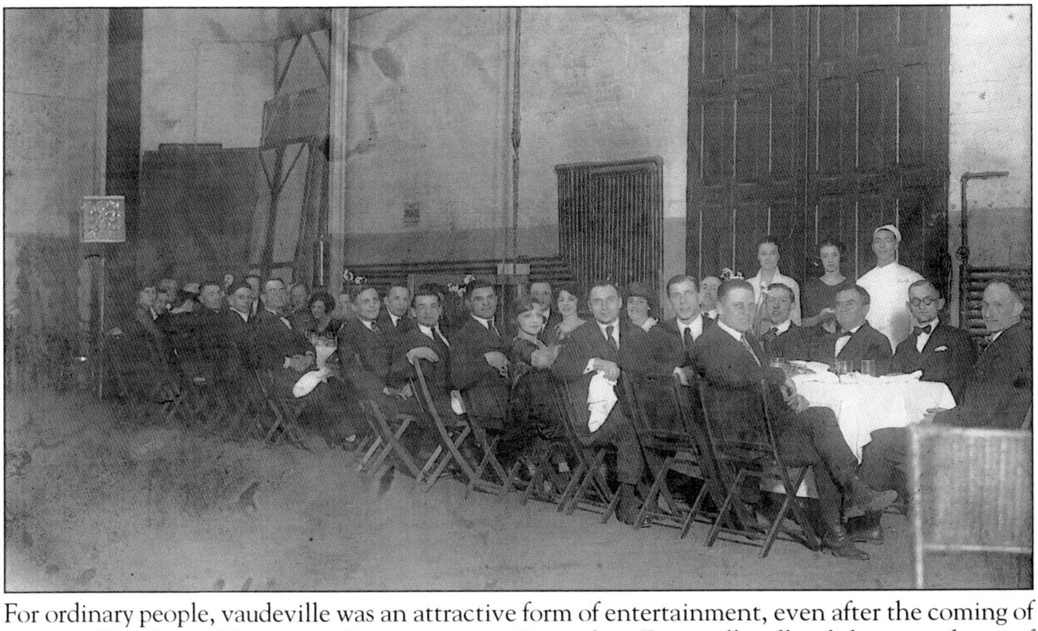

For ordinary people, vaudeville was an attractive form of entertainment, even after the coming of movies. The Grand Theater on Sycamore, near Second, in Evansville offered the most shows of any theater in the region. This is a photograph, taken sometime in the teens, of a stage Christmas party thrown by the manager for employees and vaudeville actors. (Courtesy of USI.)

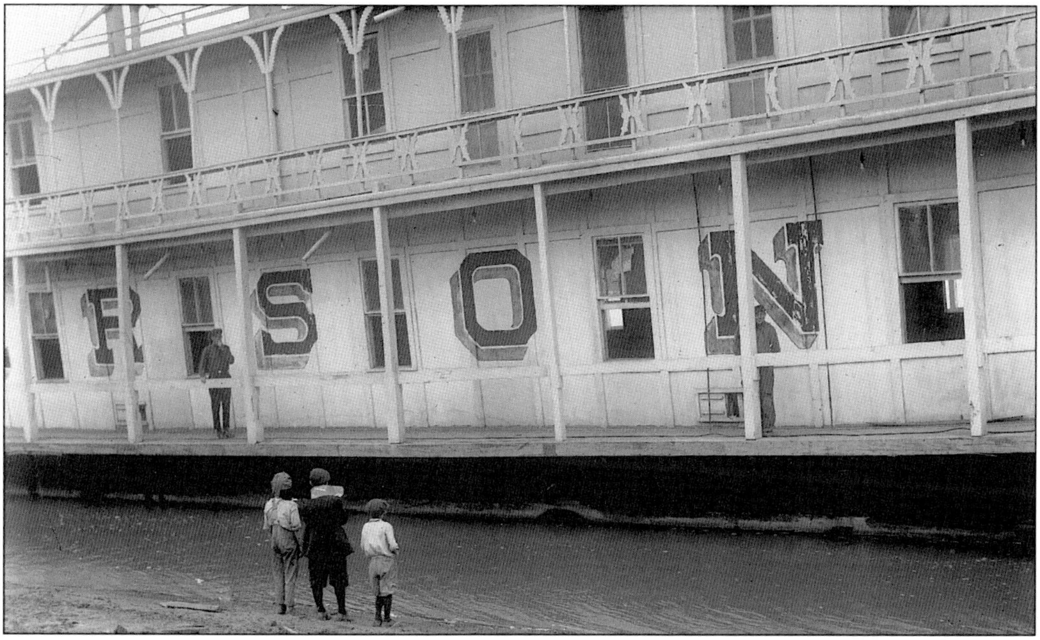

Boys standing on the bank of the Ohio at Evansville are clearly attracted to the charms of the Emerson Goldenrod Showboat. Such craft provided summertime entertainment to countless numbers of residents up and down the river. The flat-bottomed boat depended on the pushing of a steamboat for power. Like others, its theater featured balconies on the sides as well as the rear. (Courtesy of USI.)

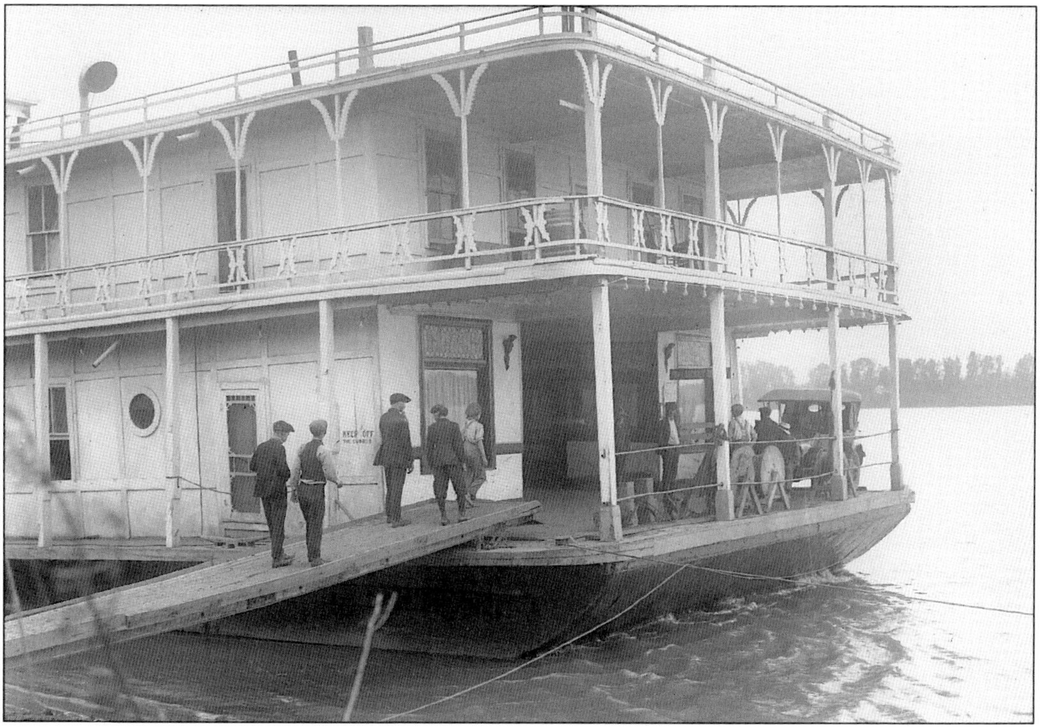

Apparently at least one of the boys was able to board. (Courtesy of USI.)

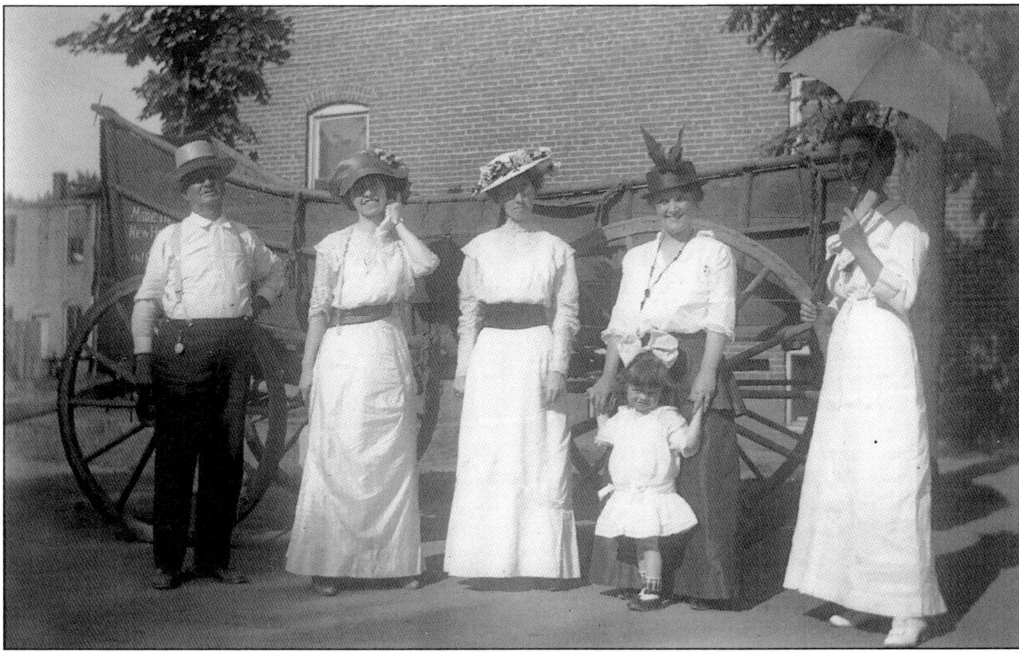

In the summer of 1914, the people of New Harmony celebrated their centennial. These are some of the participants in that special event. (Courtesy of USI.)

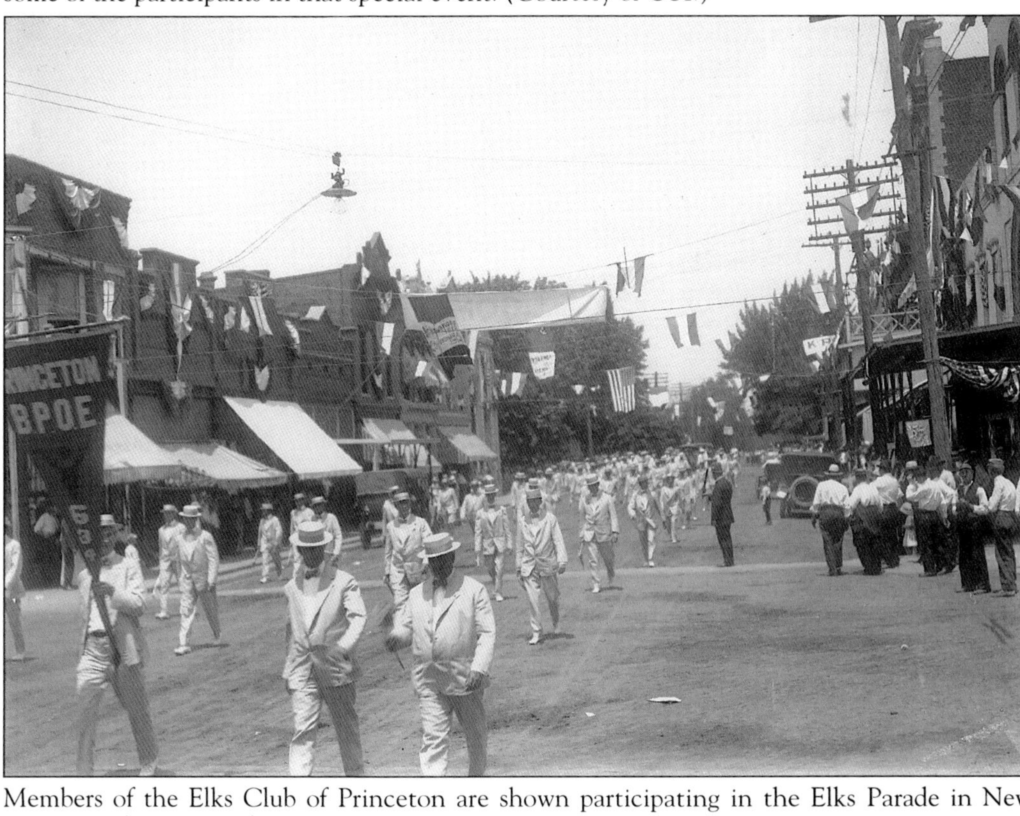

Members of the Elks Club of Princeton are shown participating in the Elks Parade in New Harmony. (Courtesy of USI.)

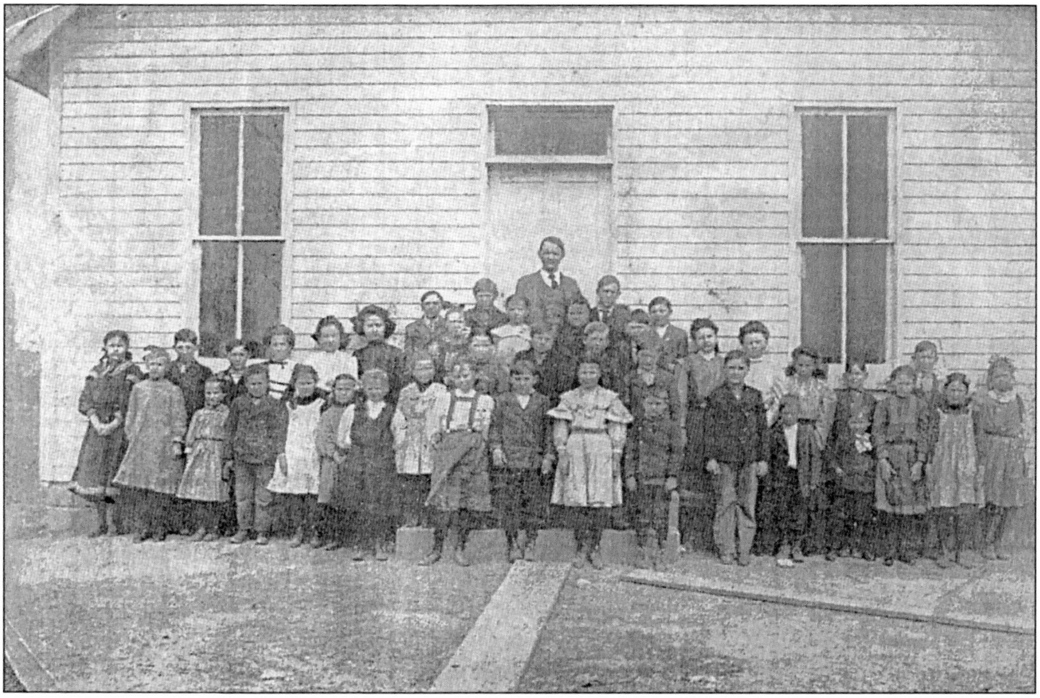

These are students at Middlefork School in 1910. The one-room schoolhouse was located in Jefferson County, Indiana, near the town of DuPont. (Courtesy of Jefferson County Historical Society.)

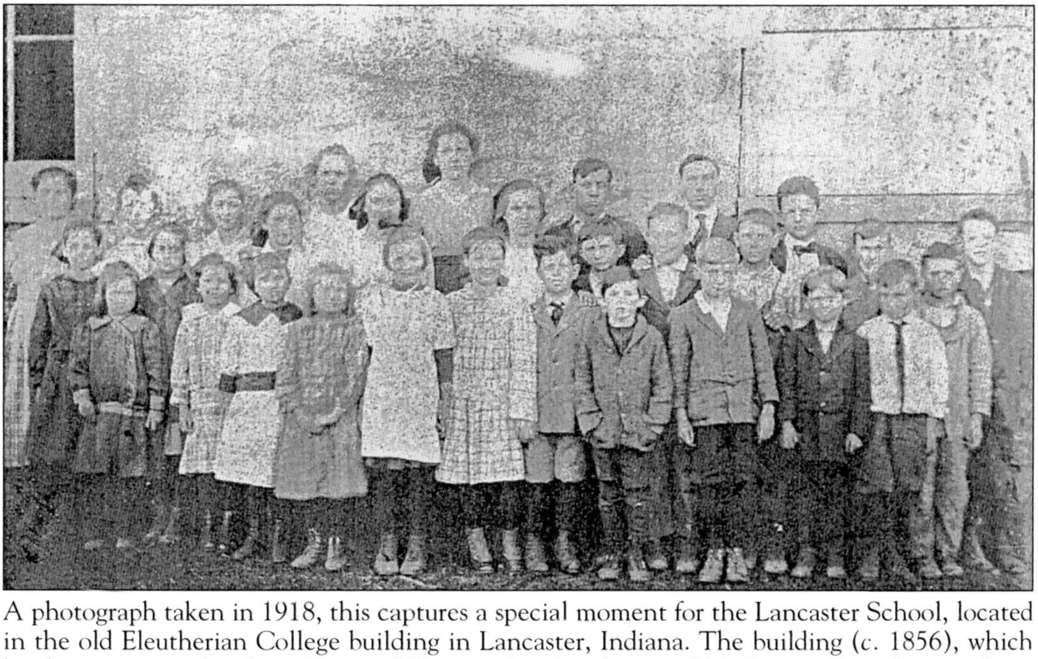

A photograph taken in 1918, this captures a special moment for the Lancaster School, located in the old Eleutherian College building in Lancaster, Indiana. The building (*c.* 1856), which has been preserved and is a National Historic Landmark, served black as well as white students in the antebellum era. (Courtesy of Jefferson County Historical Society.)

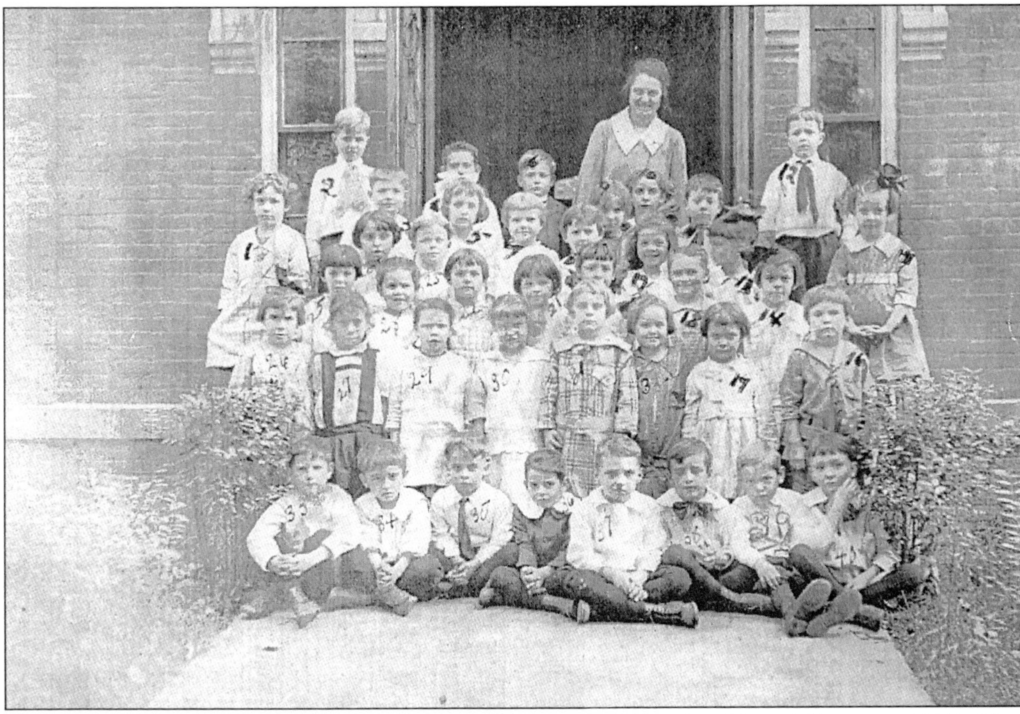

These are first-grade students at the East Market Street School in New Albany in 1917. (New Albany-Floyd County Public Library.)

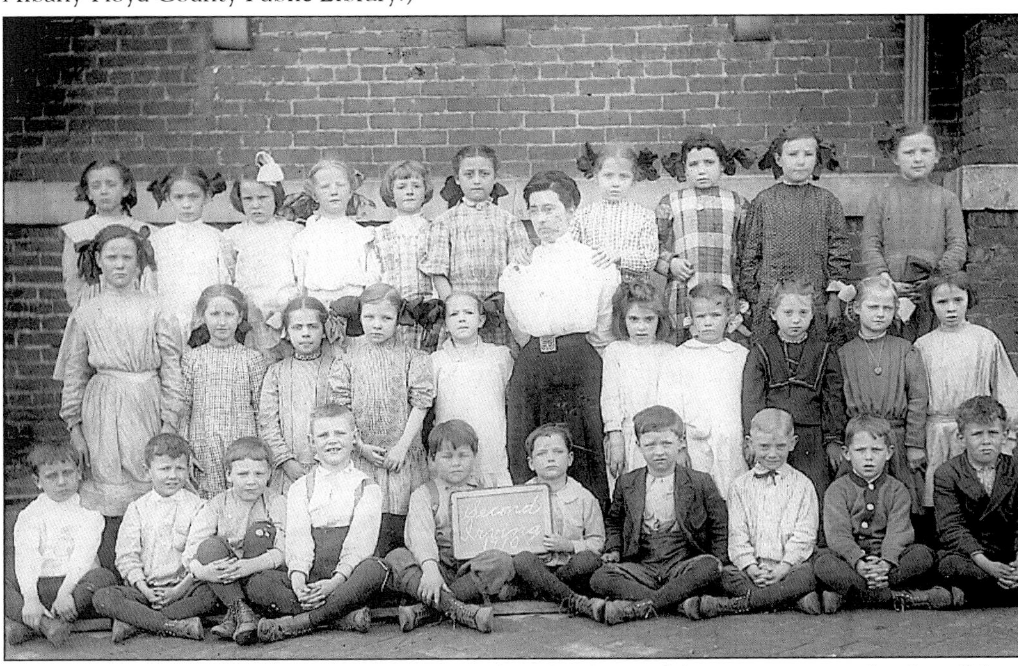

Students and their teacher were photographed in the front of their one-room school in Gibson County in 1910. Because of a state law passed in 1907 that closed schools with less than twelve students and transferred them to larger schools nearby, 3,900 one-room schools had closed by 1920. But 4,800 remained. (Courtesy of Willard Library.)

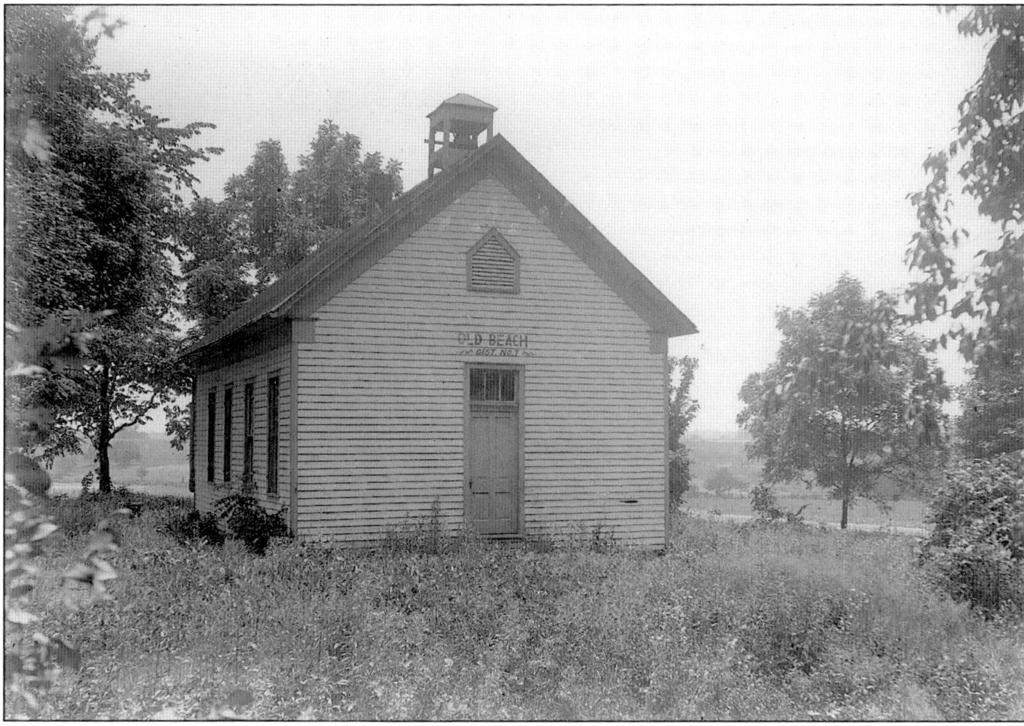

Beech School, in School District # 7 near New Harmony, was one of thousands of one-room rural schools in Indiana at the time that this photo was taken—before school consolidation. (Courtesy of USI.)

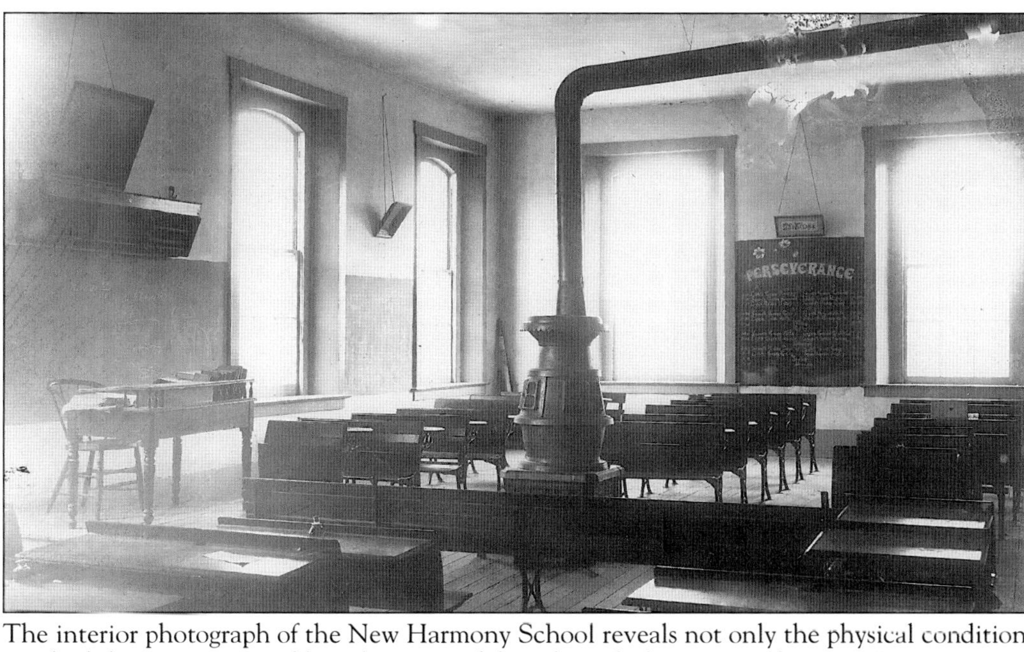

The interior photograph of the New Harmony School reveals not only the physical conditions in which learning occurred but also some of the ethos of education at the time. "Perseverance" is a virtue that the teacher clearly wants pupils to acquire. (Courtesy of USI.)

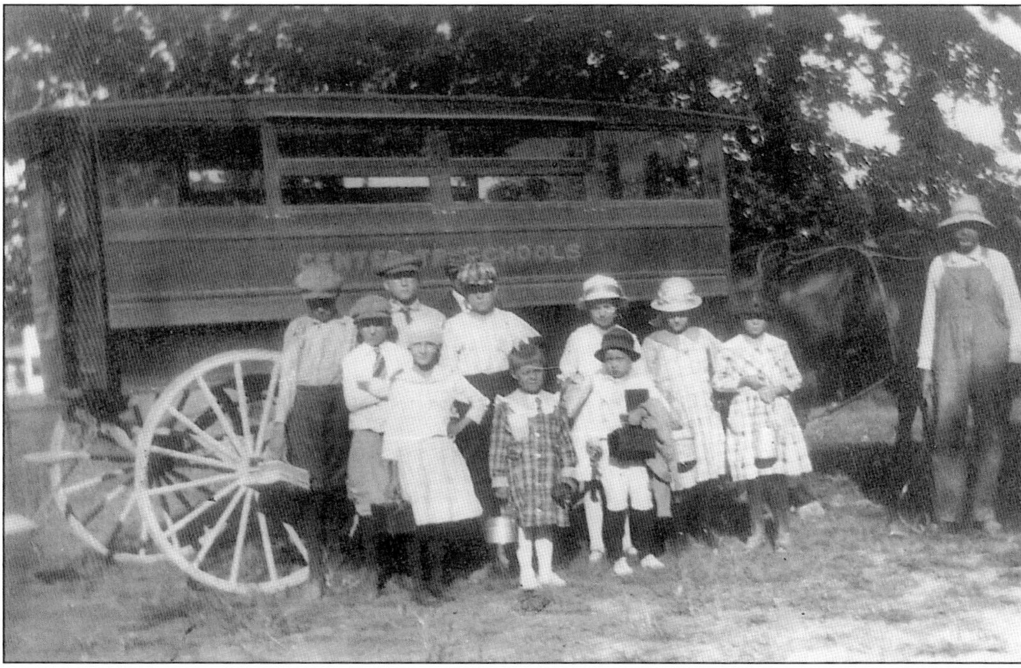

After consolidation, this school wagon transported the eleven students from the former Kansas Road School to McCutchanville School, on the north side of Vanderburgh County. This photo was taken in 1919. (Courtesy of Willard Library.)

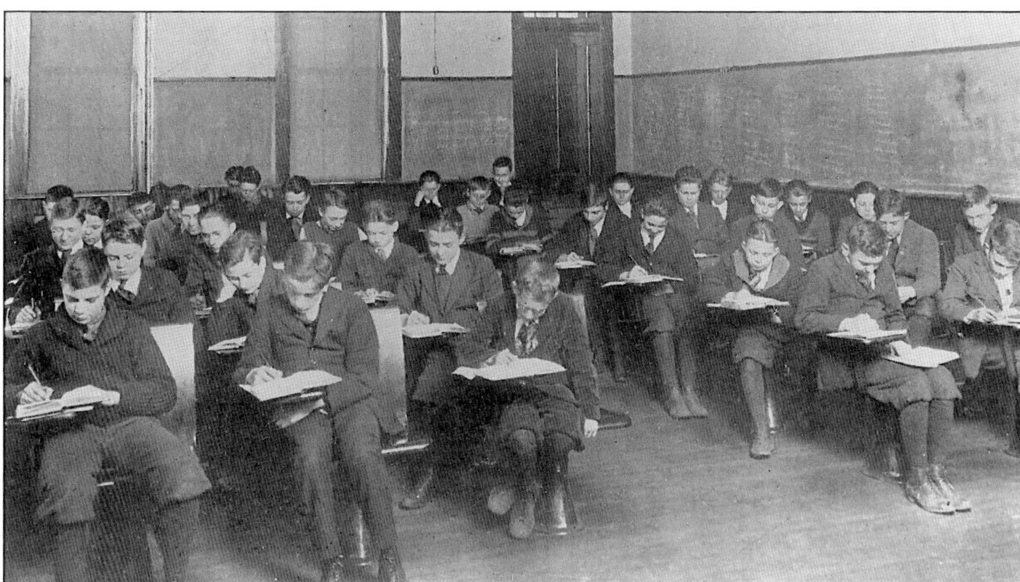

Latin students in the Holy Trinity Parish School in Evansville are pictured in 1920. The parish, established in the late 1840s with the financial assistance of industrialist and banker John A. Reitz, was located on the border between the original Evansville plat and that of Lamasco, which Evansville annexed in 1857. German-American workers were the chief residents of the region. (Courtesy of USI.)

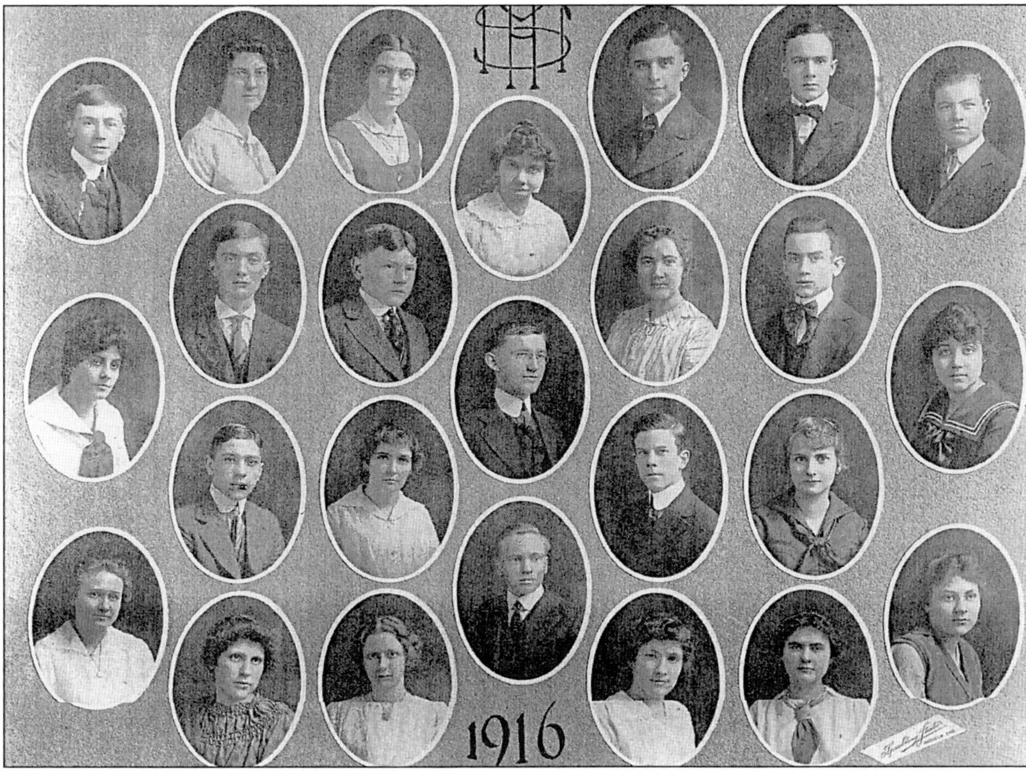

This is the photograph of Madison High School class of 1916. At far left, middle photo, is Irene Dunne, who became a famous Hollywood film star in the 1930s and 40s. Her high school yearbook called her "divinely tall and most divinely fair." (Courtesy of Jefferson County Historical Society.)

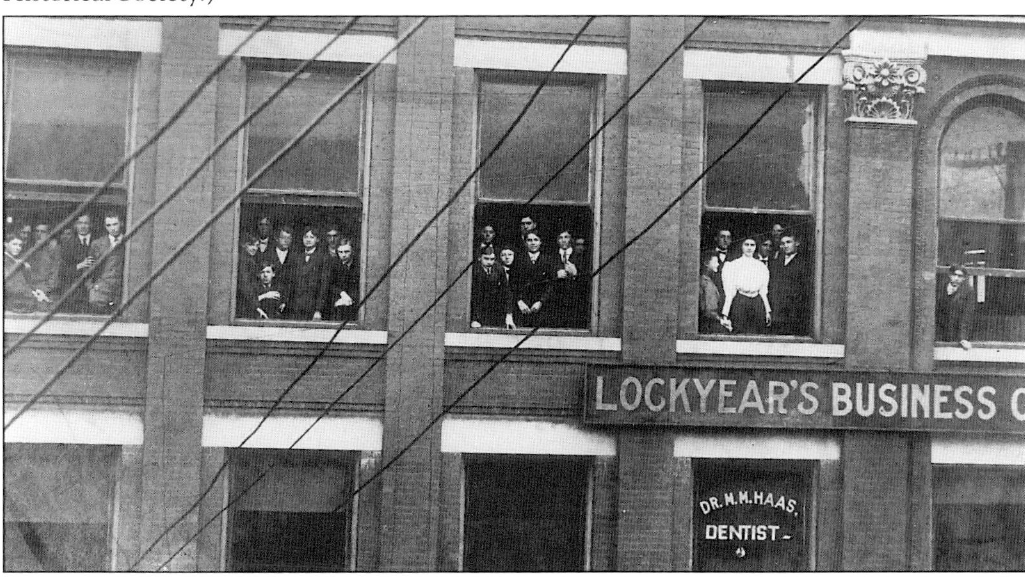

Students at Lockyear's Business College in downtown Evansville were photographed looking out of the school's windows in 1910. Most were young men—an indication that much of the clerical and managerial work in the region remained a man's enterprise. (courtesy of USI.)

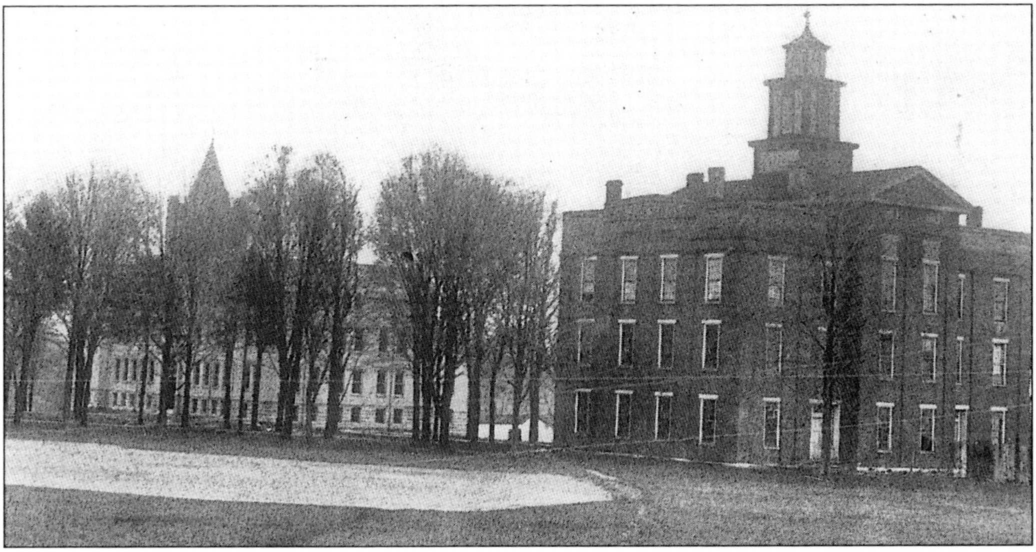

Moore's Hill College, founded in 1854, was located on the western edge of Dearborn County, near Lawrenceburg, until Mayor Benjamin Bosse led a successful campaign to move the Methodist school to Evansville for the 1919–1920 year. It became Evansville College. (Courtesy of Willard Library.)

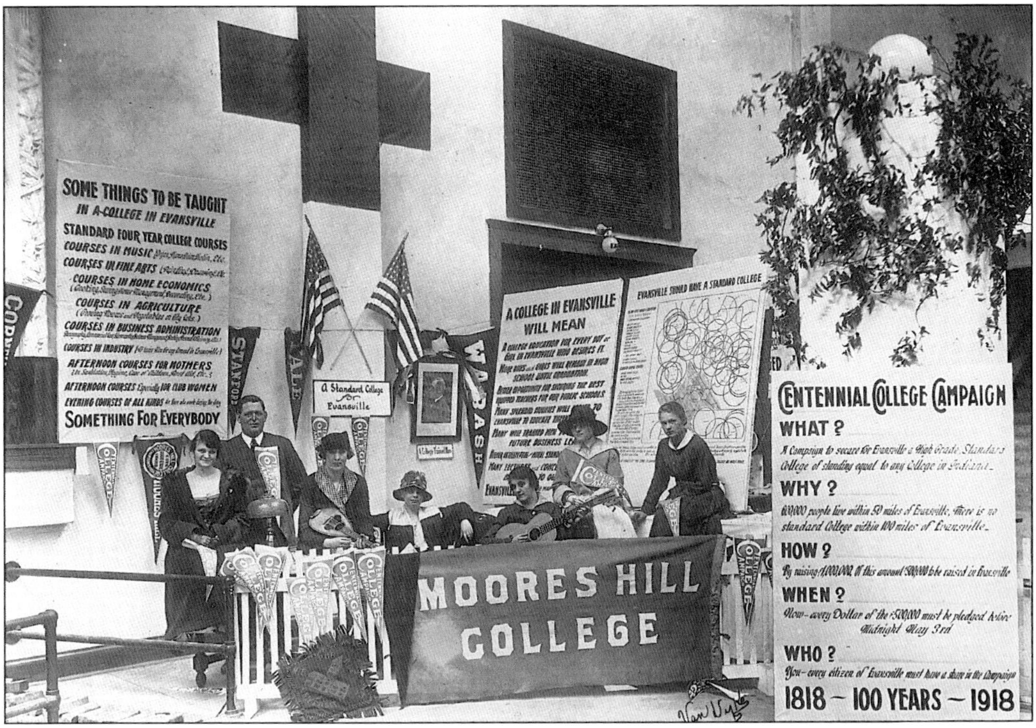

During the Great War, Mayor Bosse and other Evansville civic leaders campaigned for a college. At the time, there were only three colleges in southern Indiana. Shown here is part of a 1918 effort to raise funds to bring Moore's Hill College, a struggling Methodist institution in southeast Indiana, to Evansville. In 1919 Evansville College opened its doors. A new campus was established on Lincoln Avenue in 1922. (Courtesy of University of Evansville.)

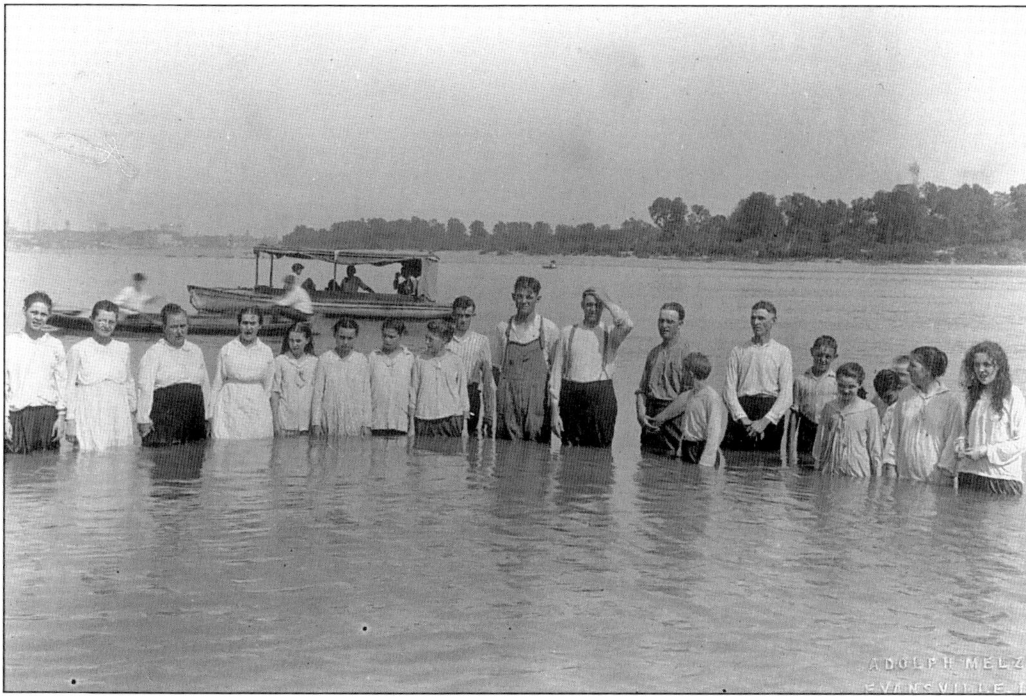

Adult baptism in the Ohio River (and its tributaries) was a fairly common practice in this era. This one occurred near Evansville. (Courtesy of Willard Library.)

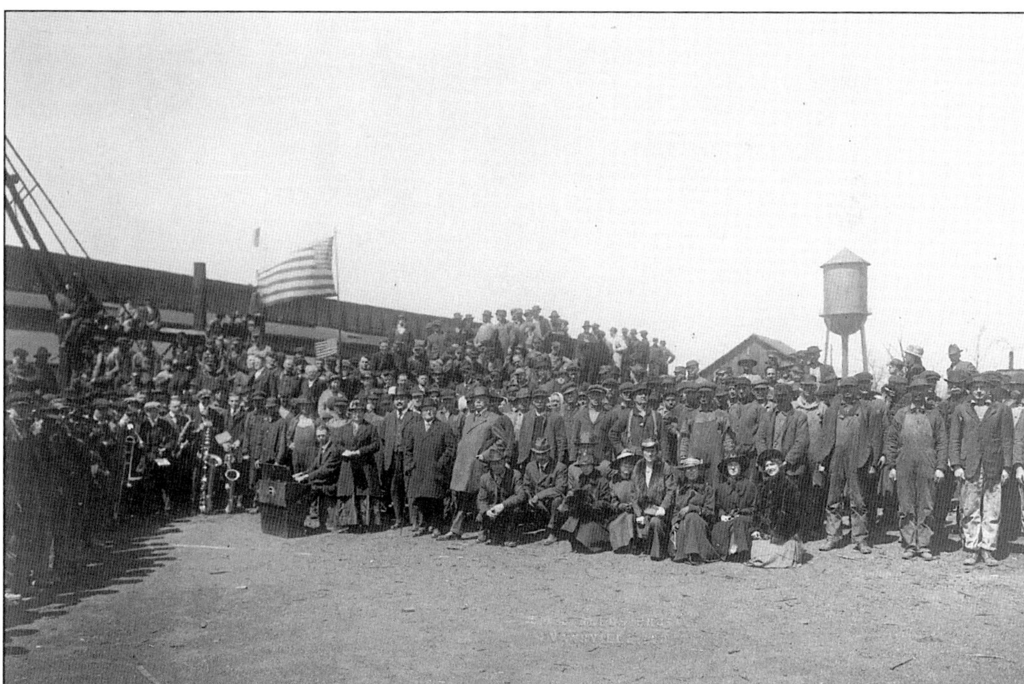

L & N Railroad workers participated in noontime evangelistic meetings in the spring of 1917 in Evansville. (Courtesy of USI.)

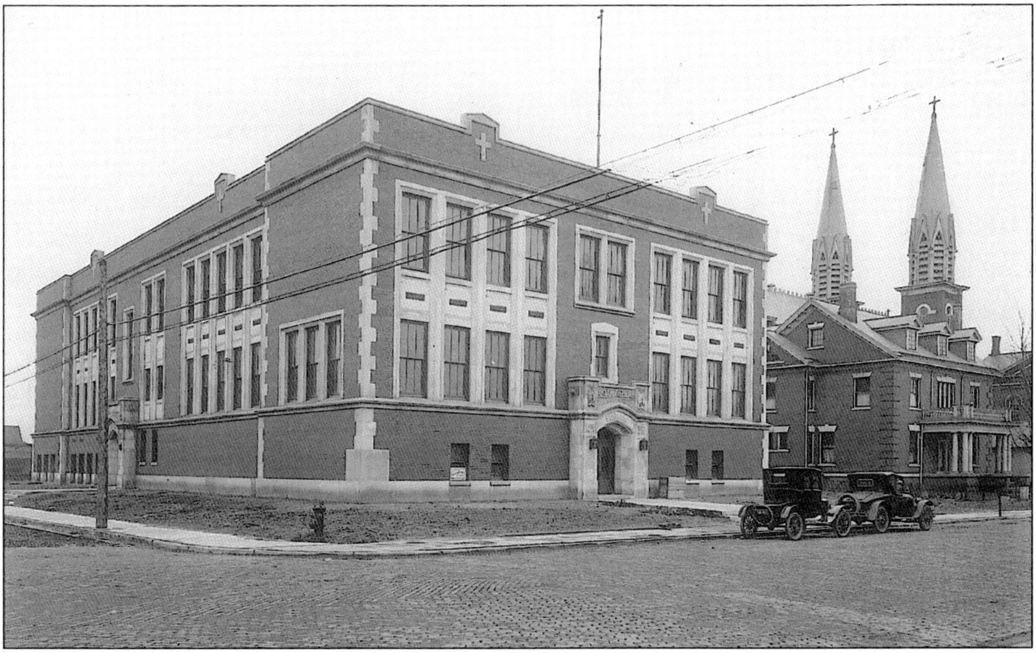

St. Boniface Church, erected in the early 1880s by German Catholic industrialists and workers on Evansville's west side, is shown here in the distance in 1910. In the foreground is its new parochial school. (Courtesy of Willard Library.)

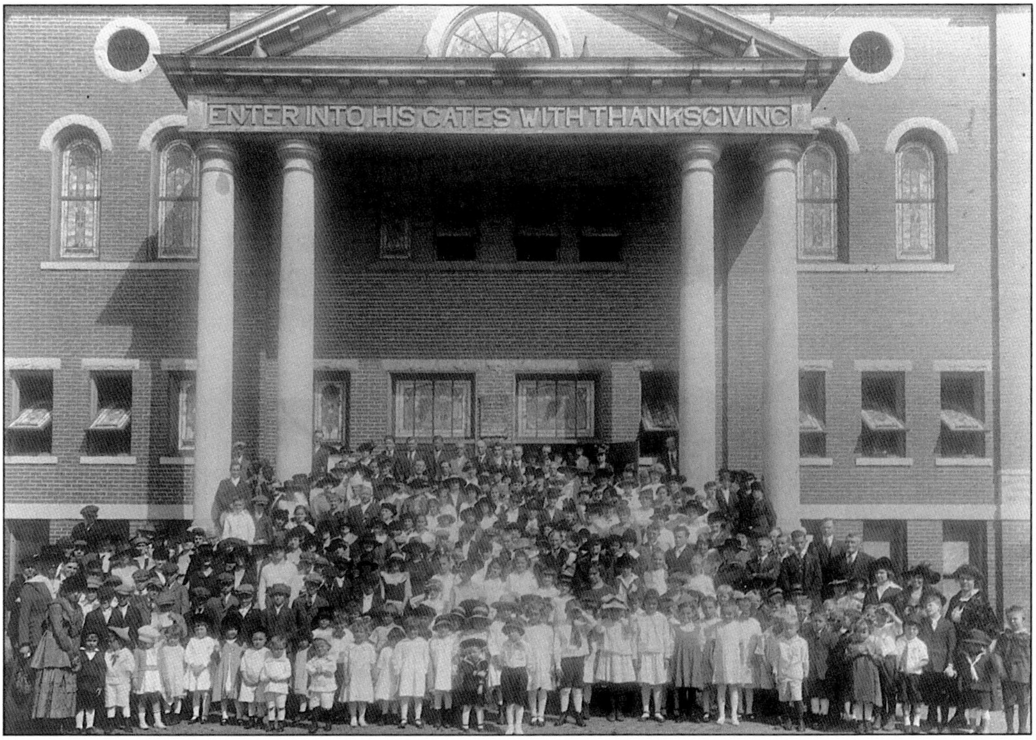

Members of the Bethany Christian Church were photographed in front of their new edifice on Columbia Street, Evansville, in 1914. (Courtesy of USI.)

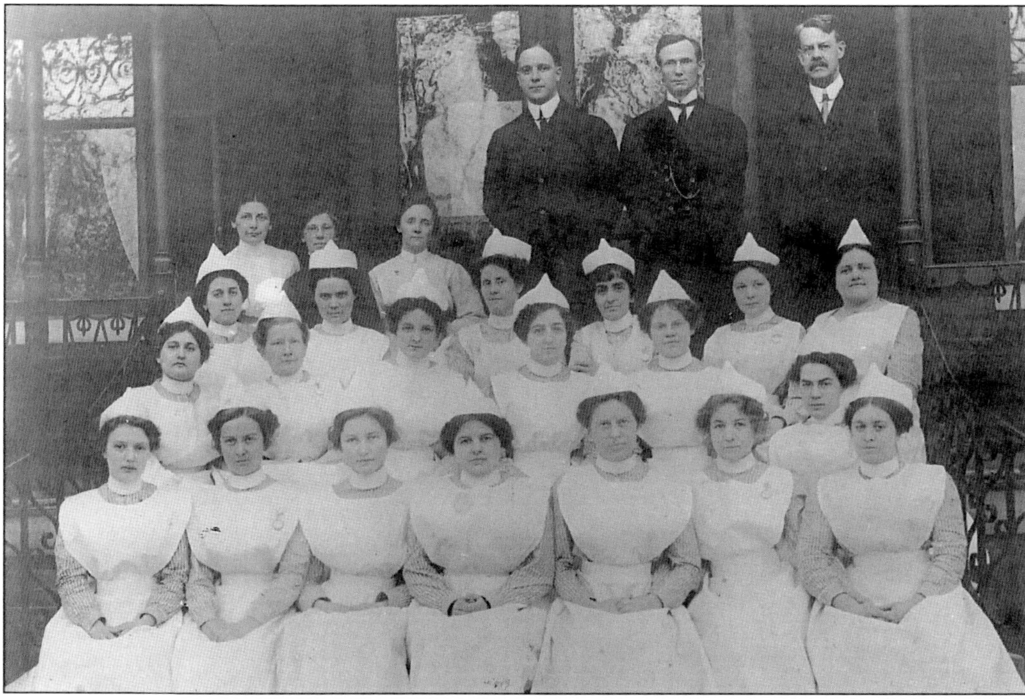

Shown here is Dr. Edwin Walker, his staff, and nursing students. Walker established a sanitarium in 1894 that was enlarged in 1914 and known as Walker Hospital. Later it was known as the Welborn-Walker, the Welborn, and after 1944 as Welborn Baptist. Nurses' training, begun here in 1894, helped to signify the emergence of medical professionalism. Evansville's other two hospitals also trained nurses. (Courtesy of USI.)

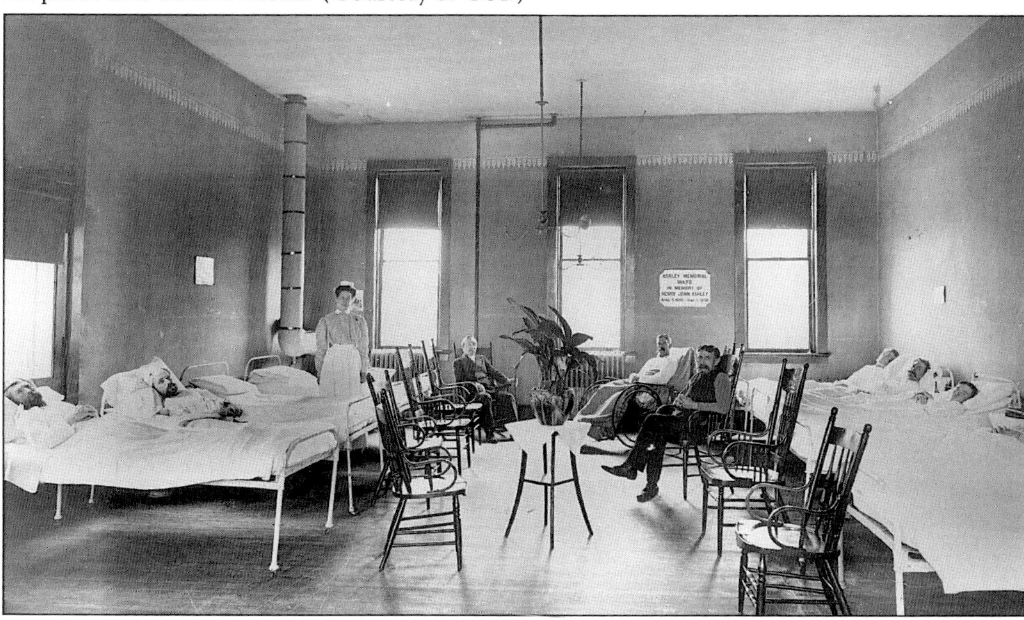

When this was taken in 1910, there were three hospitals in Evansville. This is the Ashley Memorial Ward at Deaconess Hospital. Hospital care was extremely rare in this era. (Courtesy of Deaconess Hospital.)

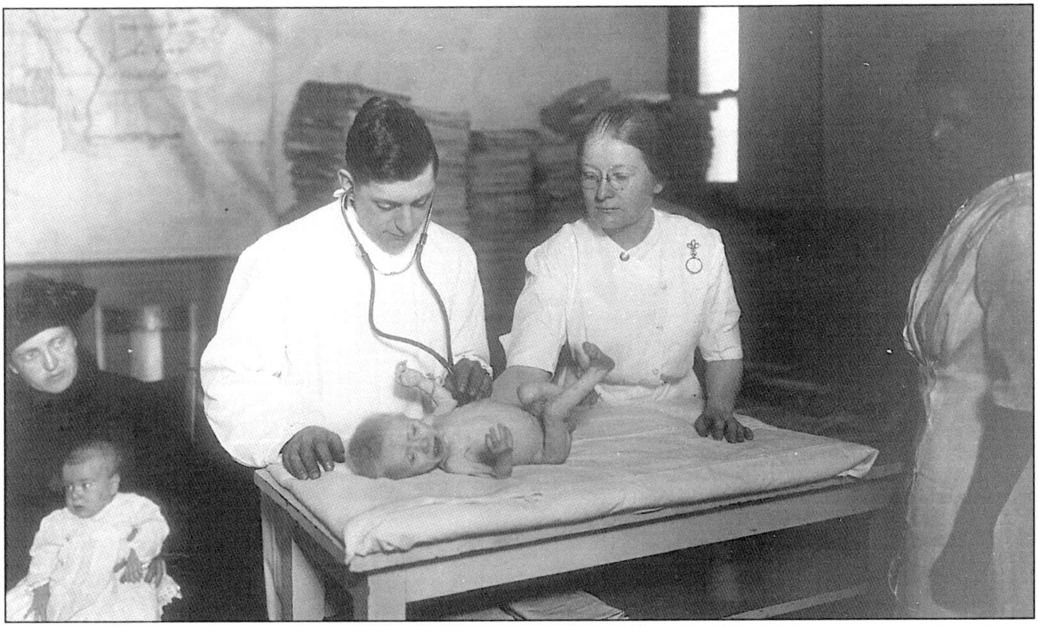

The Public Health Nursing Association, formed in Evansville in 1888, dealt with several realities of urban life—disease, malnutrition, and inadequate health care among the less fortunate. Aside from providing home health care for workers' families, the PHNA opened a clinic, shown here in 1915, that dispensed information and provided basic health care, especially for babies. (Courtesy of USI.)

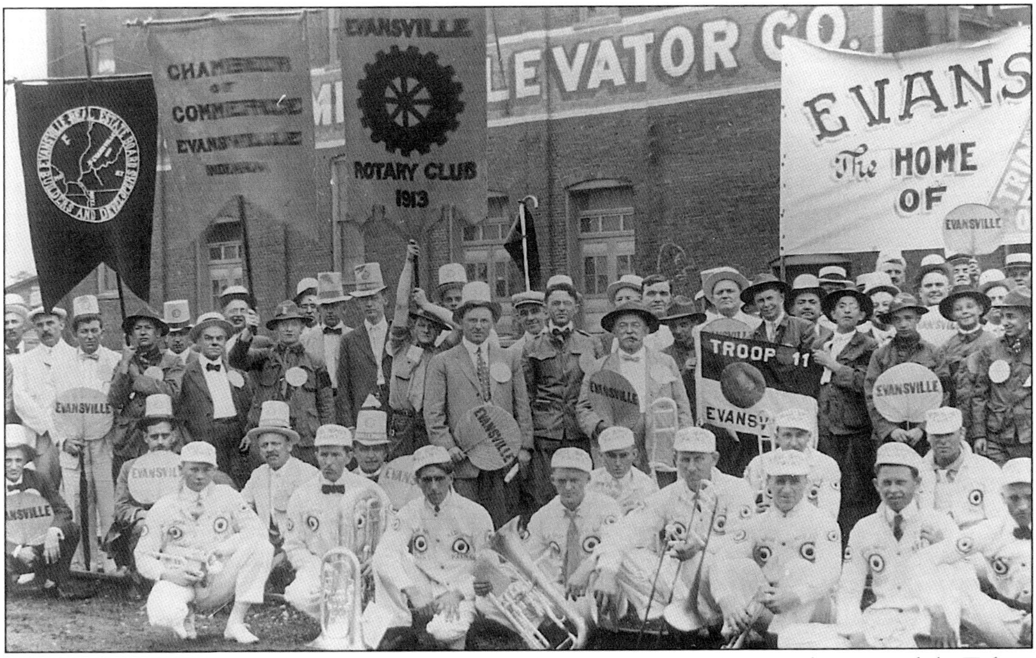

One of the newer forms of social organization in larger communities was the civic club. Taken in Carmi, Illinois, this photograph is part of a larger one documenting the visit of members of Evansville's Rotary Club (founded in 1914) and other community groups seeking to promote Evansville-made products in the Tri-State. (Courtesy of USI.)

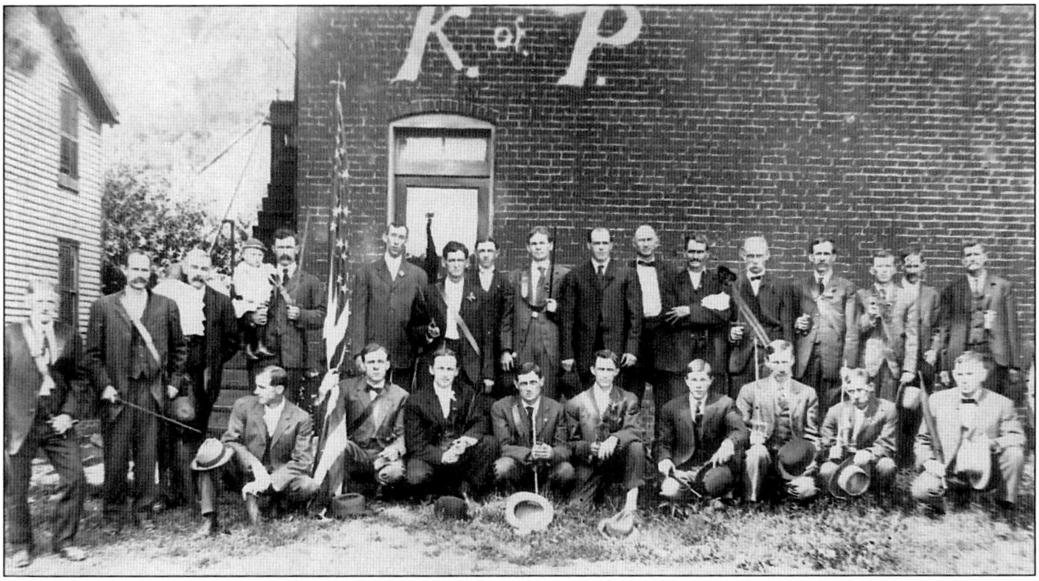

As shown by the number of men in the photo, the Knights of Pythias was an important civic organization in Leavenworth, a community of about 650 residents. The photo was taken in 1910. (Courtesy of Elaine Stephenson.)

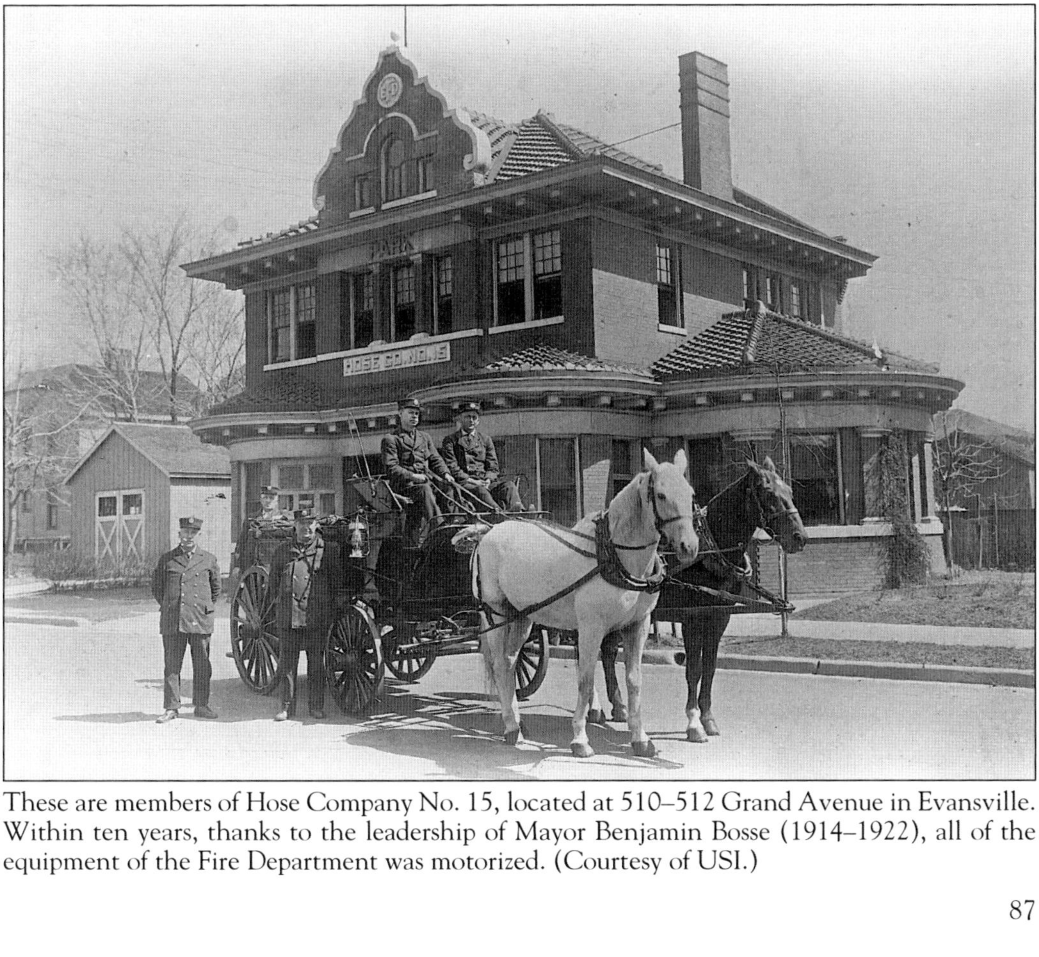

These are members of Hose Company No. 15, located at 510–512 Grand Avenue in Evansville. Within ten years, thanks to the leadership of Mayor Benjamin Bosse (1914–1922), all of the equipment of the Fire Department was motorized. (Courtesy of USI.)

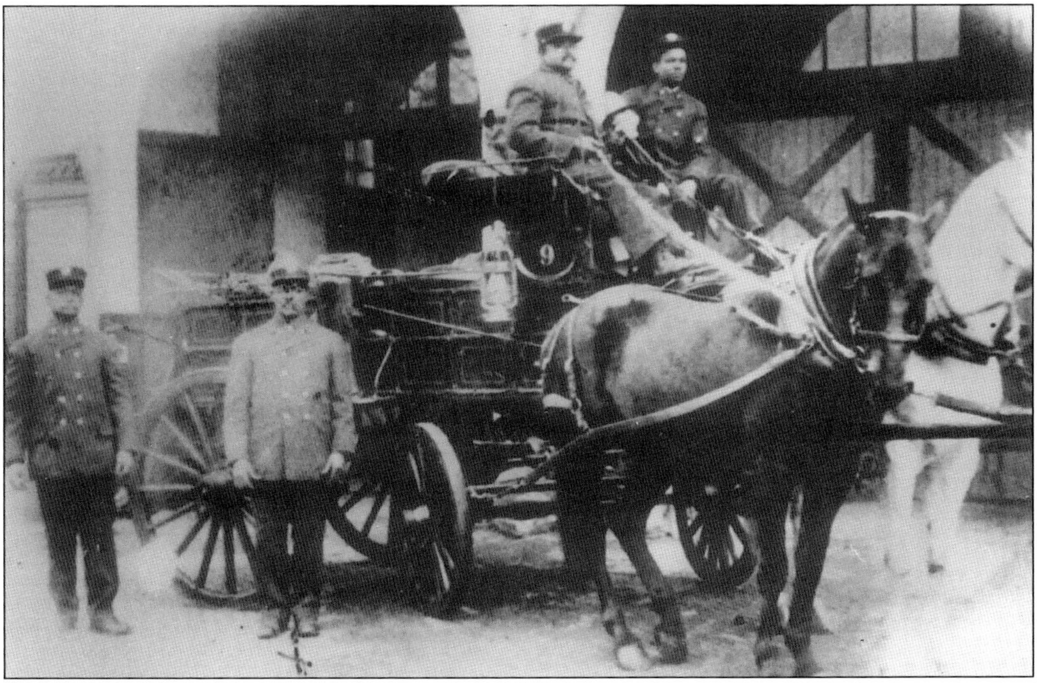

These are members of all-black Hose House No. 9 in Evansville *c.* 1910. Located in Baptisttown, the center of black community life, it was the only company in which African Americans could serve. Appointment to the fire department, like the police department, was a highly partisan process, and members held positions of high esteem in the black community. (Courtesy of USI.)

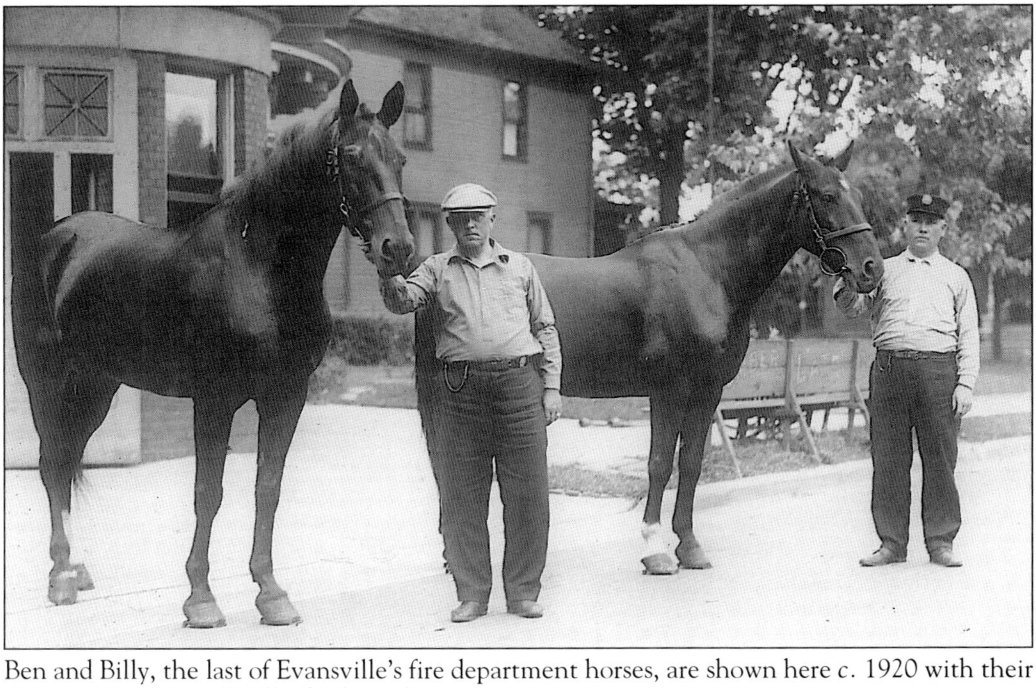

Ben and Billy, the last of Evansville's fire department horses, are shown here *c.* 1920 with their drivers. (Courtesy of Willard Library.)

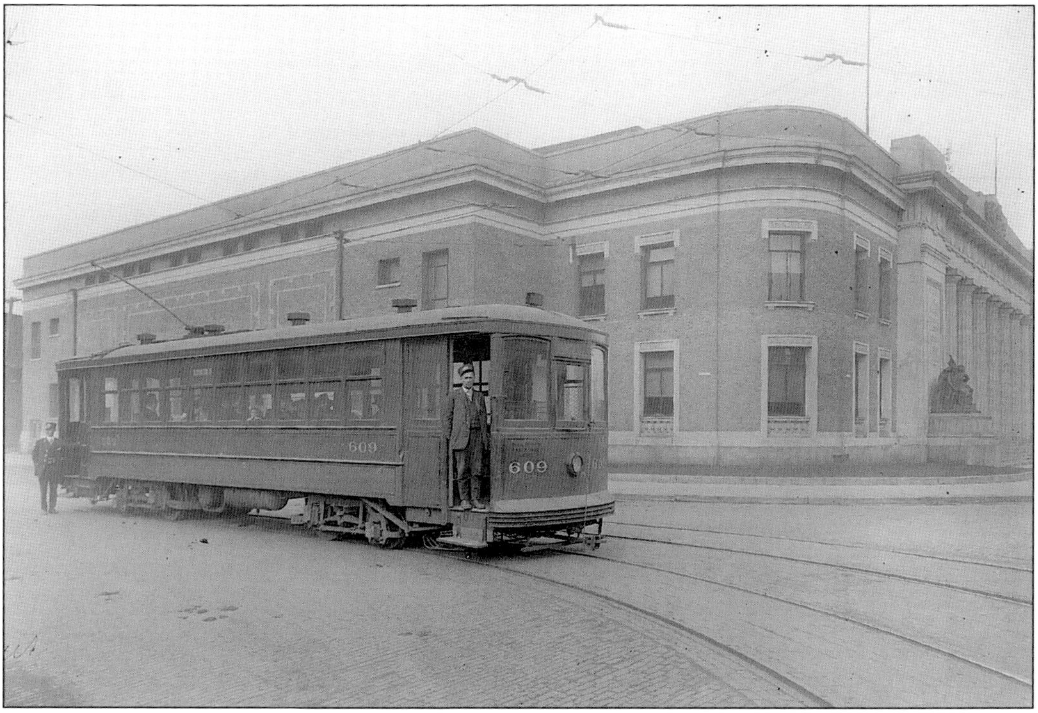

A streetcar and its operator were photographed in front of Evansville's Soldiers and Sailors' Memorial Coliseum shortly after its erection in 1916. The coliseum would be the city's chief public meeting and exhibition space until the 1960s. It is being restored and preserved through the efforts of veterans' groups. (Courtesy of Willard Library.)

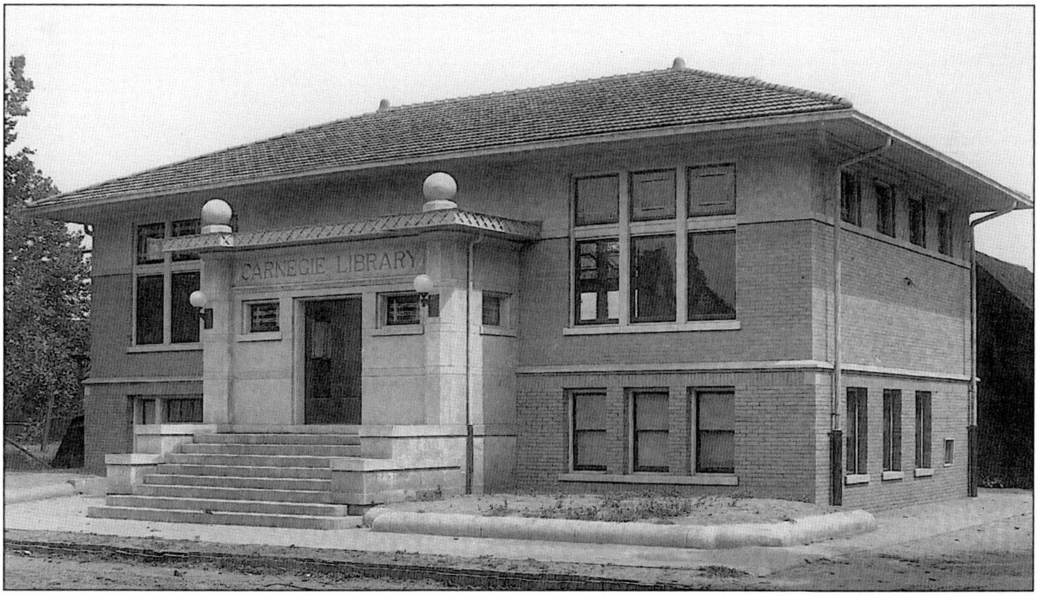

The Evansville Public Library was created, like systems in most southern Indiana towns, with a promise of buildings from Andrew Carnegie. Buildings on West Franklin Street and in Bayard Park followed, as did a segregated branch for African Americans on Cherry Street, shown here in 1912, shortly after the system opened. (Courtesy of Willard Library.)

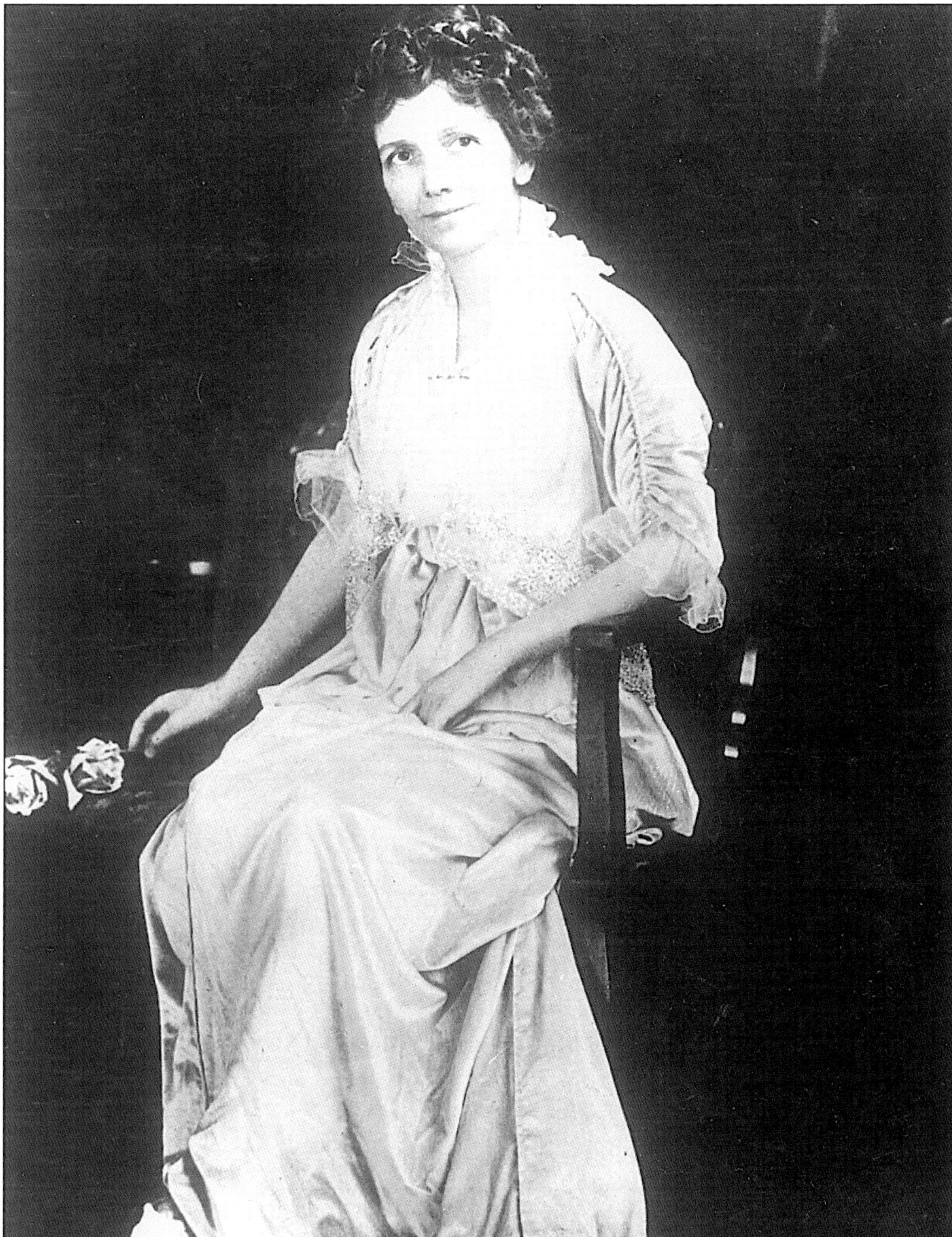

Albion Fellows Bacon (1865–1933) was in this time the most prominent white woman in Evansville's civic affairs. Daughter of the pastor of Trinity Methodist Episcopal Church, and wife of merchant Hilary E. Bacon, she spearheaded a number of local and state-wide philanthropic efforts and social improvement projects. She was perhaps most noted for leading the successful initiative to enact the state's first tenement housing law in 1911. (Courtesy of USI.)

Albion Fellows Bacon's counterpart among Evansville's blacks was Sallie Wyatt Stewart, longtime educator and civic leader. Among others, she formed the Day Nursery Association, the City Federation of Colored Women's Clubs, and the "colored auxiliary" of the county tuberculosis association. She helped to found the Evansville branch of the National Association for the Advancement of Colored People. She would head the National Association of Colored Women's Clubs in the 1930s. (Courtesy of USI.)

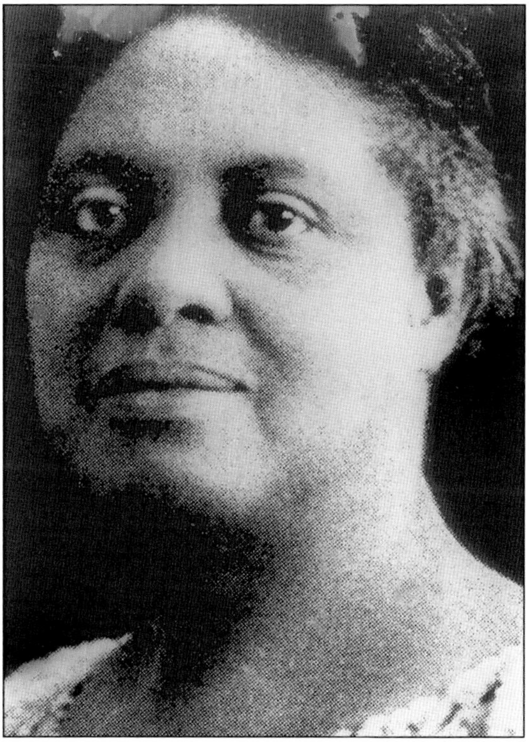

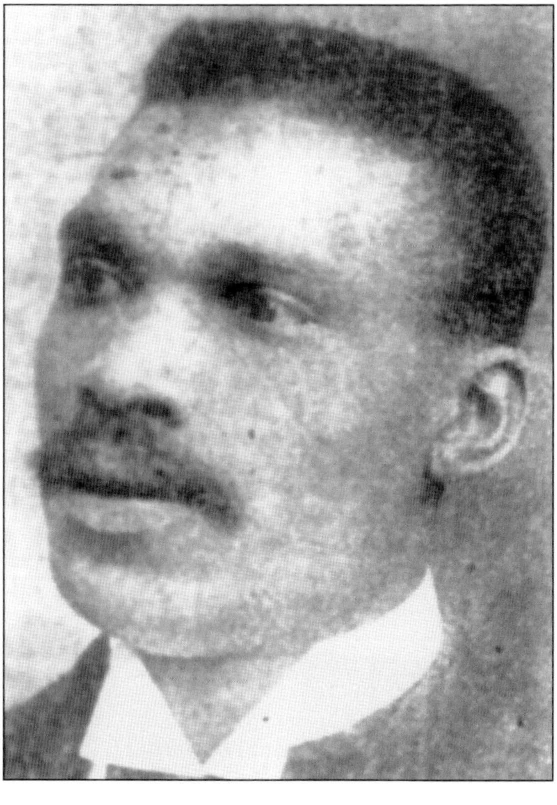

S. S. Dupee, Evansville physician between 1899 and his premature death in 1913, was, like his business and professional counterparts in southern Indiana cities and towns, also heavily involved in fraternal and benevolent societies, church work, and politics. A graduate of Fisk University and the Freedmen's Hospital at Howard University, he was also, among other things, an officer of the Indiana Knights of Tabor and author of the "colored column" for the Republican *Evansville Journal-News*. (Courtesy of USI.)

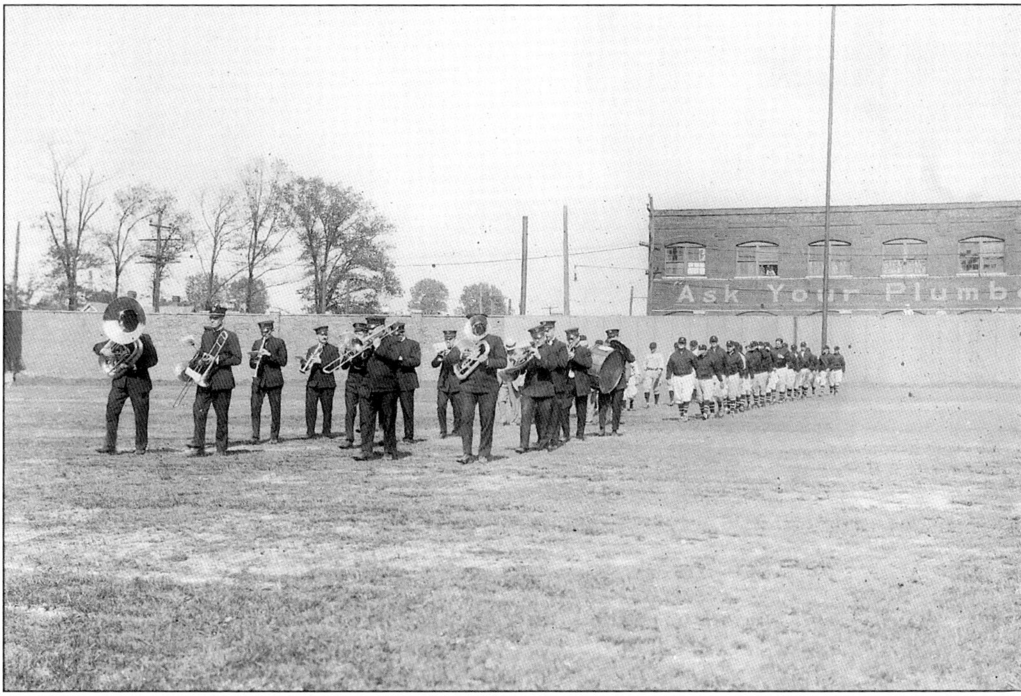

This is opening day for the Evansville Evas, shortly after the city constructed Bosse Field in 1915. The field was touted as the only municipally-owned baseball field in the nation. (Courtesy of Willard Library.)

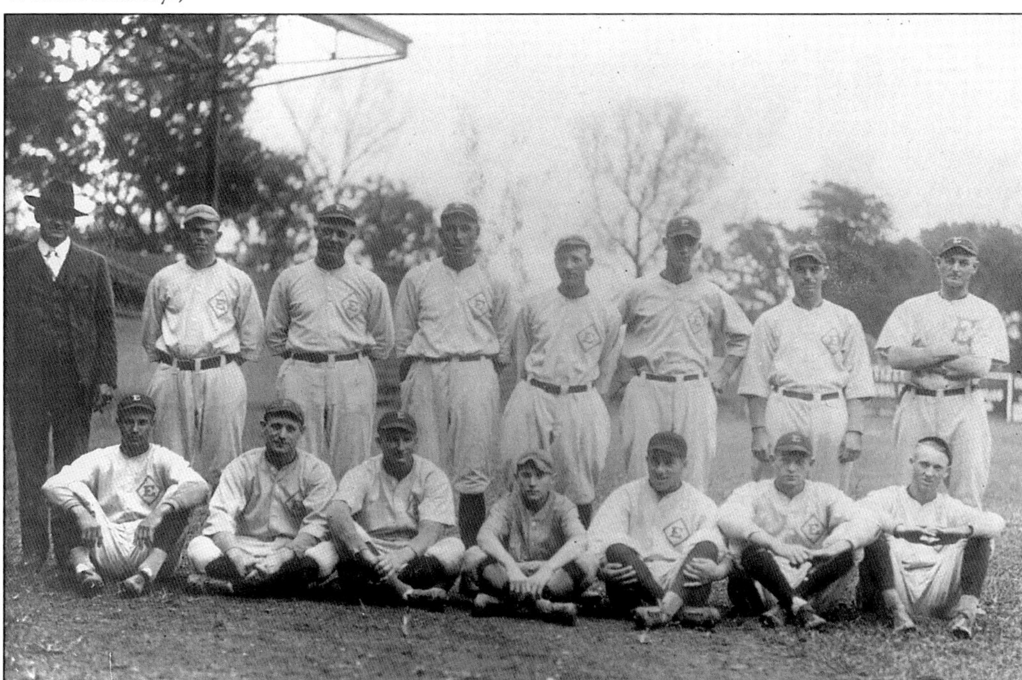

Members of the Evansville Evas, who competed in the Kitty League, are shown here in 1920. (Courtesy of USI.)

The Woodlawn baseball team was comprised of staff from the state hospital for the mentally disabled in Evansville. Most institutions and organizations in southern Indiana cities and towns fielded amateur nines. Baseball was on the cusp of its golden age as national pastime. (Courtesy of Willard Library.)

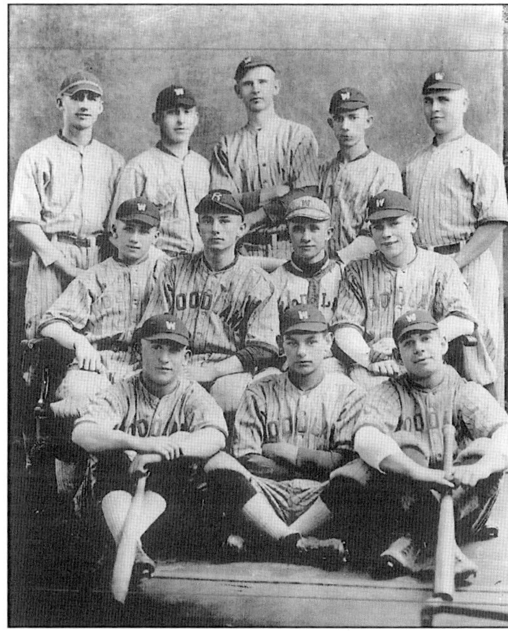

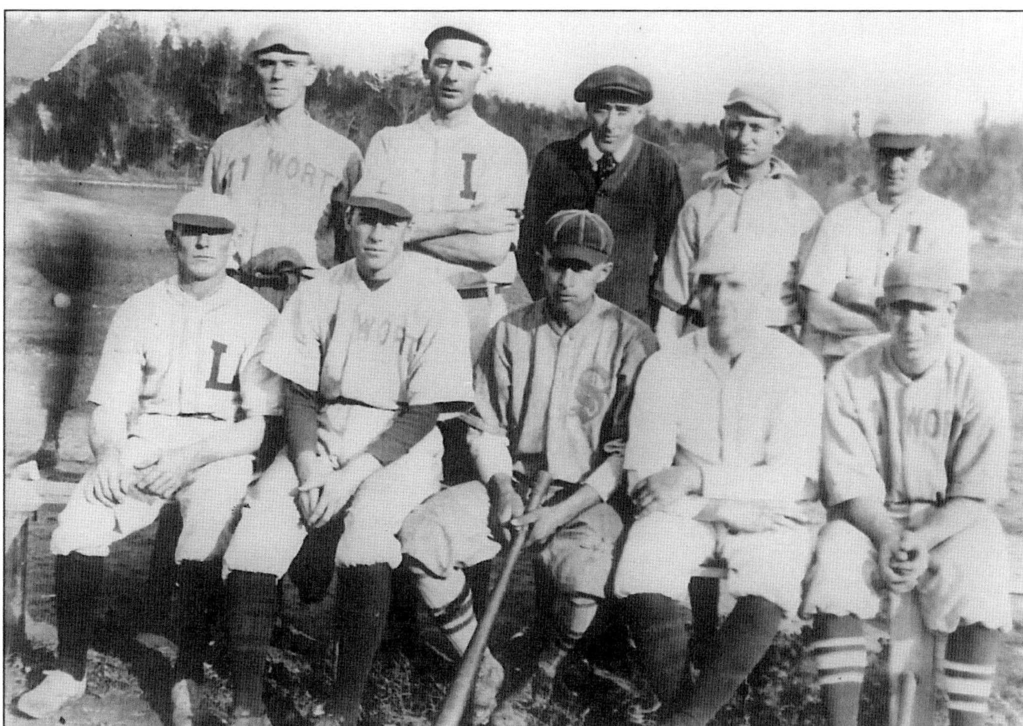

Members of the Leavenworth Merchants Baseball Team are shown here c. 1922. Most were veterans of the AEF. Tom Stephenson, manager, is third from the left in the back row. Their home field was two miles east of the town. They played teams from surrounding counties and construction workers on lock and dam sites 43, 44, and 45. Their greatest moment was a closely fought loss to the Louisville Colonels. (Courtesy of Elaine Stephenson.)

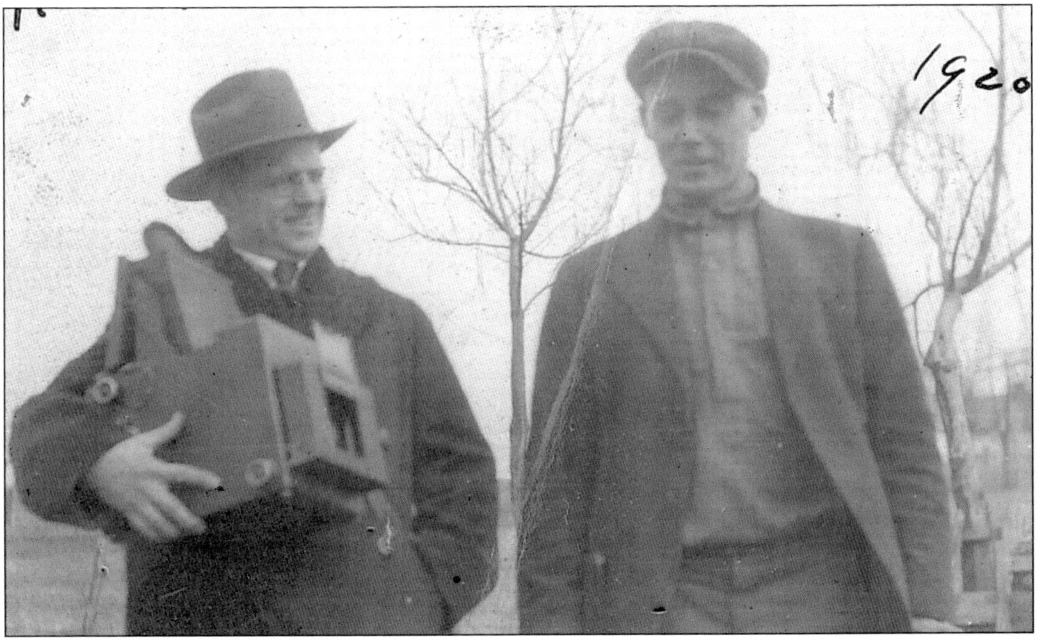

Edd Roush, all-star centerfielder of the Cincinnati Reds, was a native of Oakland City. He is with *Evansville Courier* photographer Karl Kae Knecht in 1920. In the previous year he gained the batting title and his team won the World Series (the "Black Sox" scandal). He started in professional baseball with Evansville in 1912. He spent his first full year in Cincinnati in 1917. (Courtesy of Willard Library.)

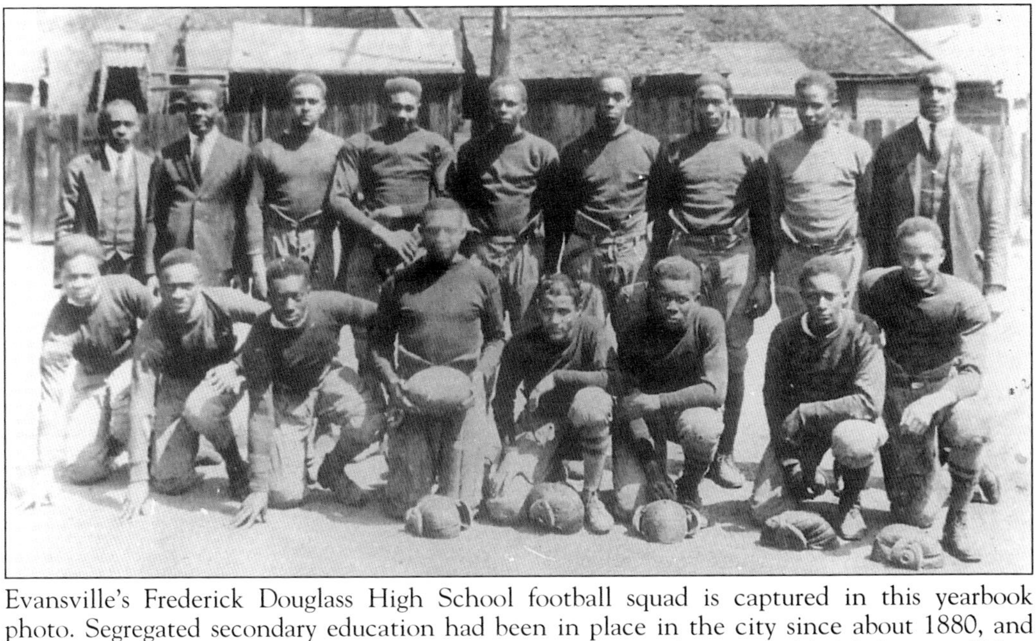

Evansville's Frederick Douglass High School football squad is captured in this yearbook photo. Segregated secondary education had been in place in the city since about 1880, and was also practiced in other larger communities in southern Indiana, notably Madison and New Albany. This team played only other black squads in the region, and was totally dependent for equipment and travel arrangements on supportive teachers, parents, and fans. (Courtesy of USI.)

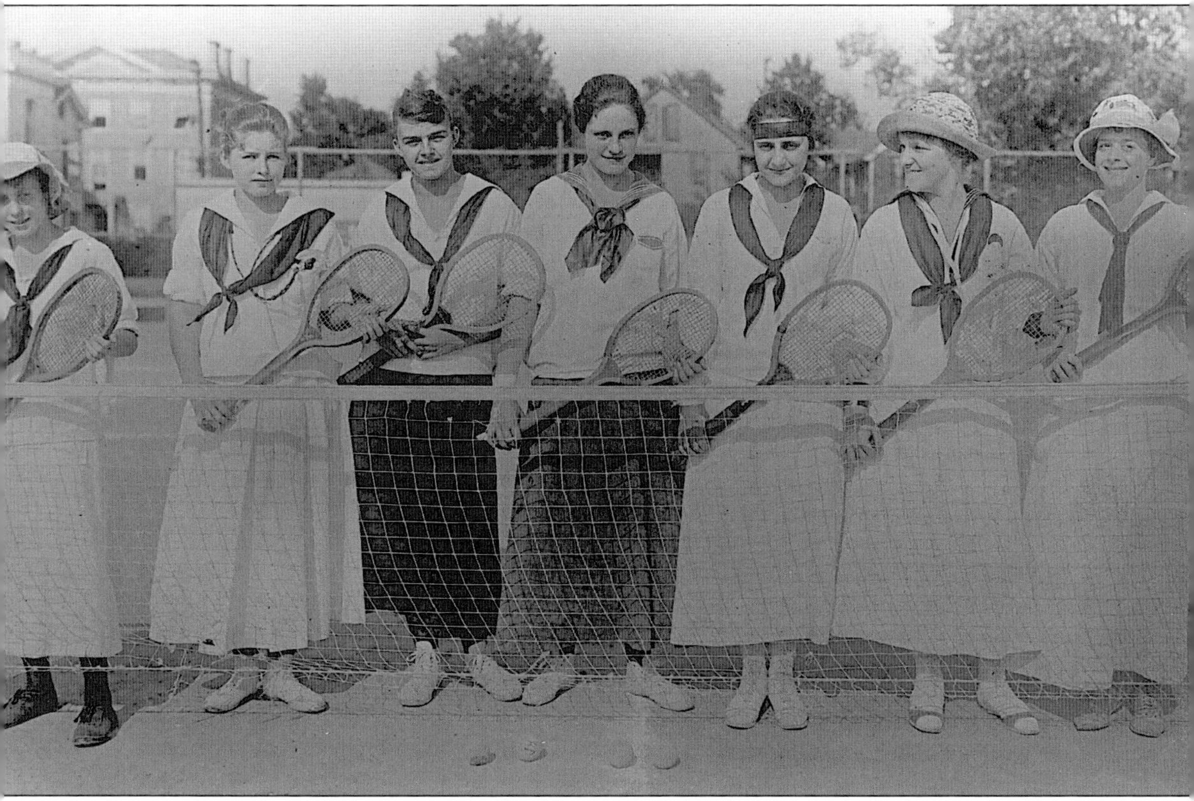

These are participants in the first Evansville girls' tennis tournament, held in September of 1916 in Sunset Park. It was one indication of the liberalization of gender roles in the teens and after. Those identified are, from left to right, unidentified, Anna Louise Thurgood, Agnes McConnel, Nell Chese[elro?], Aline Ellis, Marjorie (surname unidentified), and Florita Eichel. (Courtesy of USI.)

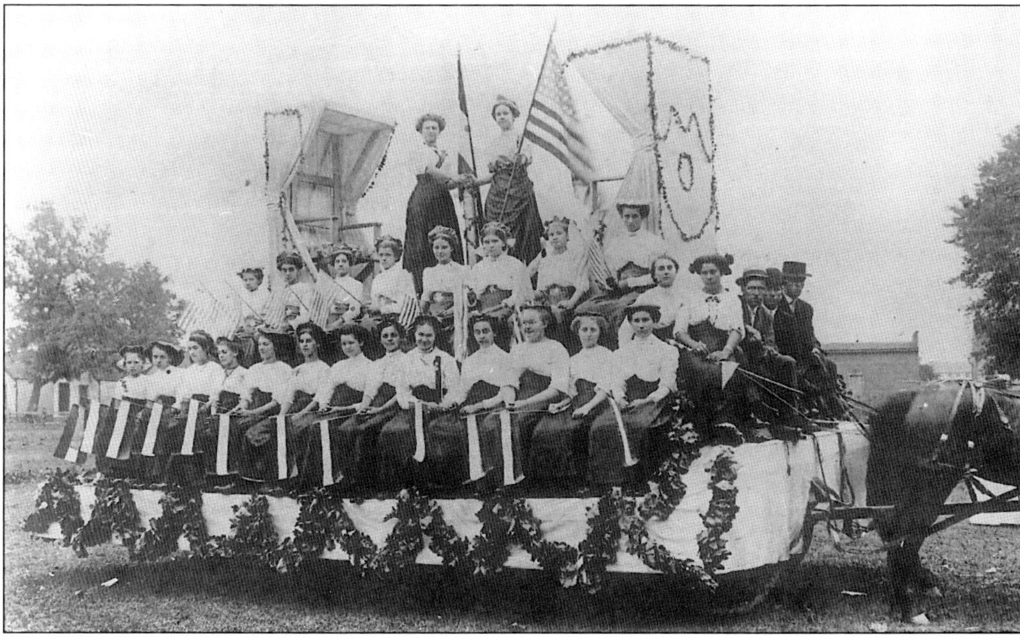

Parades provided recreation, fostered competition among civic and business organizations, and engendered a sense of community. These are workers on the Fendrich Company float for a German Day parade, about 1914. German Day, established in the early 1890s in heavily German-American Evansville, was second in importance only to Independence Day. World War I brought an end to that. (Courtesy of Willard Library.)

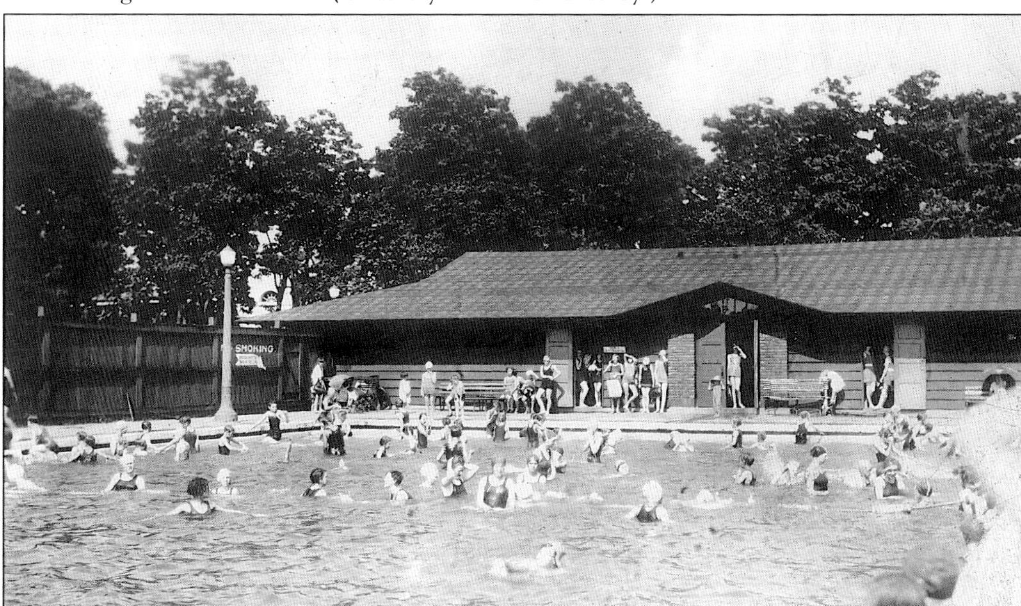

The swimming pool at Garvin Park was once central to the summertime recreation of children and adults on Evansville's north side. The park, named for long-time civic leader Thomas Garvin, became part of the city's park system during the administration of Benjamin Bosse. (Courtesy of Willard Library.)

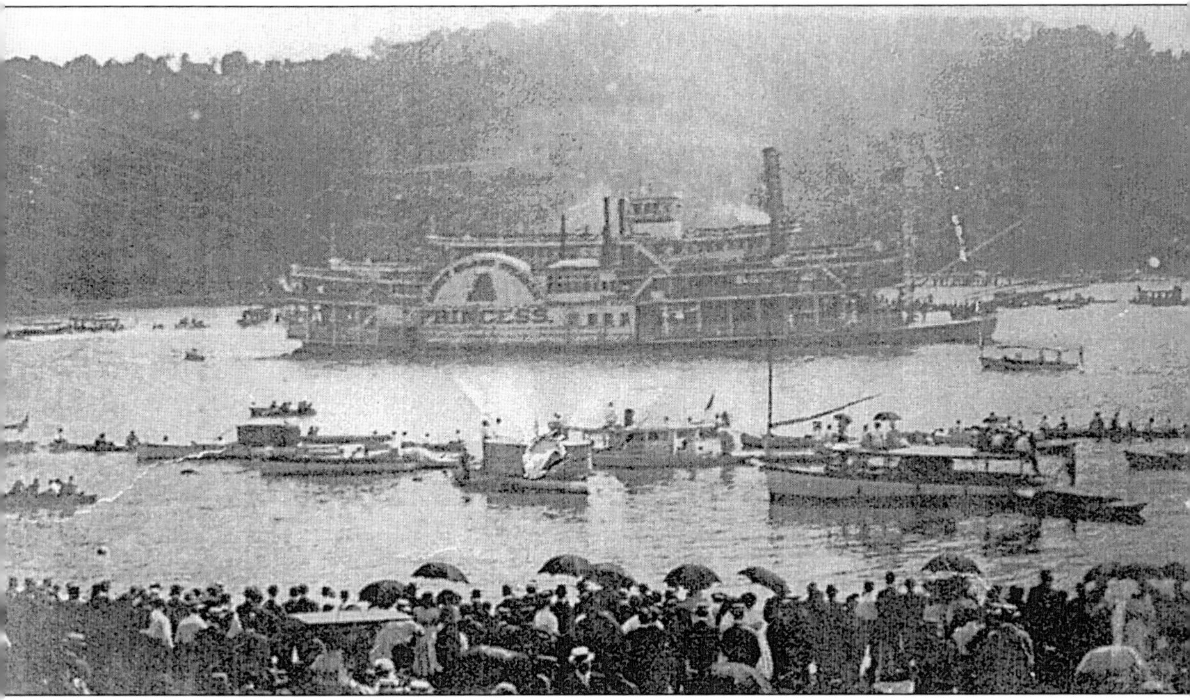

The third annual Powerboat Regatta was held in Madison in September of 1916. Speedboats racing at speeds up to 30 miles an hour drew large crowds from Cincinnati and Louisville to watch the action on the Madison Riverfront. The annual Regatta today still draws large crowds, with hydroplanes racing at speeds over 150 miles per hour. (Courtesy of Jefferson County Historical Society.)

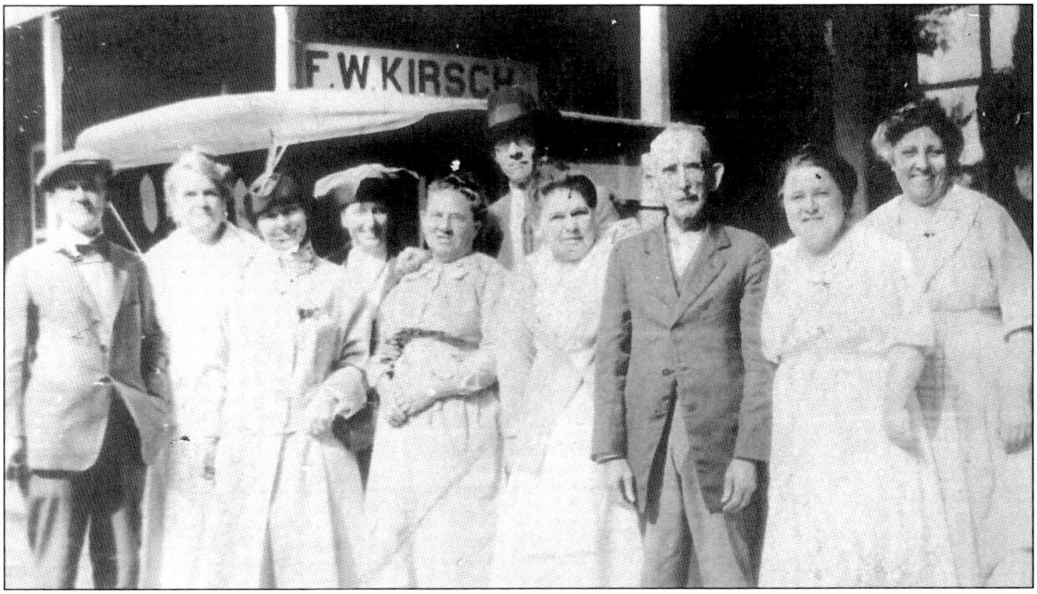

Probably the most common form of relaxation was gathering with friends at a local public place. This group of Leavenworth residents was photographed in the front of the F.W. Kirsch Store. The proprietor, Fred Kirsch, is sixth from the left. On the left is Stewart Hollcroft, driver of the town's lone (Model T) taxi. (Courtesy of Elaine Stephenson.)

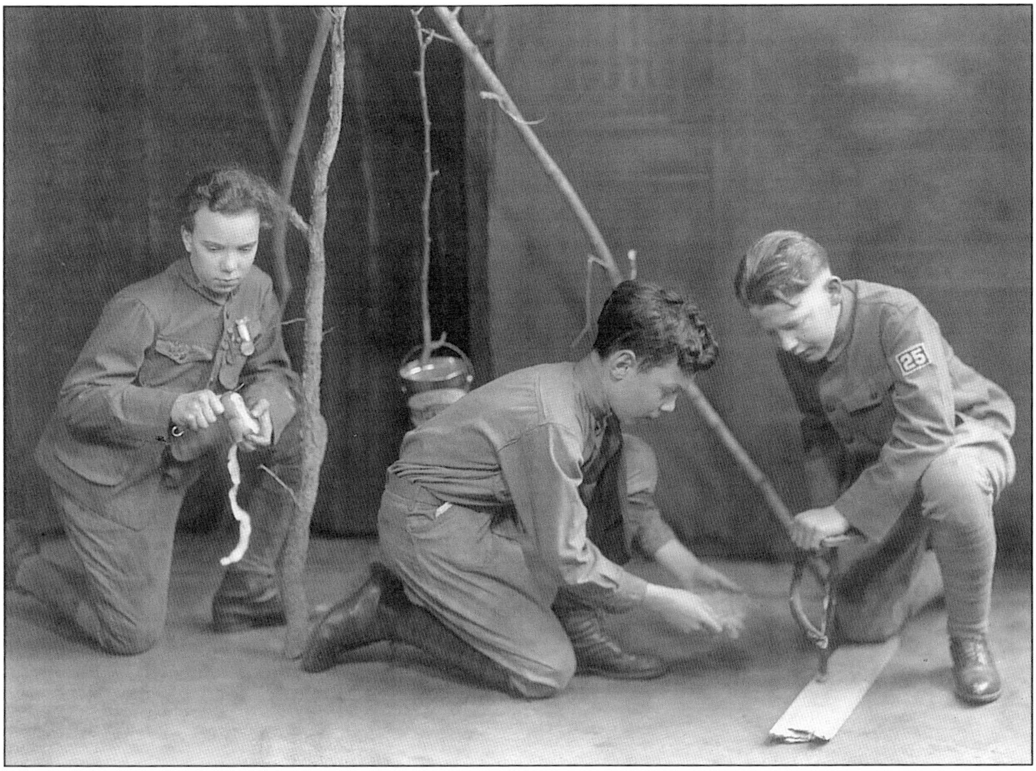

Participation in the Boy Scouts—in this case, three unidentified young men from southwestern Indiana—was increasingly popular in the World War I era. (Courtesy of Willard Library.)

Six

Going to War

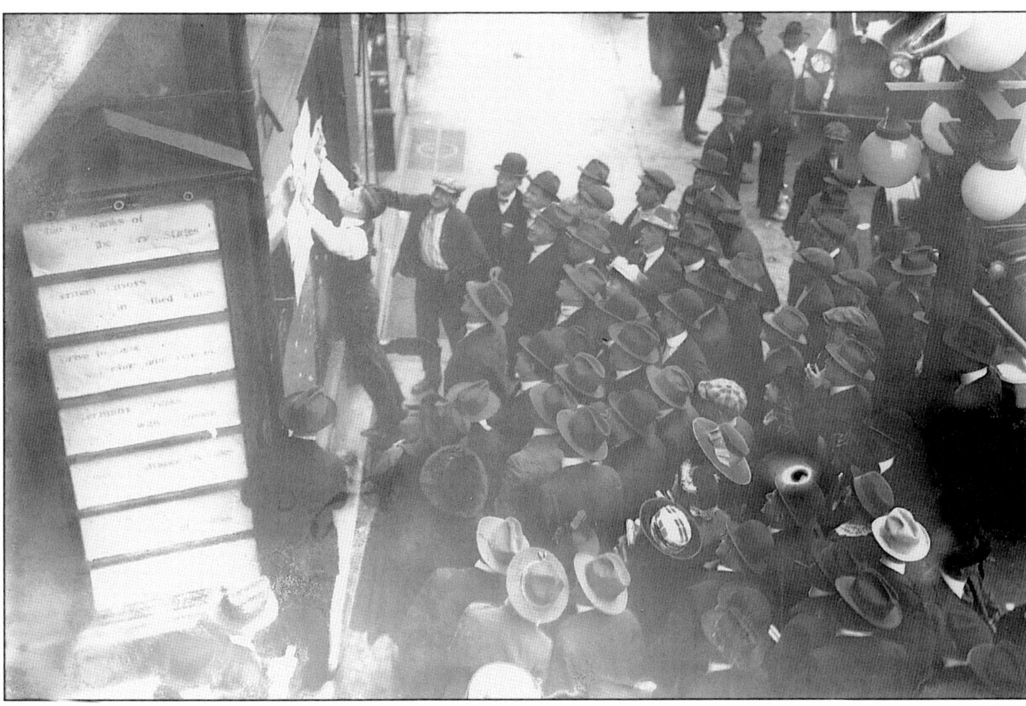

Draft numbers have just been posted in downtown Evansville in 1917, a consequence of the Selective Service Act passed after the declaration of war on Germany in April of that year. Men were called up by a random drawing of the numbers assigned to them when they were enrolled for potential service. (Courtesy of USI.)

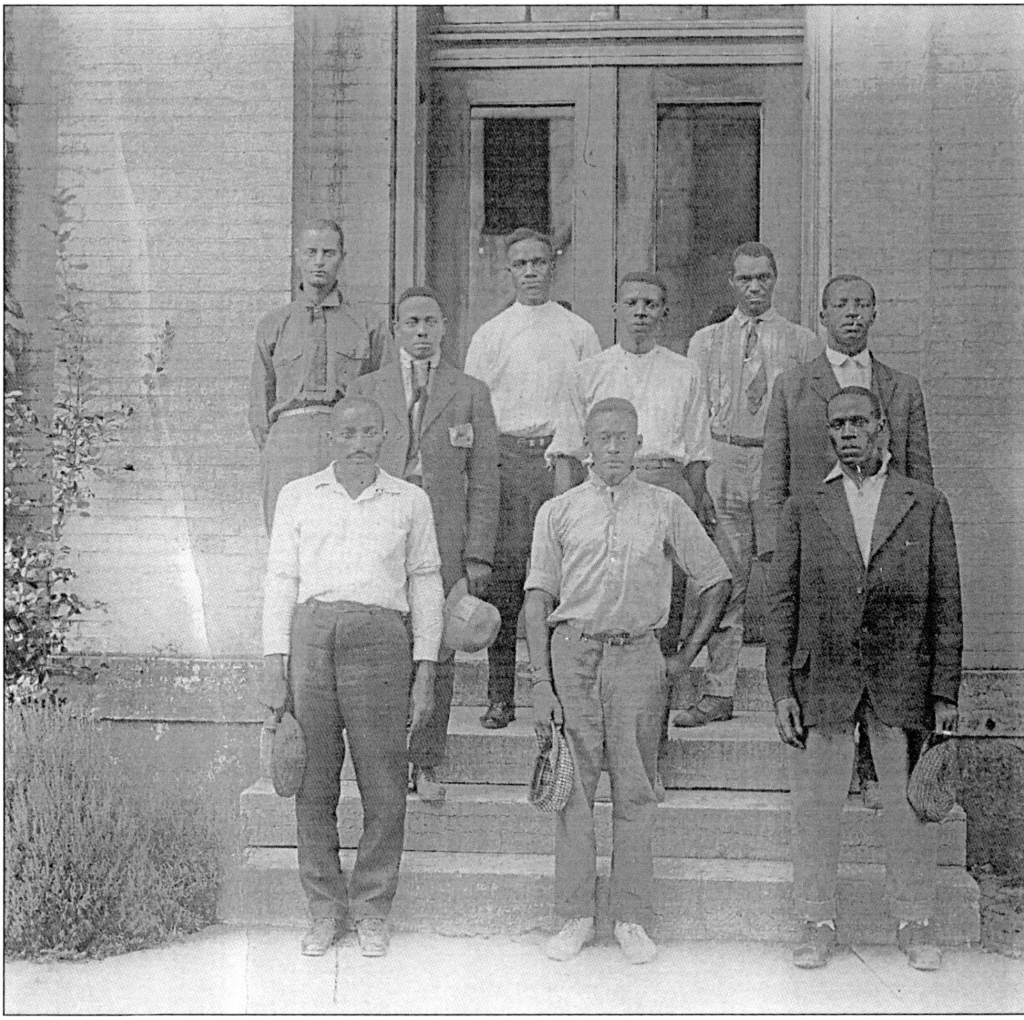

Madison photographer Louis Cohen recorded each group of World War I recruits that departed from Madison for training camp. Draftees came from surrounding counties as well as Jefferson County, gathering at Madison for transportation to training camps in Indiana or Kentucky. These black recruits were photographed on the rear steps of the county courthouse. Several other white groups were photographed there also. (Courtesy of Jefferson County Historical Society.)

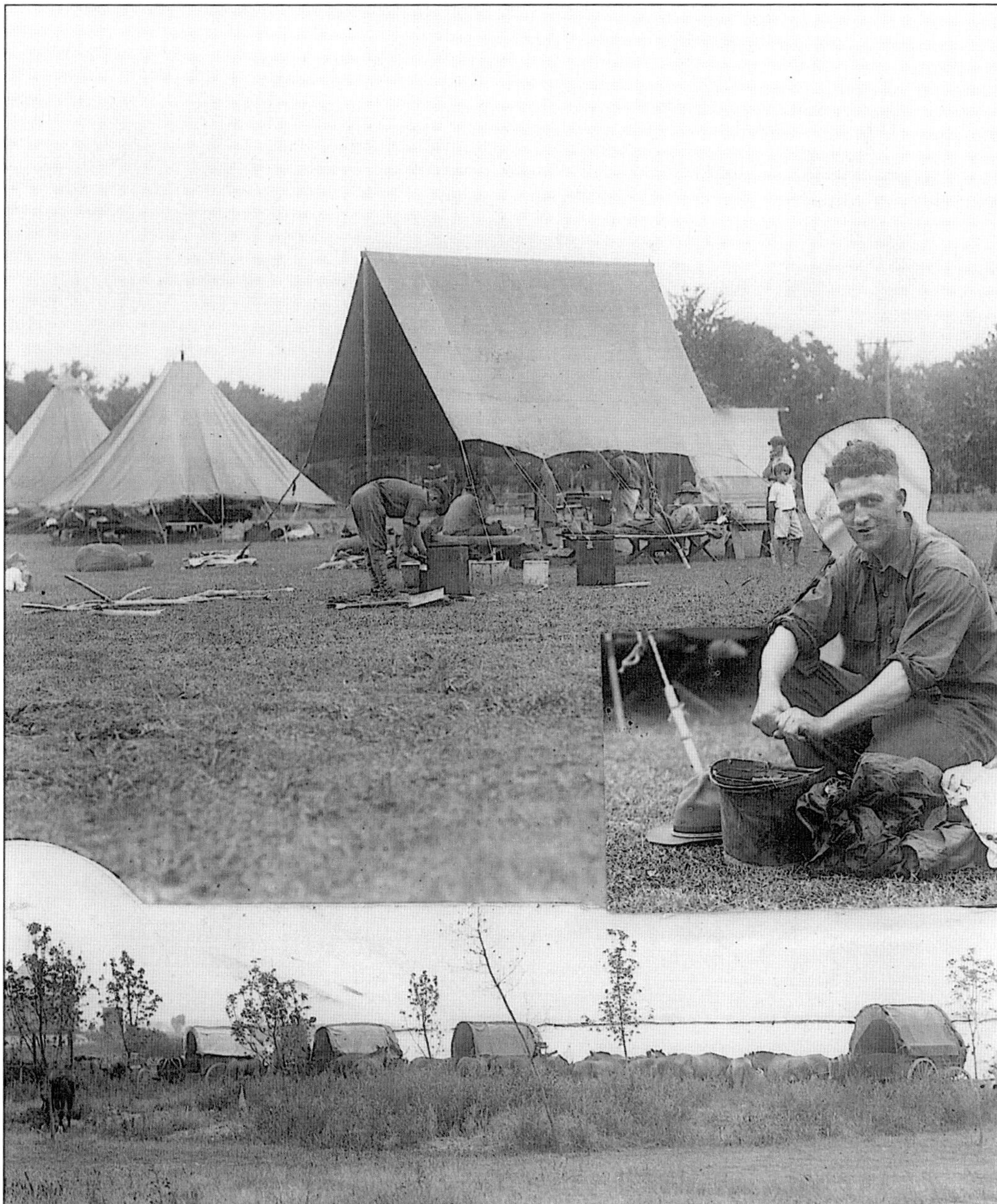

Sunset Park in Evansville served during World War I as an encampment site for boys going off to war. This is one of *Courier* photographer Karl Kae Knecht's composites. (Courtesy of Willard Library.)

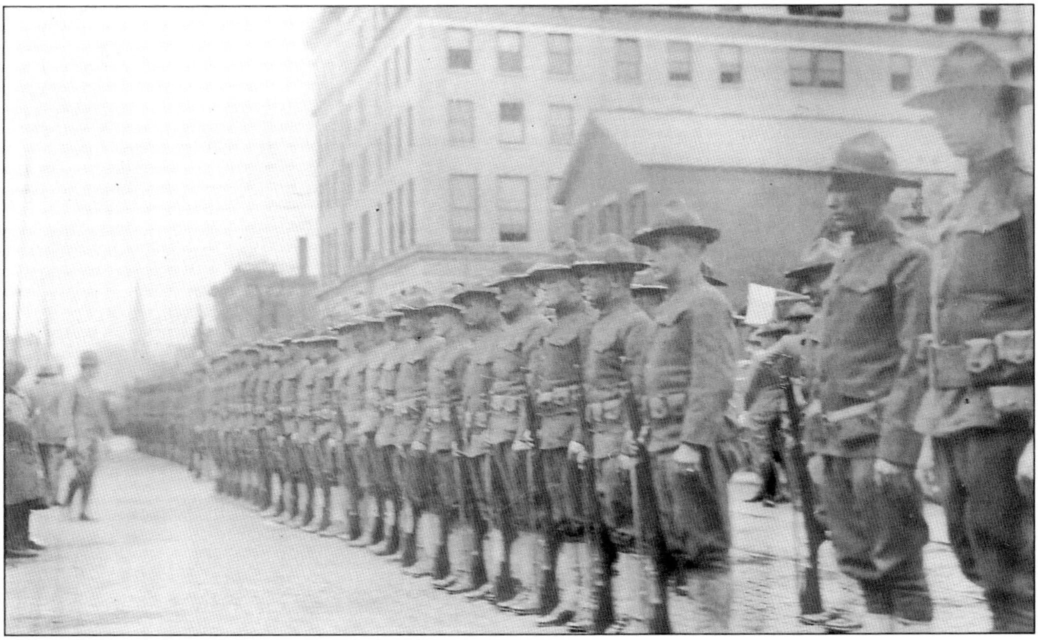

Company A is shown drilling in the fall of 1917 on Fifth Street, near the new YMCA in Evansville, before shoving off for training. (Courtesy of Willard Library.)

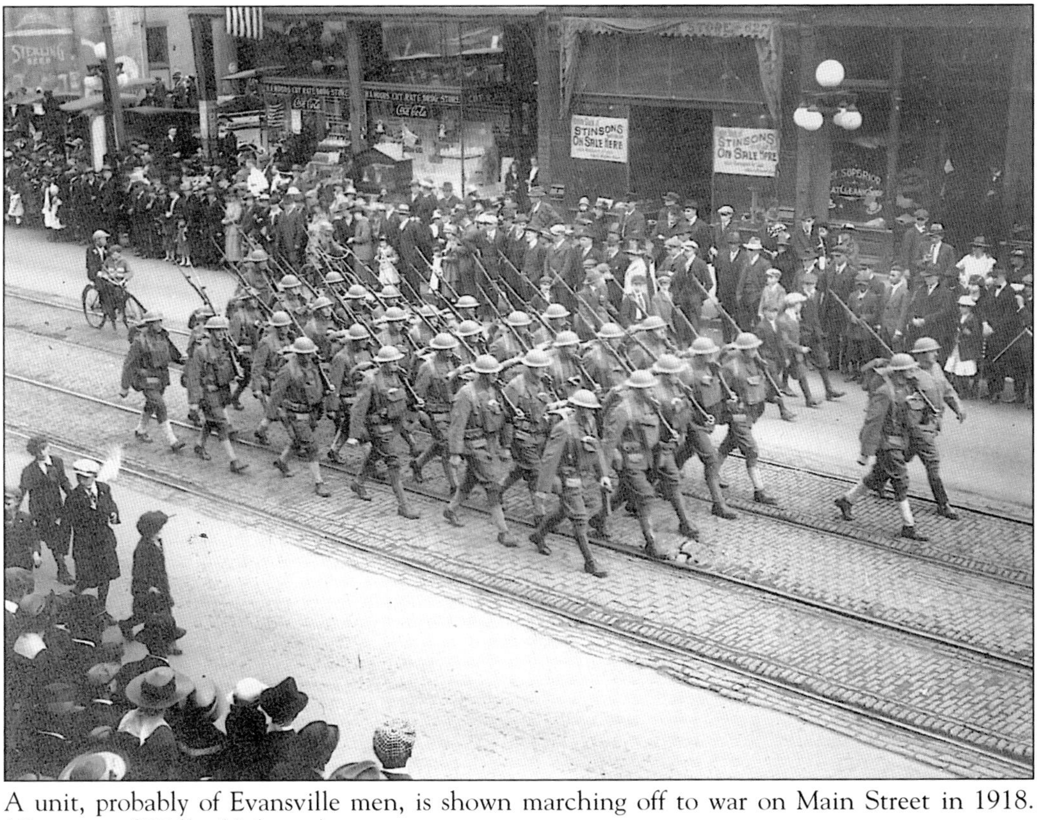

A unit, probably of Evansville men, is shown marching off to war on Main Street in 1918. (Courtesy of Willard Library.)

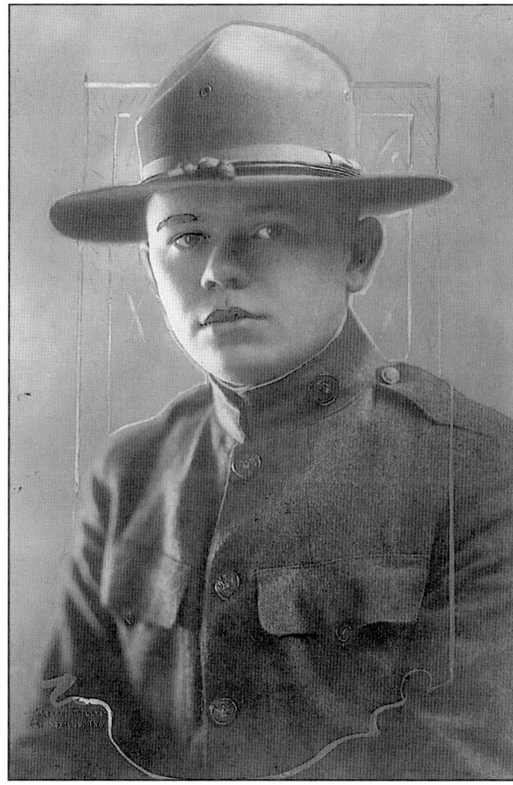

William Boehne, recently inducted into the Ordnance Corps of the United States Army, was one of a number of young men from prominent Vanderburgh County families who performed military service in World War I. (Courtesy of Willard Library.)

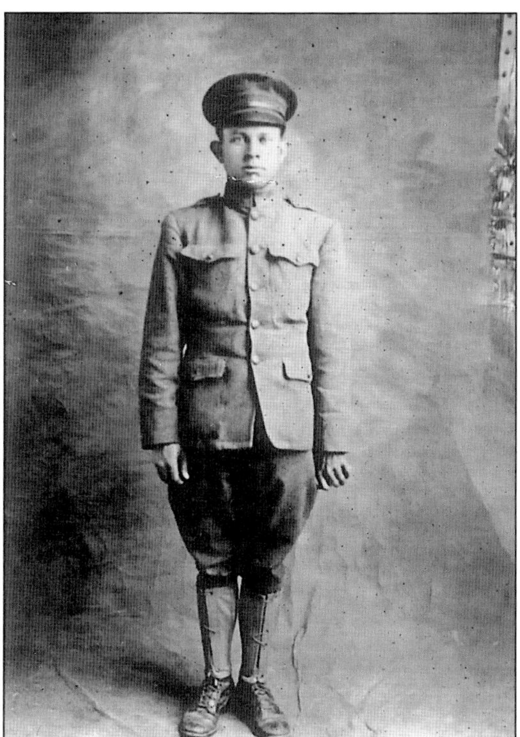

Perhaps the most celebrated of local men who served was James Bethel Gresham of Evansville, a native of Kentucky. Gresham, a corporal in Company F of the Sixteenth Infantry of the First Division of the American Expeditionary Corps, is believed to be the first member of the AEF killed in France. He died November 3, 1917. (Courtesy of Willard Library.)

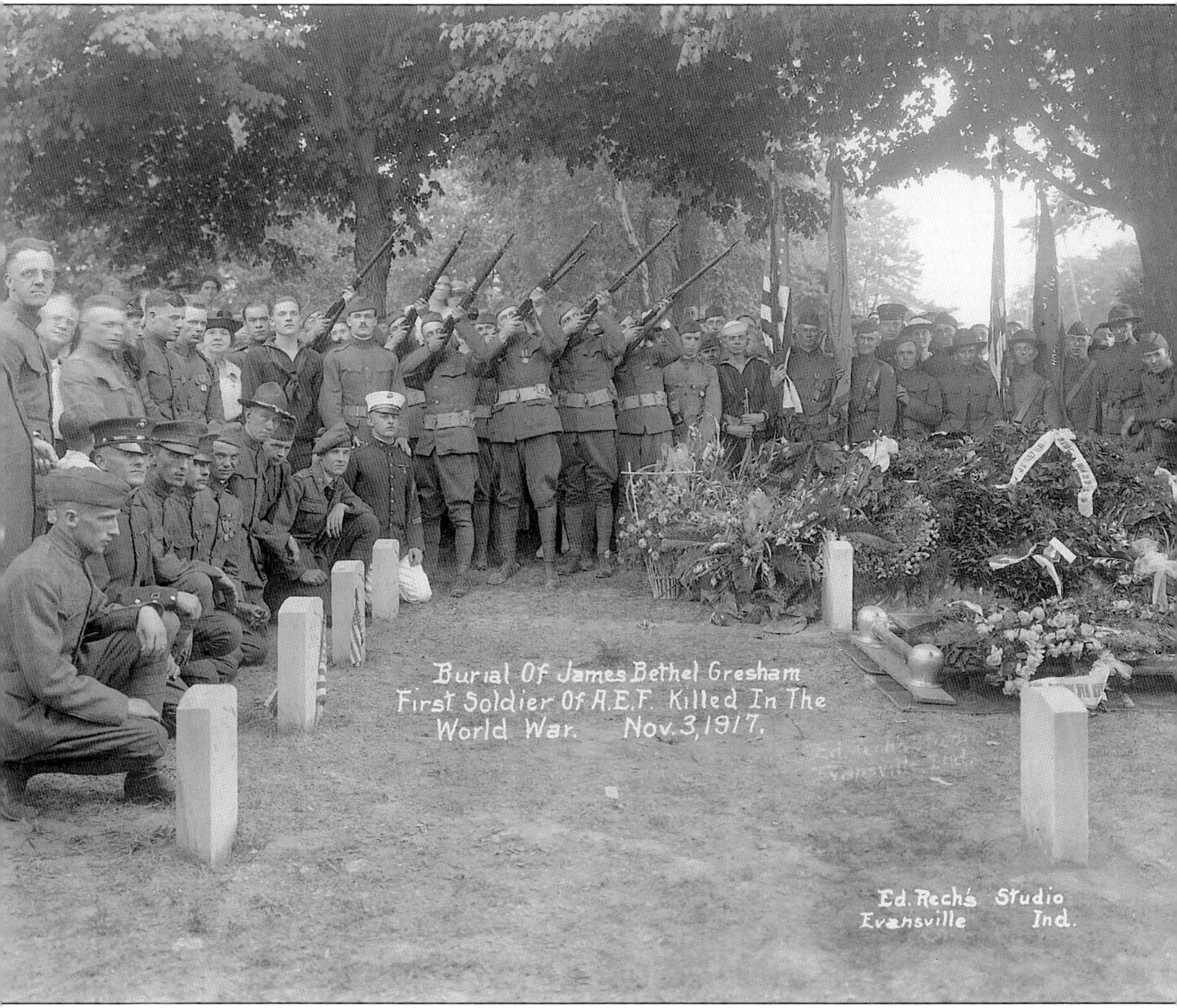

This was the scene as veterans honored the sacrifice of James Bethel Gresham, when his remains were re-interred at Evansville's Locust Hill Cemetery after the ending of the war. (Courtesy of USI.)

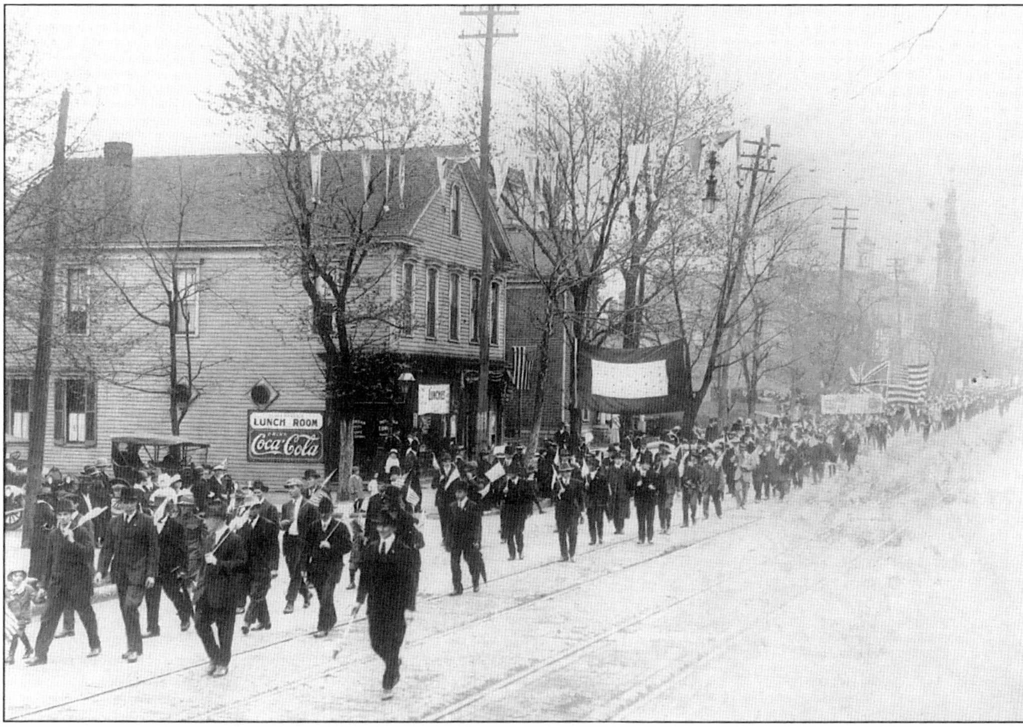

Public parades increased in frequency and enthusiasm during the war, especially in 1918. This patriotic parade was photographed at Fifth and Spring Streets in New Albany, probably during a Liberty Loan drive in the spring of 1918. Flags of the Allies are evident in the distance. (Courtesy of Carnegie Center for Art and History.)

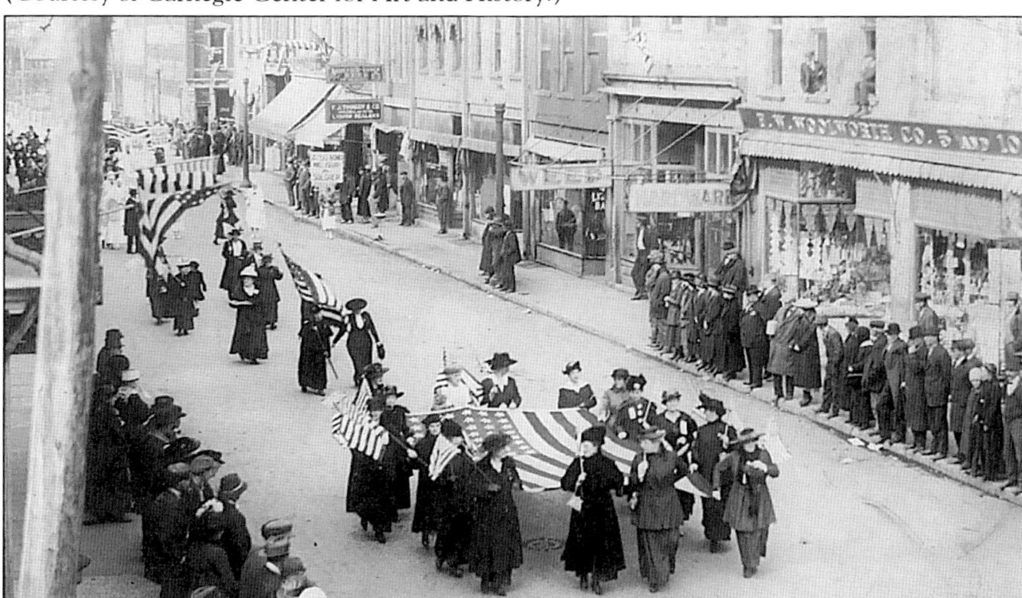

These are women in a Liberty Loan parade in Vincennes on October 24, 1917. So many (seven thousand or so) took part that there were few residents left to watch. This is Main Street, between First and Second Streets. (Courtesy of Lewis Library.)

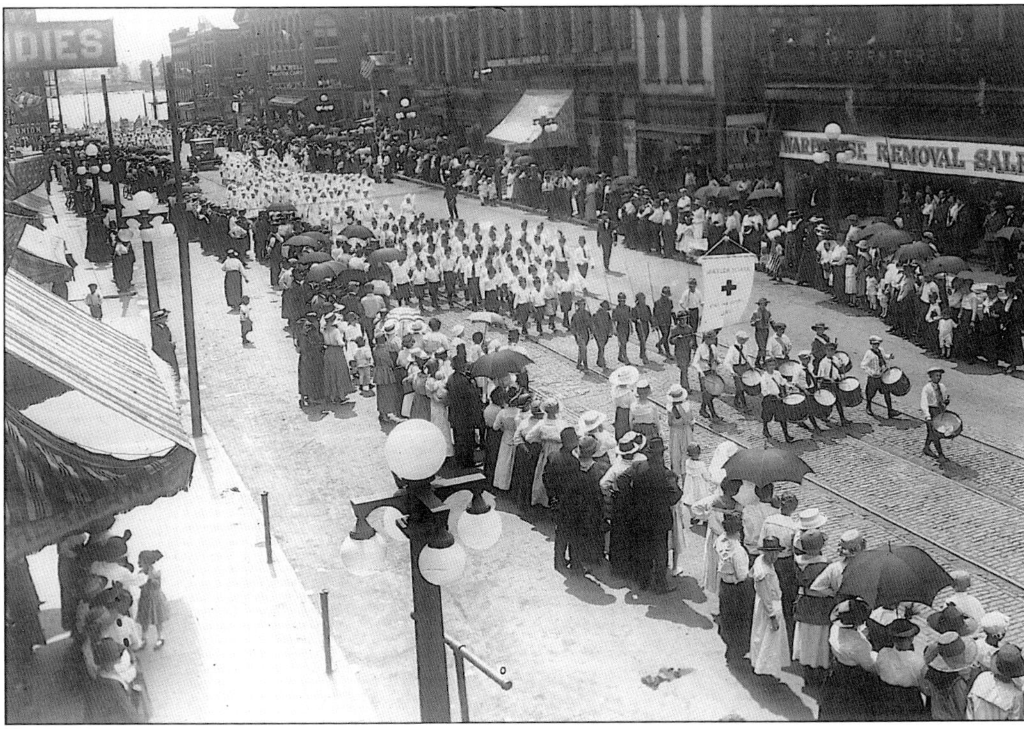

This is a unit representing the Junior Red Cross of Wheeler School in Evansville participating in a Liberty Loan drive parade on Main Street in the spring of 1918. (Courtesy of Willard Library.)

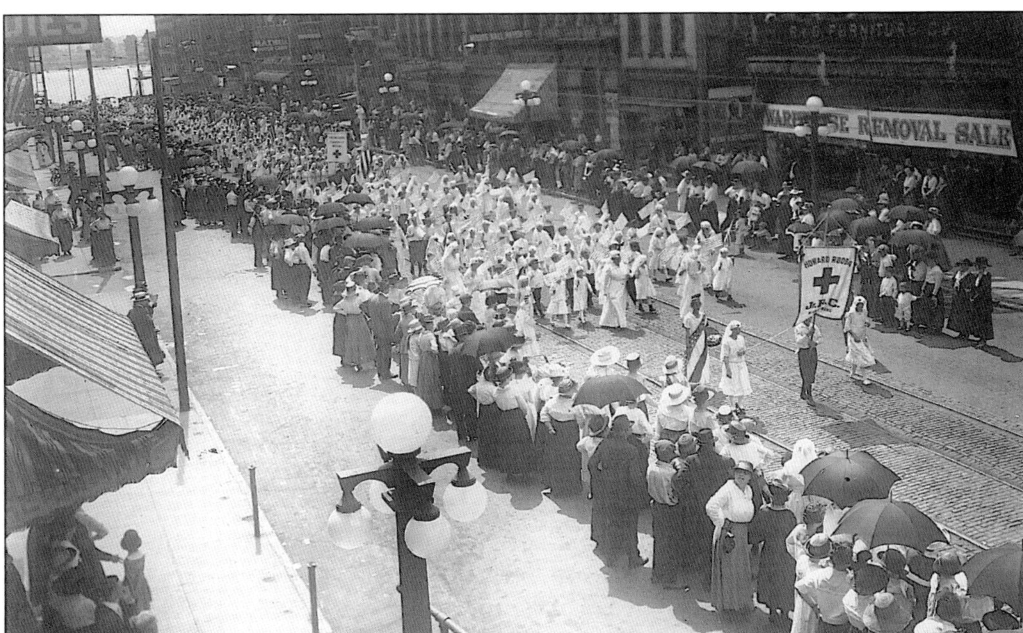

Howard Roosa School of Evansville also had a unit in that parade. (Courtesy of Willard Library.)

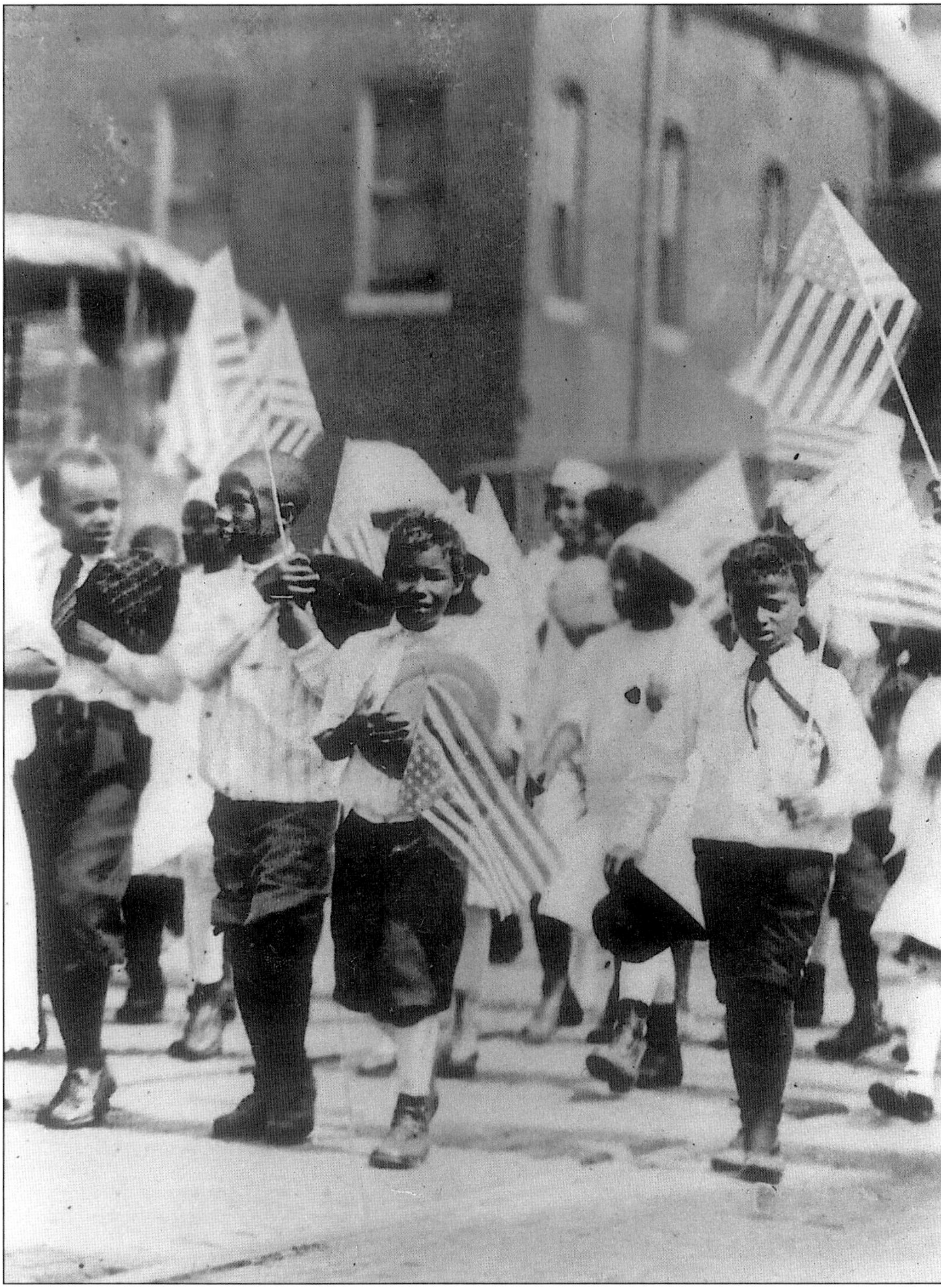

Despite pervasive racism, African Americans in southern Indiana towns and cities approached World War I with hope that loyal participation would be rewarded with racial justice. Induction of black troops, though, was delayed until late summer in 1918. These youth in a 1918 Evansville parade were probably oblivious to the vagaries of race, which would haunt their generation and those who went to war in 1942 as well. (Courtesy of USI.)

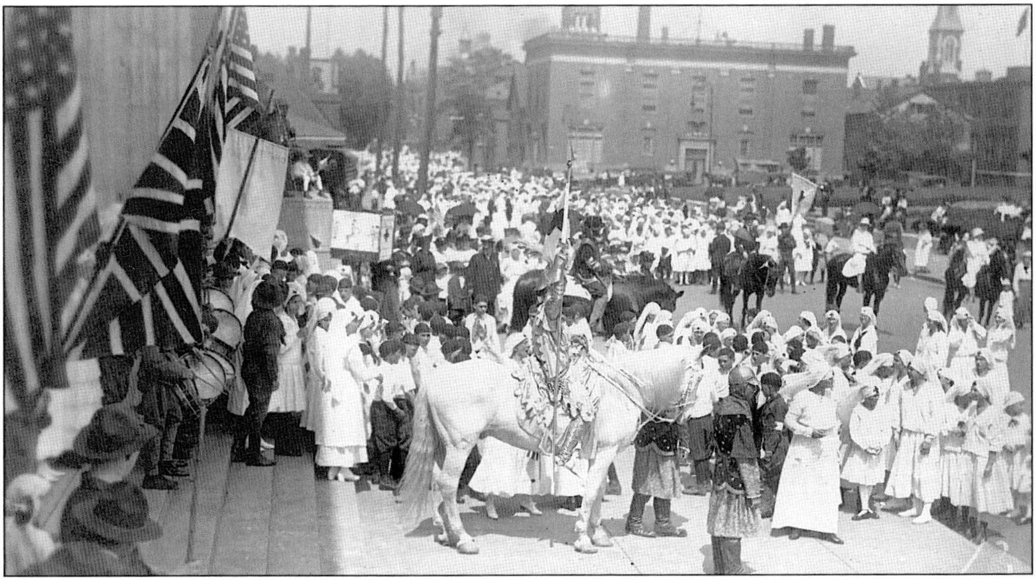

Probably part of the same massive parade, pictured here are three children dressed as knights. One, in white and probably intended to be Joan of Arc, is mounted on a white horse. (Courtesy of Willard Library.)

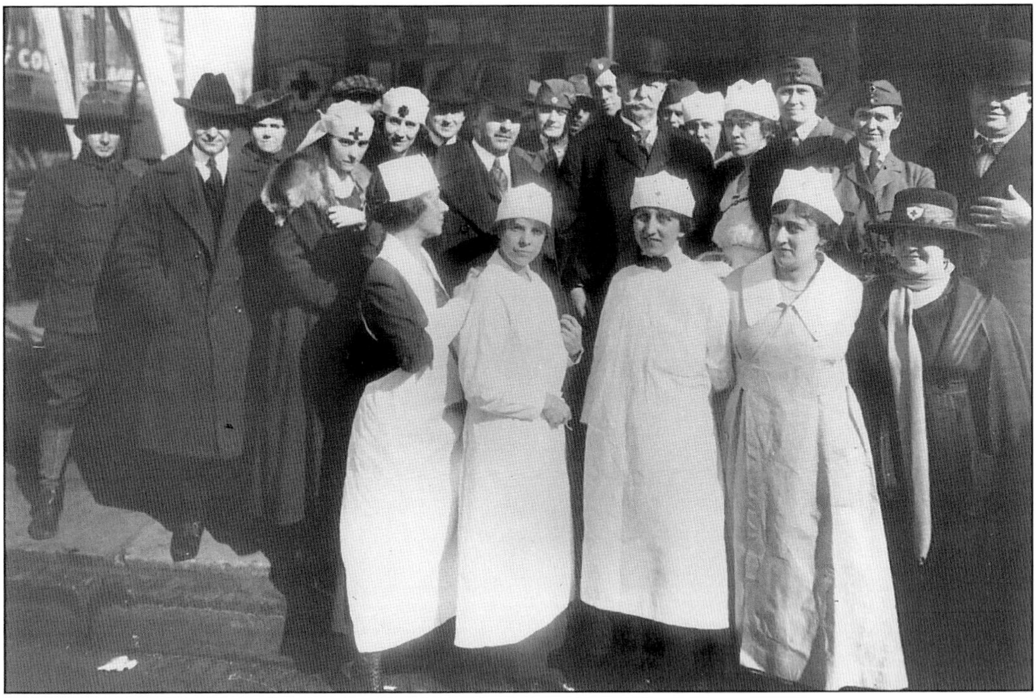

Posed in front of a Red Cross canteen in Evansville in the spring of 1918 are a number of supporters, including Mayor Benjamin Bosse (second row, right). Their special visitor (center) was former president William Howard Taft. The Evansville chapter raised $125,000 between May 1917 and July 1919. Volunteers prepared 305,000 surgical dressings and served coffee and sandwiches to 104,000 men at the canteens, located at the two railroad stations. (Courtesy of USI.)

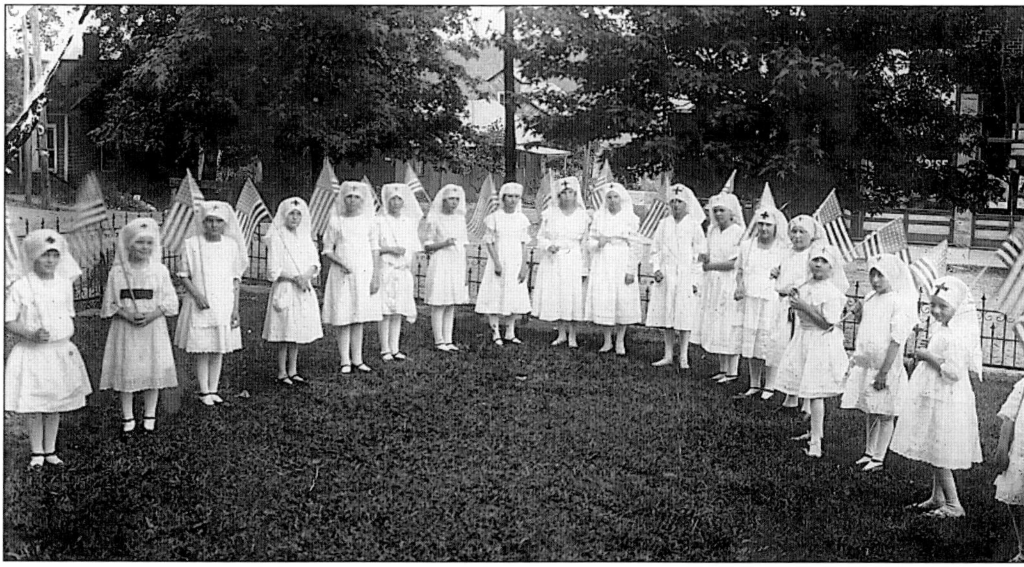

This group of youthful Red Cross workers was photographed in Ella Wright's yard in Tunnelton in 1918. (Courtesy of Maxine Kruse.)

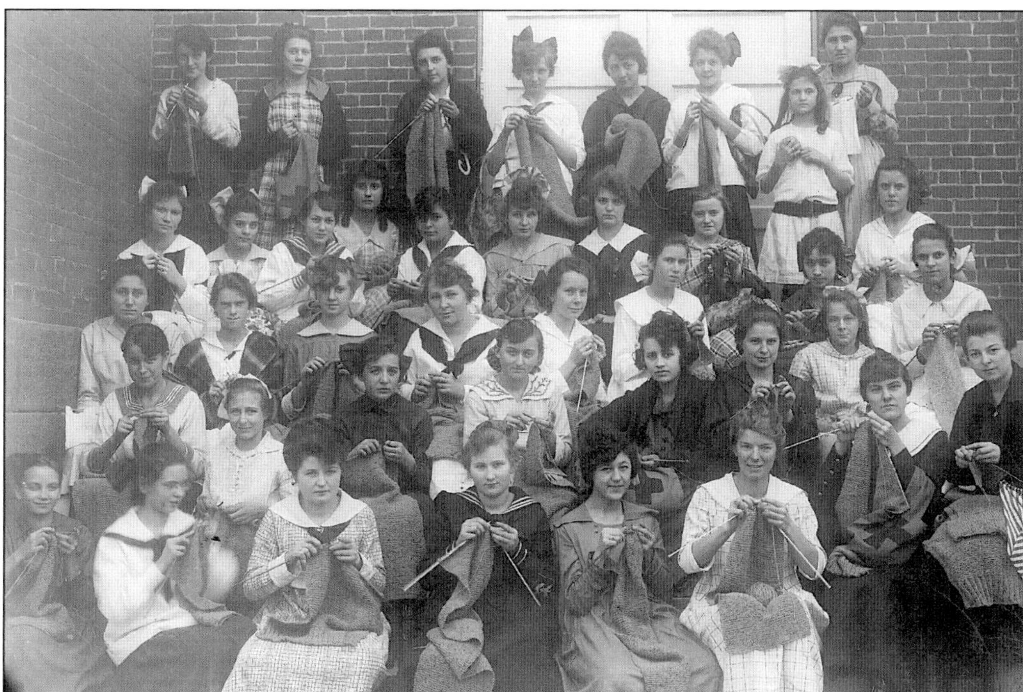

Jasper's Junior Red Cross members are knitting for the AEF. In this predominantly German community, declared *Dubois County in the World War*, "the American-German had to be taught that he was a German-American, and…just a plain natural-born American, who had failed to realize he was an American." Perhaps this explained Jasper's exuberant patriotism. Dubois County residents subscribed nearly $1.9 million in Liberty Loans, well above quota. (Courtesy of John Fierst.)

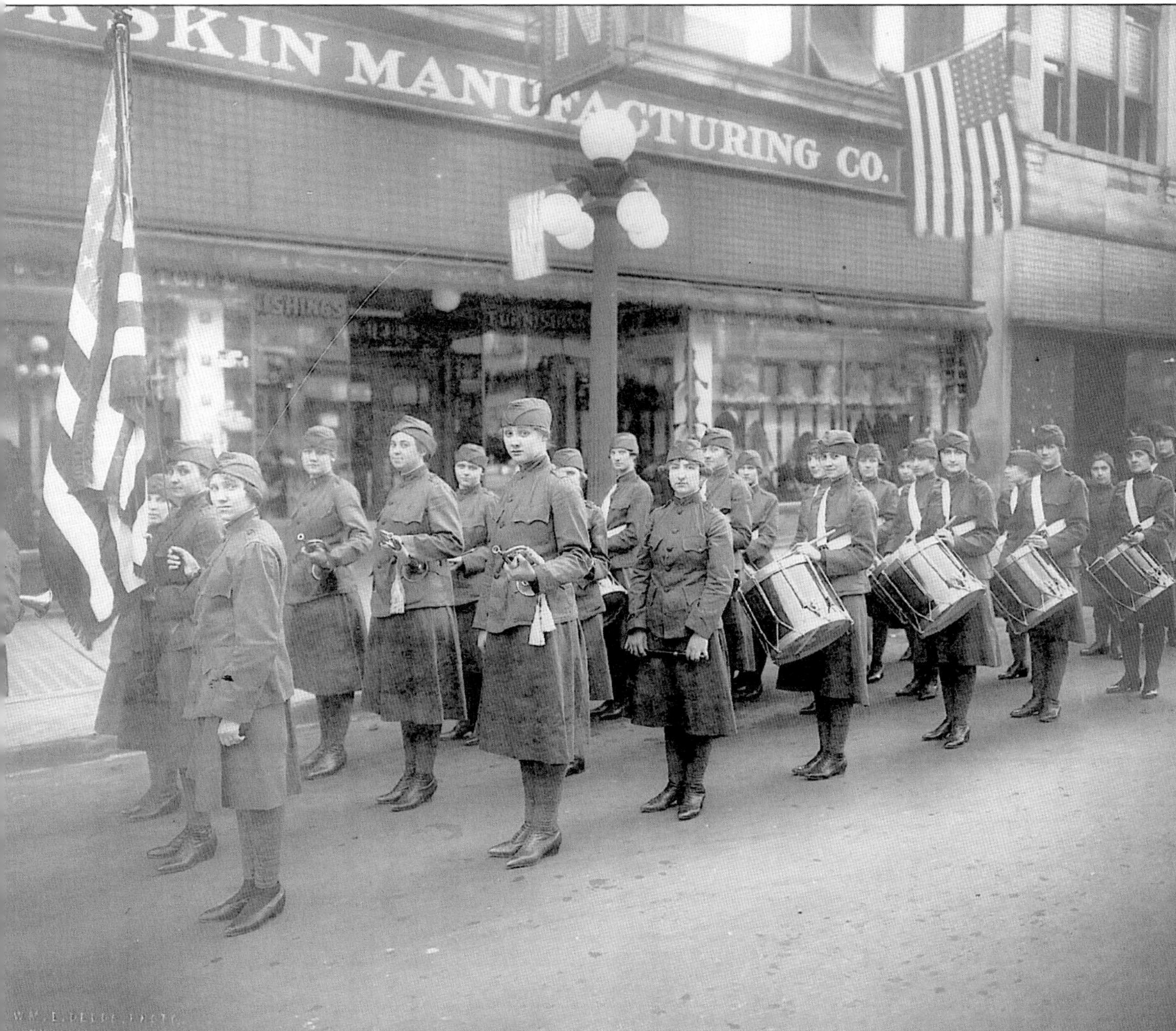

Also showing their patriotism were workers at the Buckskin Manufacturing Company, located at 111–115 Main Street in Evansville. They formed a drum corps, shown here in front of the factory store in 1918. Buckskin manufactured men's trousers and suits. (Courtesy of Willard Library.)

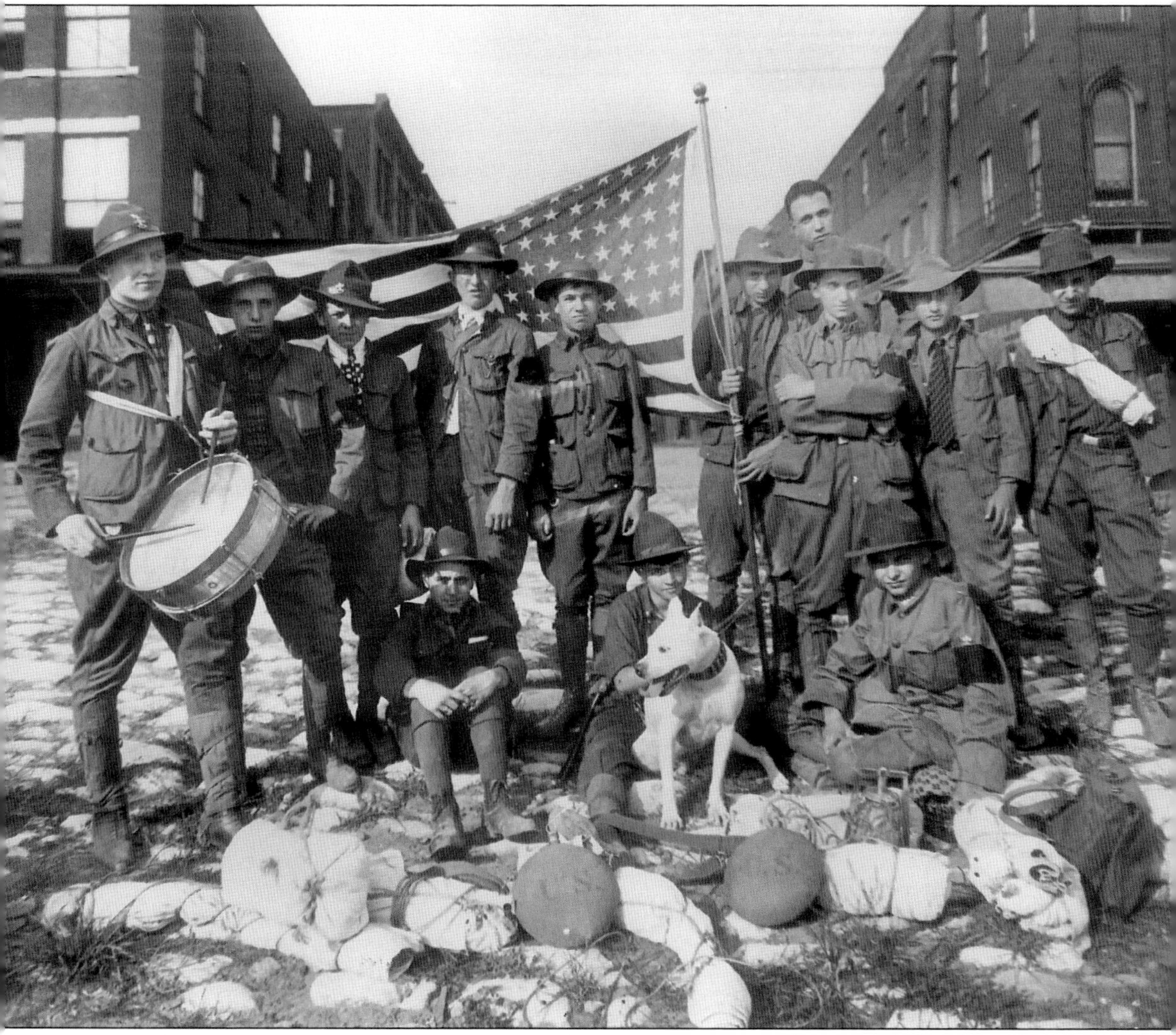

Patriotic fervor generated during the war touched every corner of Evansville and southern Indiana society. Members of the Boy Scout troop formed at Temple B'nai Israel are shown here standing at the riverfront in 1917. Holding the flag is William Drucker, later a prominent clothing merchant. Also in the photo are "Lanky" Heiman, Fred Newman, Alex Eichel, Jacob Weil, Stanley Hamner, Phil Loewenthal, Sid Gumberts, Edgar Weil, Ben Stein, H. Salm, and Rudy Schear. (Courtesy of USI.)

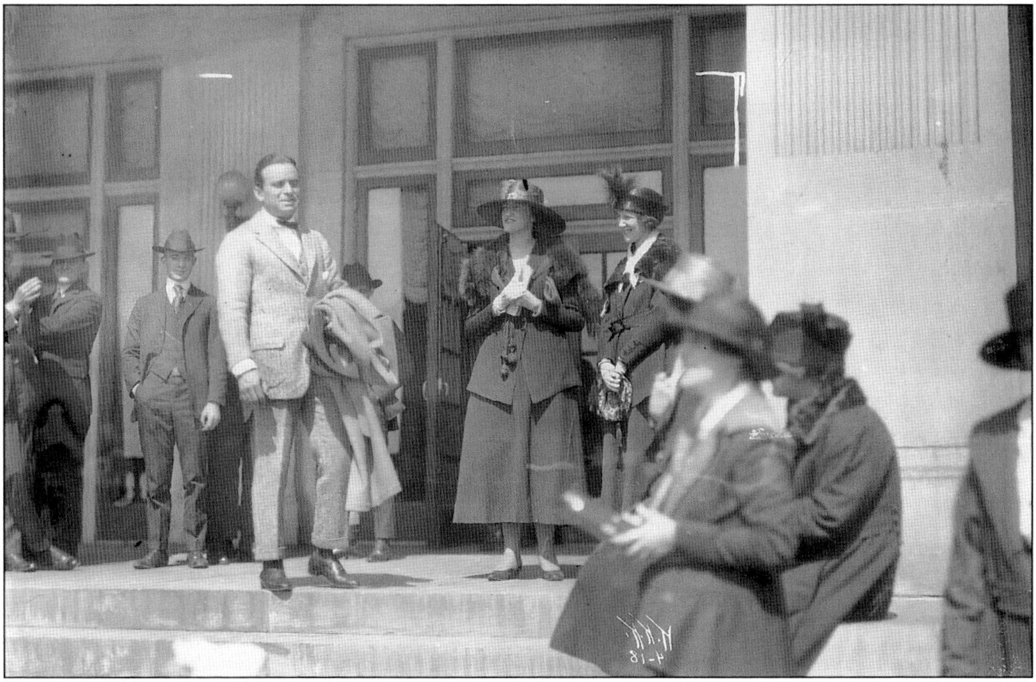

Popular silent film star Douglas Fairbanks Sr. stopped in Evansville on April 14, 1918, to promote the sale of war bonds. The site is probably the new Coliseum. (Courtesy of USI.)

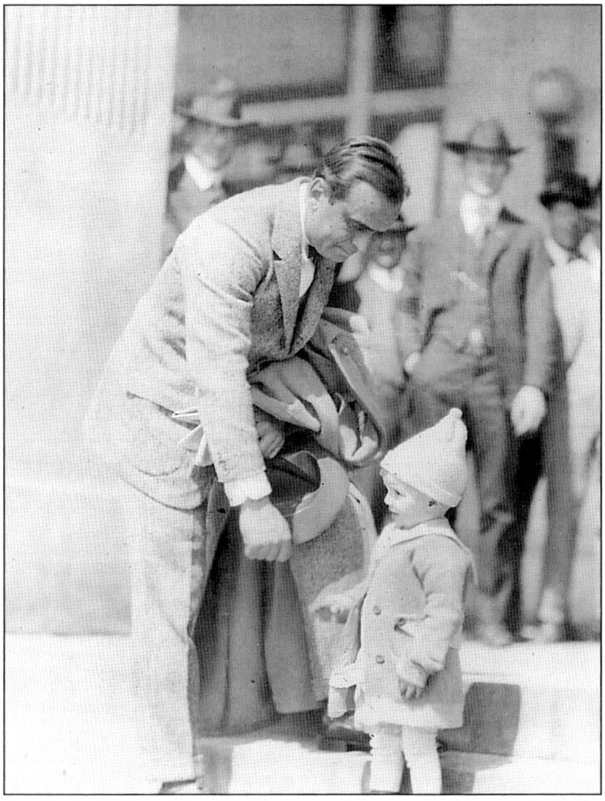

Fairbanks is shown here with an unidentified child. (Courtesy of Willard Library.)

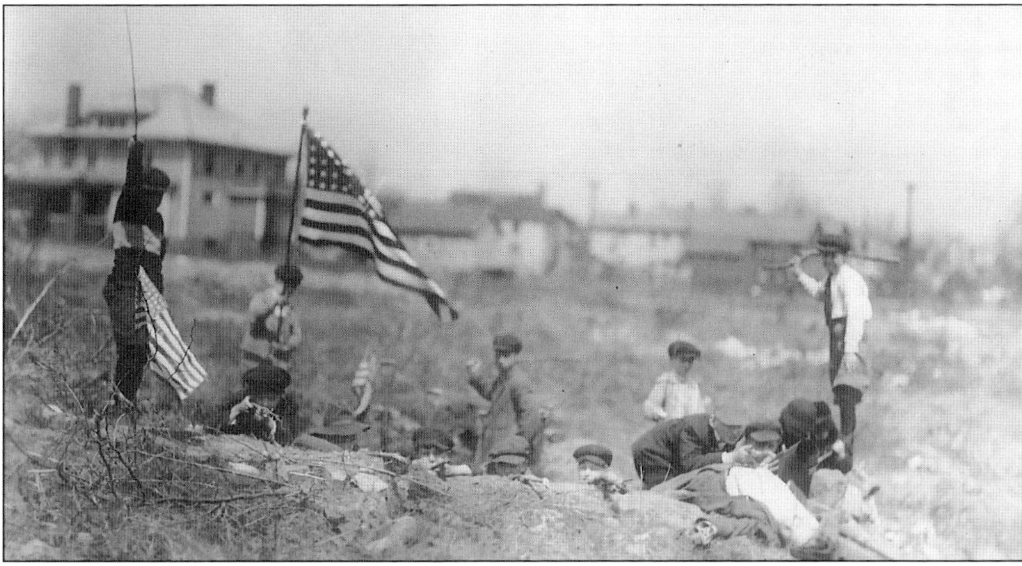

In all wars—in this case, World War I—boys play war games to mimic their elders. This shows such play near the riverfront in Evansville. (Courtesy of Willard Library.)

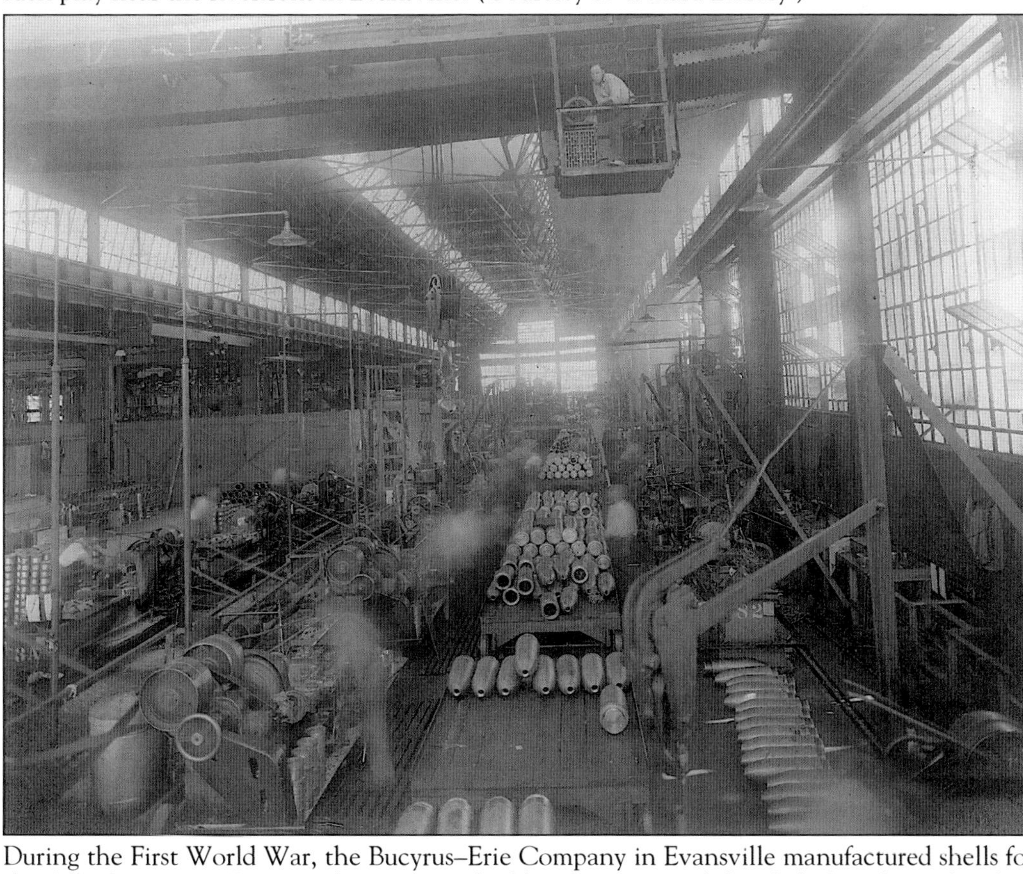

During the First World War, the Bucyrus–Erie Company in Evansville manufactured shells for the Allied armies in Europe. This structure had been constructed shortly before the outbreak of the war for the fabrication of heavy construction equipment. (Courtesy of USI.)

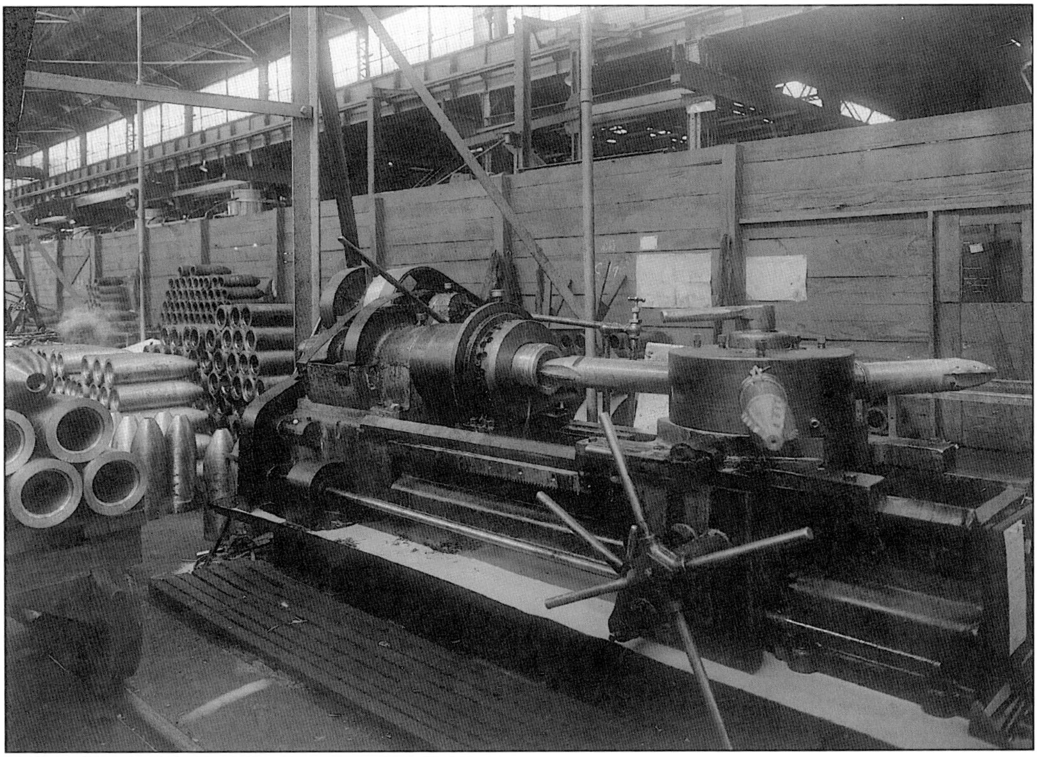

A close-up of some of the machinery used to make shells at Bucyrus–Erie is provided here. (Courtesy of Willard Library.)

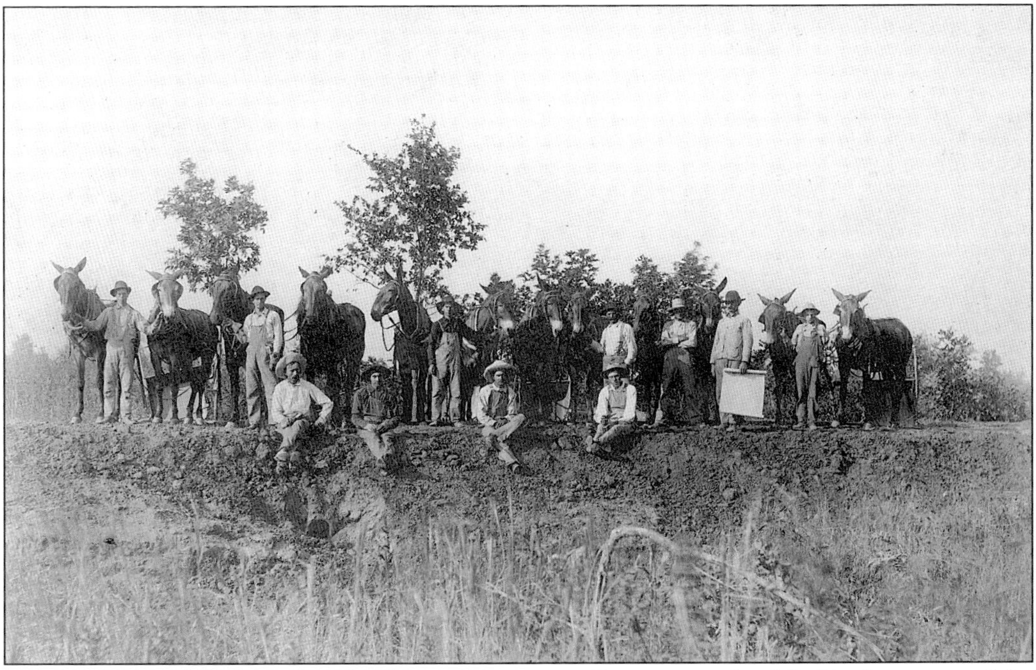

The Myles Standish farm in old Palestine, Lawrence County, south of Bedford, was noted for raising mules for the coal mines and for the army in World War I. (Courtesy of Maxine Kruse.)

Seven

FACING THE FUTURE

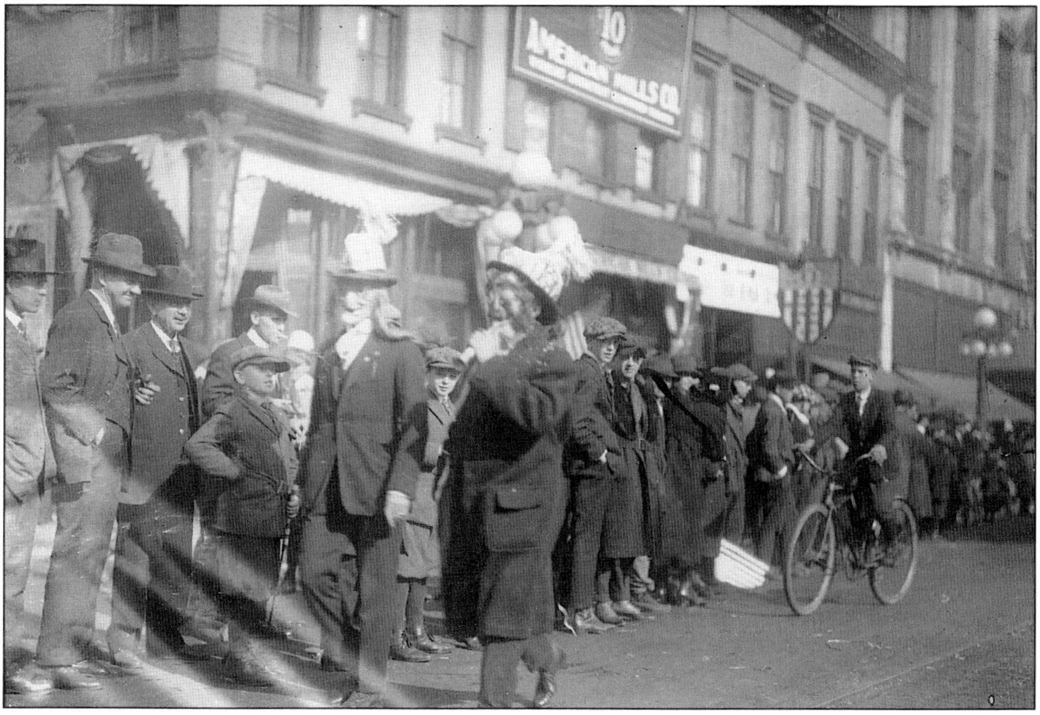

Celebrating the Armistice on November 11, 1918, in Evansville were these two paraders, at least one of whom clearly wanted to ridicule the defeated Kaiser and his Germans. (Courtesy of USI.)

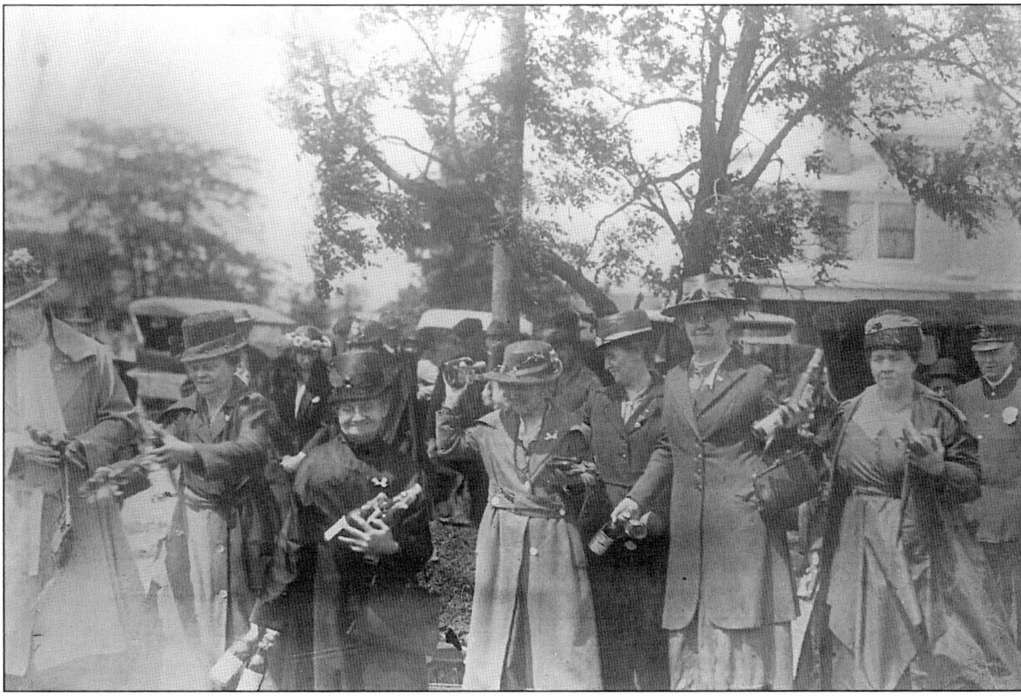

Indiana enacted statewide prohibition in February 1917 and ratified the Eighteenth Amendment proposing national prohibition in January 1919. Members of an Evansville temperance society happily greeted the institution of the latter in 1920 by pitching bottles of demon rum into the city dump. Evansville's location and culture—heavily Upper Southern and German—would make their efforts difficult to enforce in the 1920s. (Courtesy of USI.)

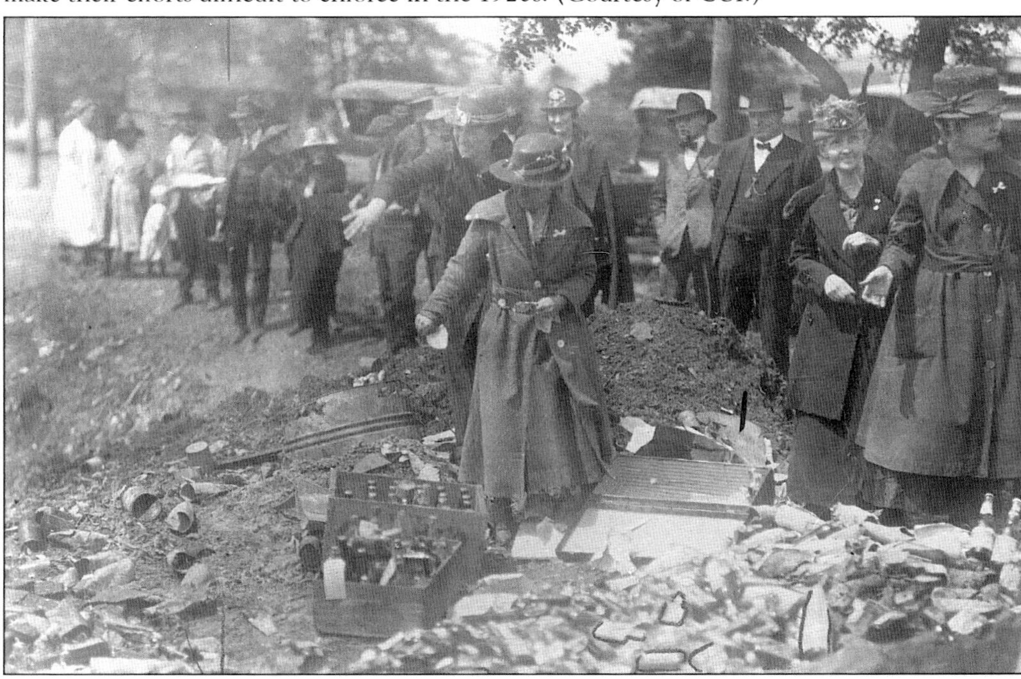

Here is another perspective on the Evansville prohibition inaugural. (Courtesy of USI.)

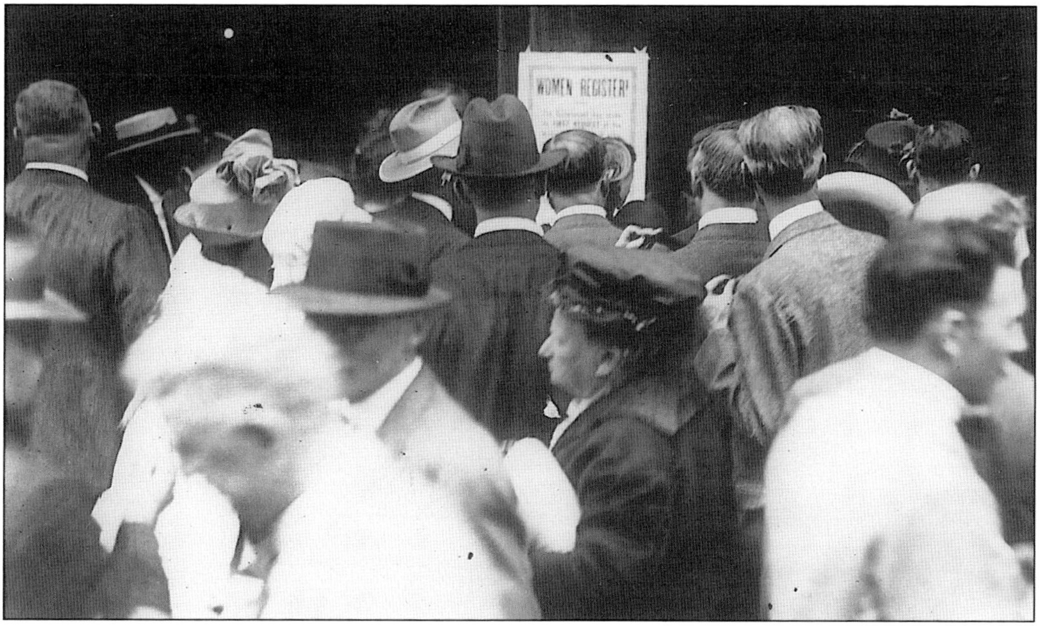

A crowd gathers around a poster urging Evansville women to register to vote. The General Assembly passed a partial suffrage bill in 1917 allowing women the right to vote immediately for presidential electors, municipal officials, and delegates to a proposed constitutional convention. Opponents sued, though, and the Indiana Supreme Court invalidated the law later that year. After the Nineteenth Amendment was ratified, Indiana's legislators adopted the amendment in January 1920. (Courtesy of Willard Library.)

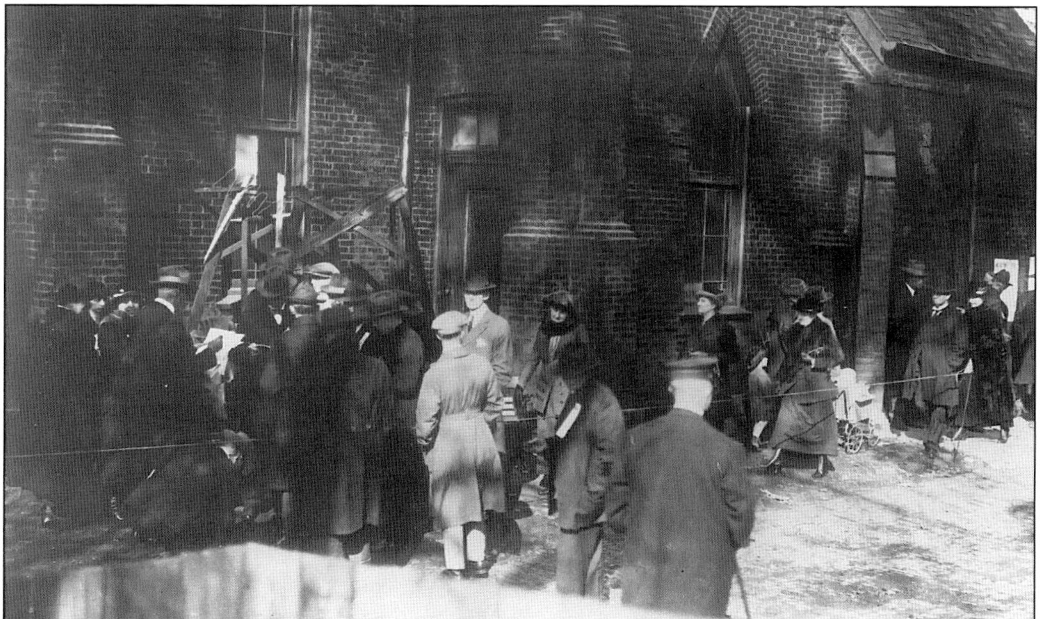

Evansville women are shown voting for the first time in November, 1920, thanks to the ratification of the Nineteenth Amendment. Many assumed that women would vote as a bloc. They would not. (Courtesy of USI.)

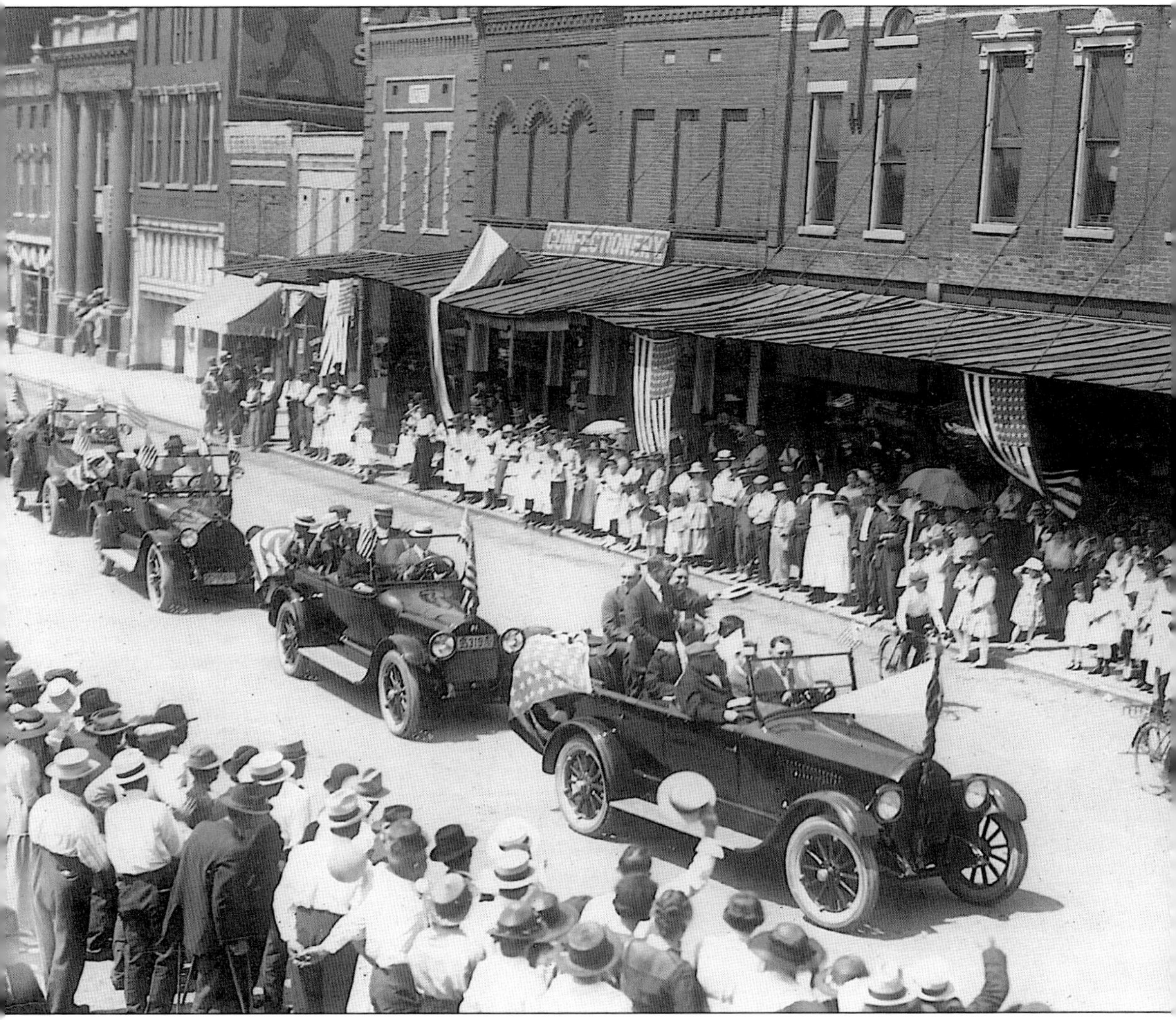

Democratic presidential candidate James Cox is seen standing in an open car on the main street of Princeton on August 25, 1920. With him are national Democratic leader Tom Taggart of French Lick and Evansville mayor Benjamin Bosse, state Democratic chair. This was a landmark national election, pitting progressivism and the League of Nations versus Warren Harding's "normalcy."(Courtesy of Willard Library.)

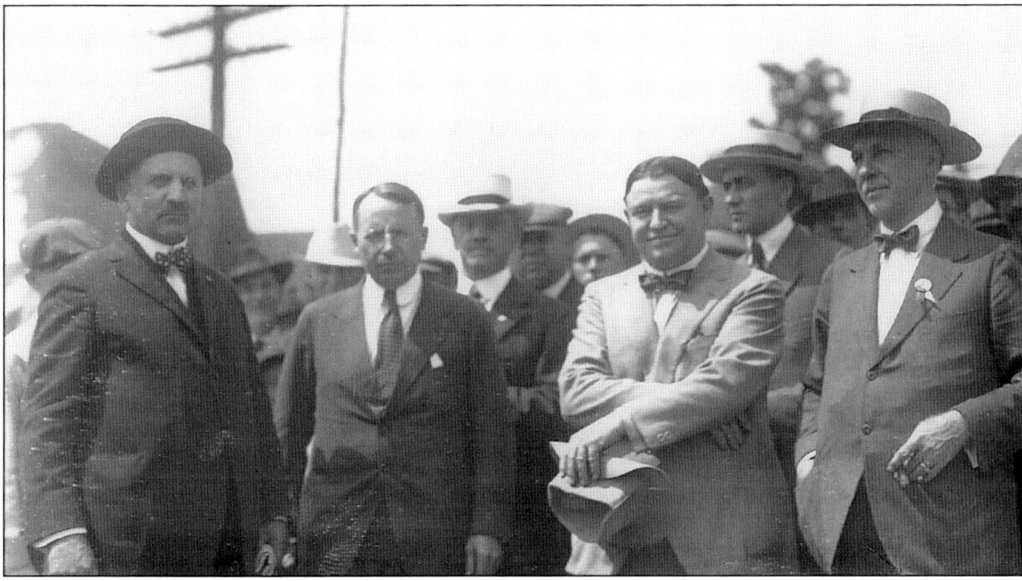

Presidential candidate James Cox (second from left) was photographed with national Democratic leader Thomas Taggart of French Lick (far right) and state Democratic leader Benjamin Bosse, mayor of Evansville (second from right), in Princeton. (Courtesy of USI.)

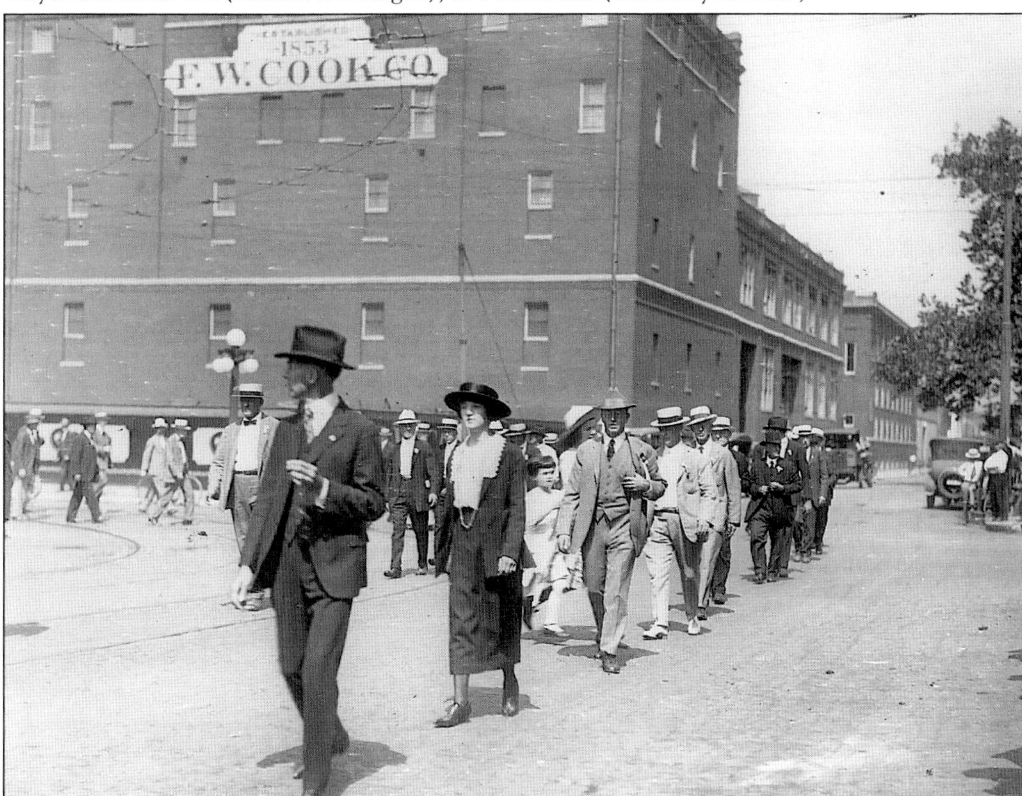

Cox also campaigned in Evansville. This group of supporters is seen marching near Seventh and Main Streets. (Courtesy of Willard Library.)

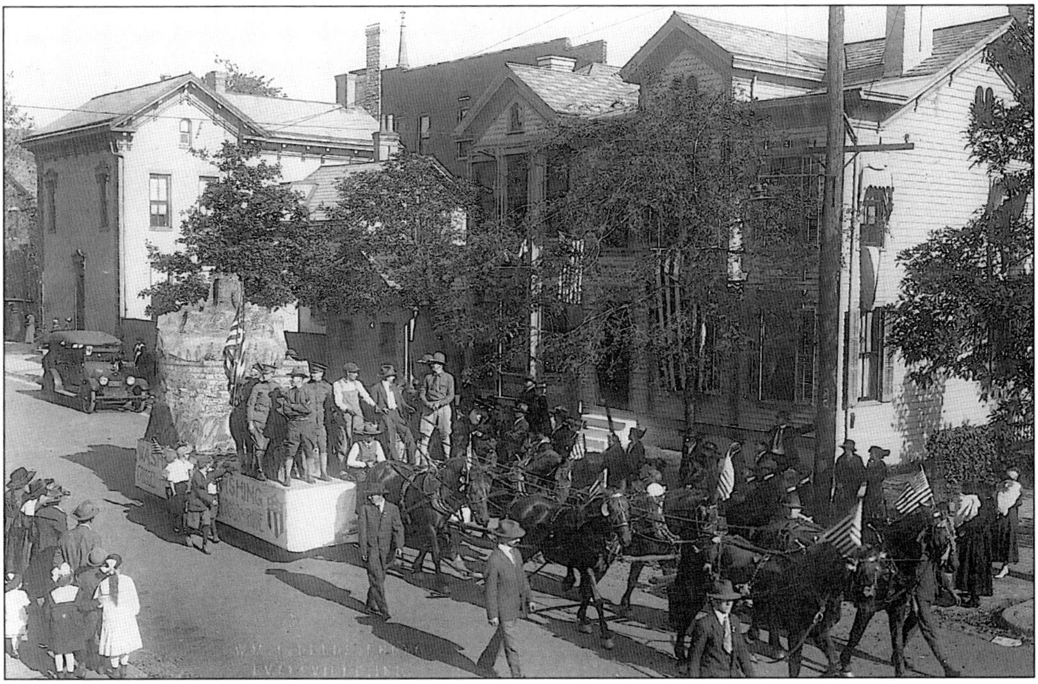

After the war, veterans were an important factor in American society, culture, and politics. Here an Evansville group is shown on a float praising Washington and Pershing—one for crossing the Delaware, and the other for crossing the Rhine. A chapter of the newly-formed American Legion was established in the city in January 1919. (Courtesy of Willard Library.)

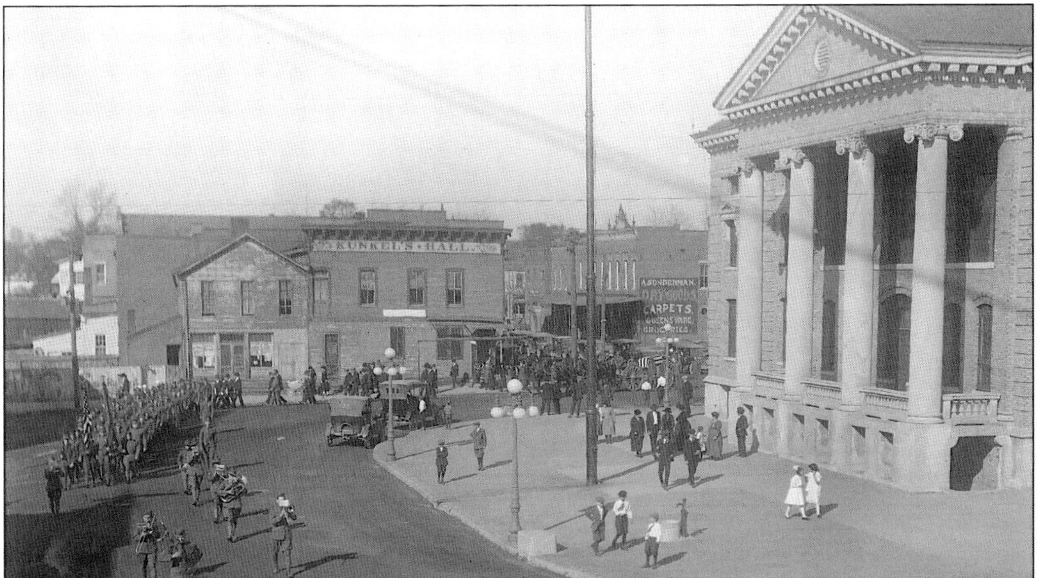

This is the funeral cortege for Clyde Line of Jasper, an army stenographer killed in France a few weeks before the armistice of November 11, 1918. The 24-year-old man was inducted June 24 and arrived in France about a month before his death. Interment in his hometown occurred in the fall of 1921. (Courtesy of John Fierst.)

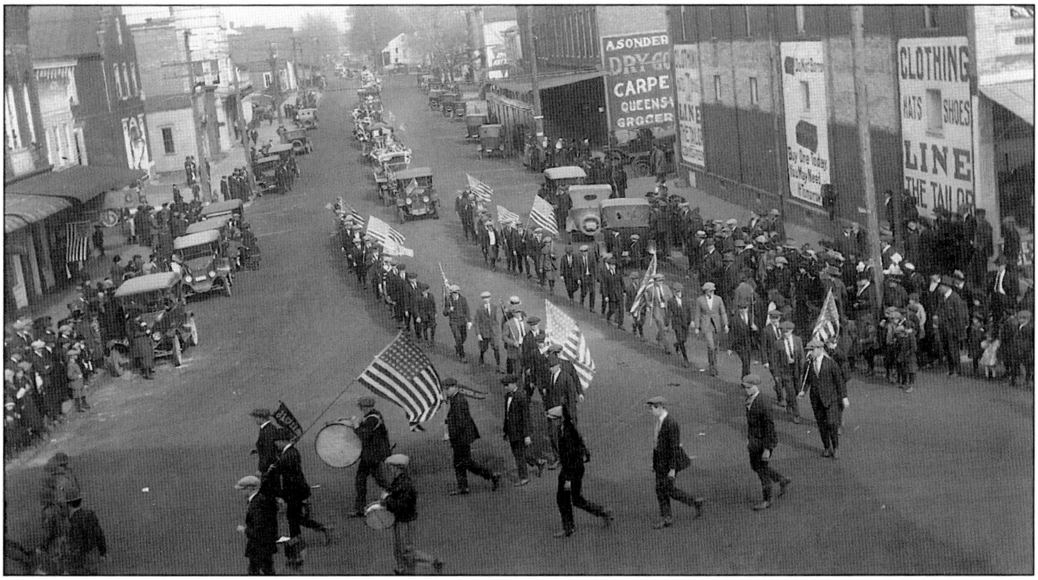

Armistice Day parades after the Great War were an essential part of civic rituals in southern Indiana, as in the nation. This one occurred in Jasper on November 11, 1921. (Courtesy of John Fierst.)

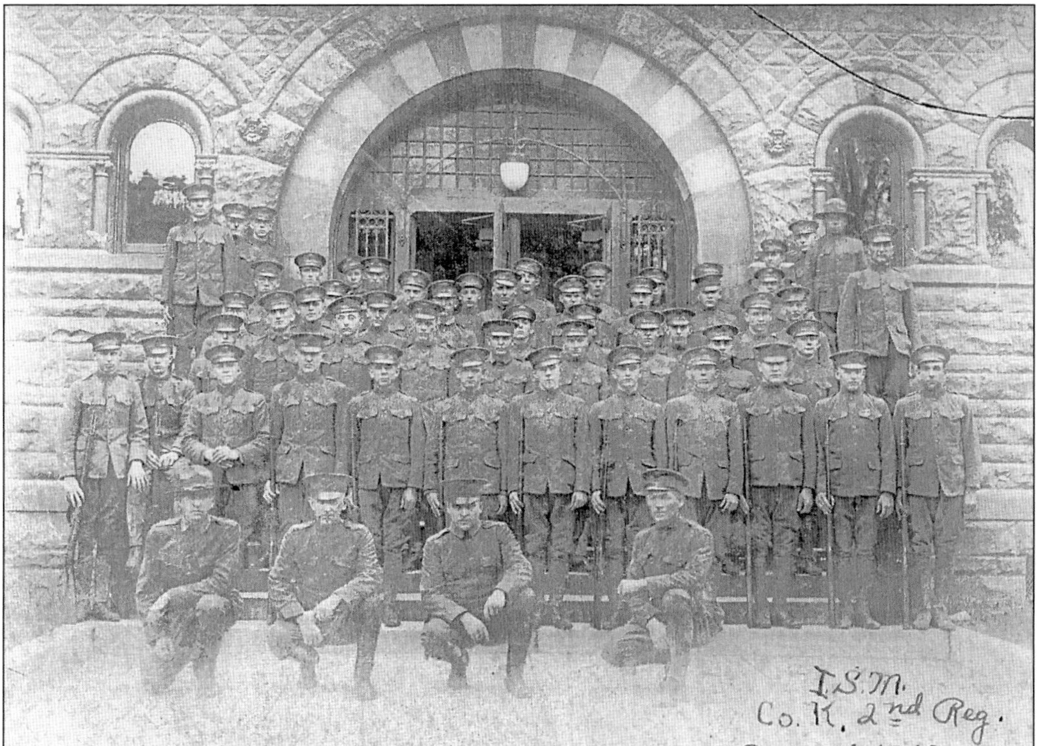

This photograph of Company K, 2nd Regiment, of the Indiana State Militia, was taken on the front steps of the Old Post Office building in Madison. (Courtesy of Jefferson County Historical Society.)

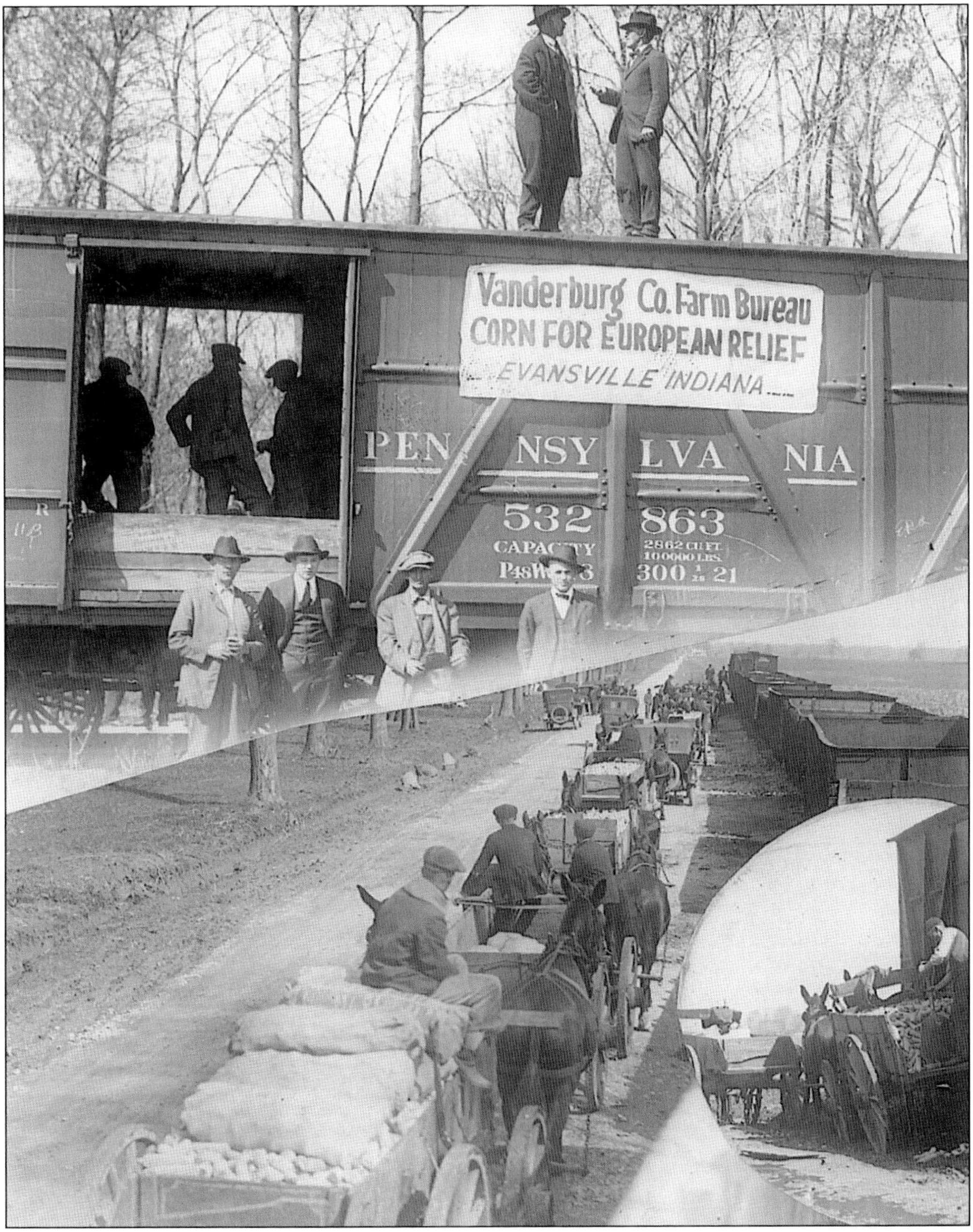

These rail cars, being loaded in Evansville in 1919, were destined to alleviate post-war suffering in Europe. This was the first community-wide relief effort for continental Europeans in the city's history, and a reminder of how the war had altered America's role in the world. (Courtesy of Willard Library.)

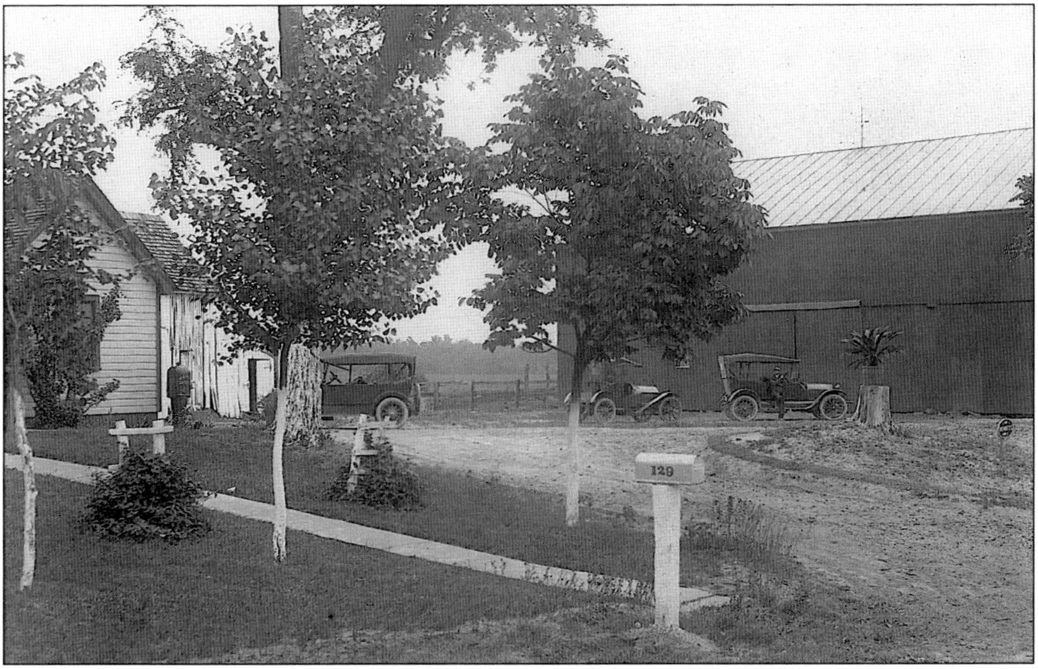

The first automobile club serving southwestern Indiana was established in 1918 on Darmstadt Road, near Clearcrest Country Club, on the north side of Evansville. It was one of many marks of the coming of the auto age. (Courtesy of Willard Library.)

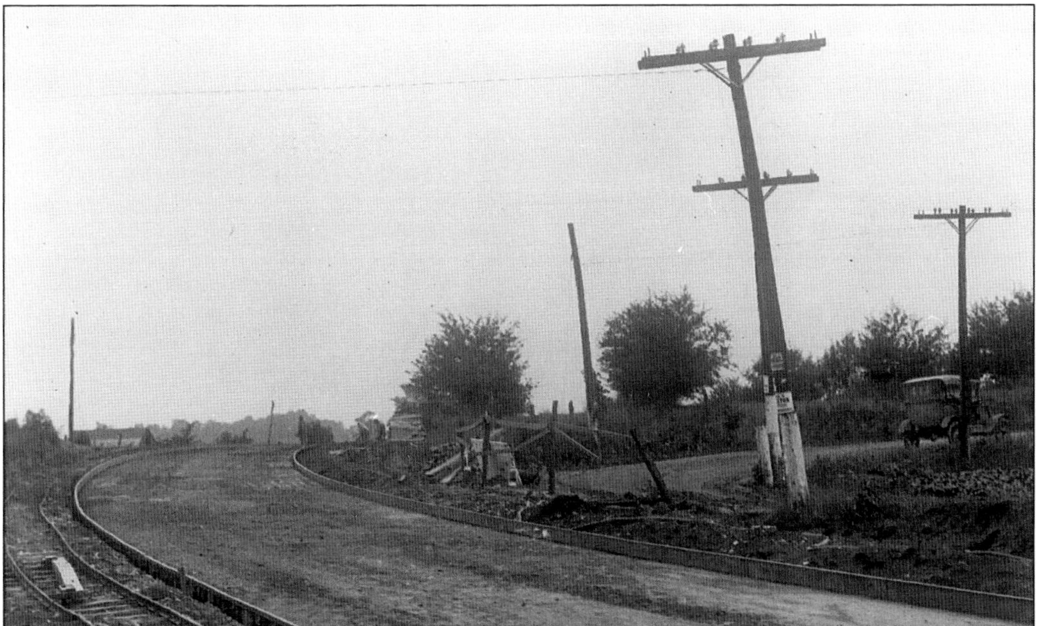

A harbinger of modern times, this is construction work on the new state highway at the Vanderburgh–Warrick county line in the early 1920s. Four years after the adoption of the Federal Highway Act of 1916, the Indiana Department of Highways created a state highway plan. This is probably what would become State Road 62. (Courtesy of USI.)

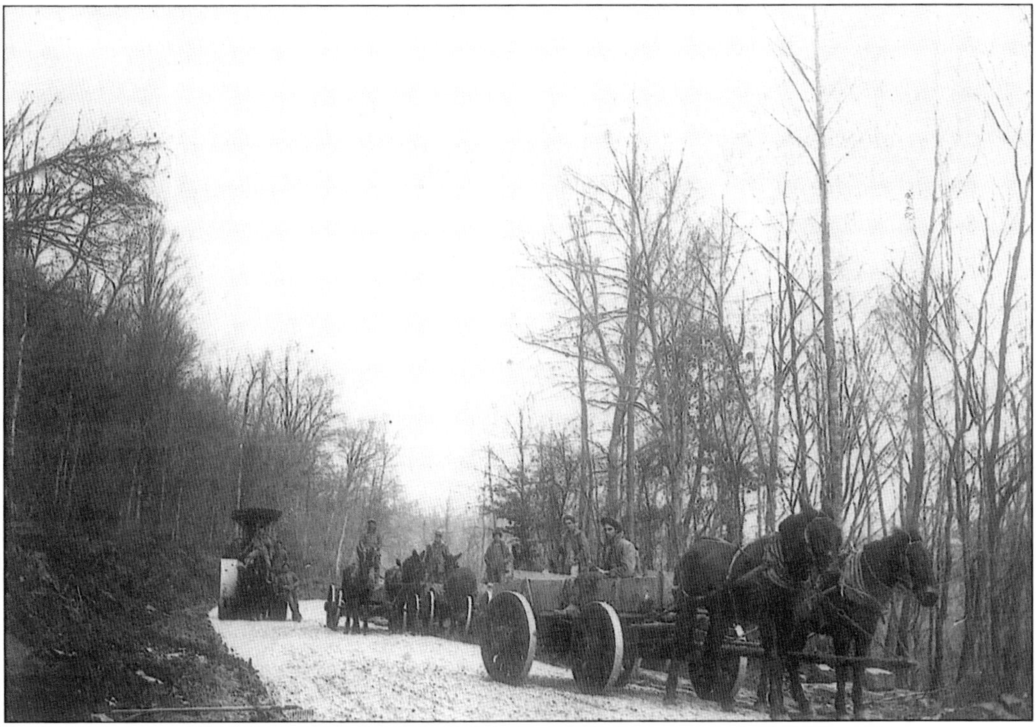

A crew of men with heavy equipment was photographed building State Road 37 in Crawford County after World War I. (Courtesy of Harold and Sheila Horn.)

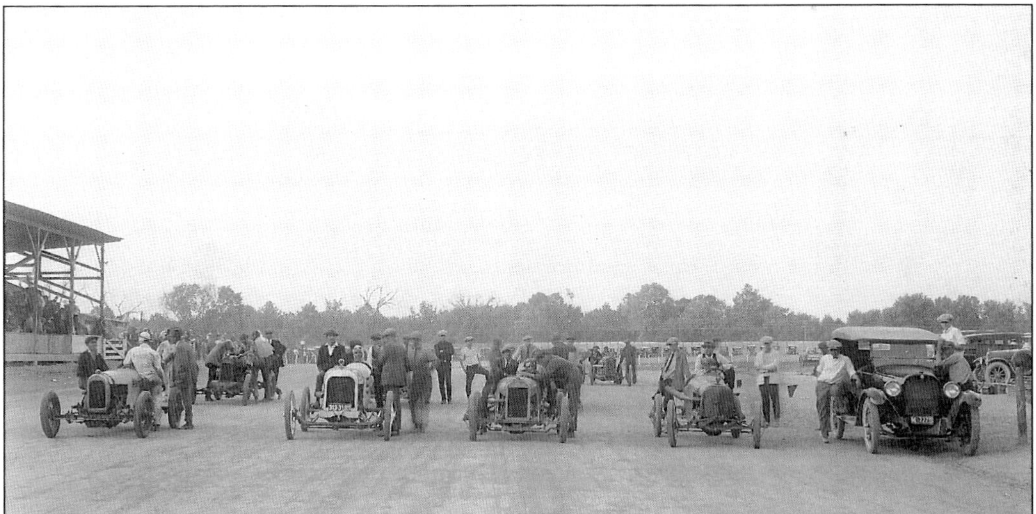

The Salt Creek Race Track, between Bedford and Oolitic, was by the time of this 1923 photograph an essential part of automobile culture. Auto speedways, which had their roots in Carl Fisher's Indianapolis racetrack over a decade earlier, were an integral part of the growing fascination with cars and their recreational potential. (Courtesy of Maxine Kruse.)

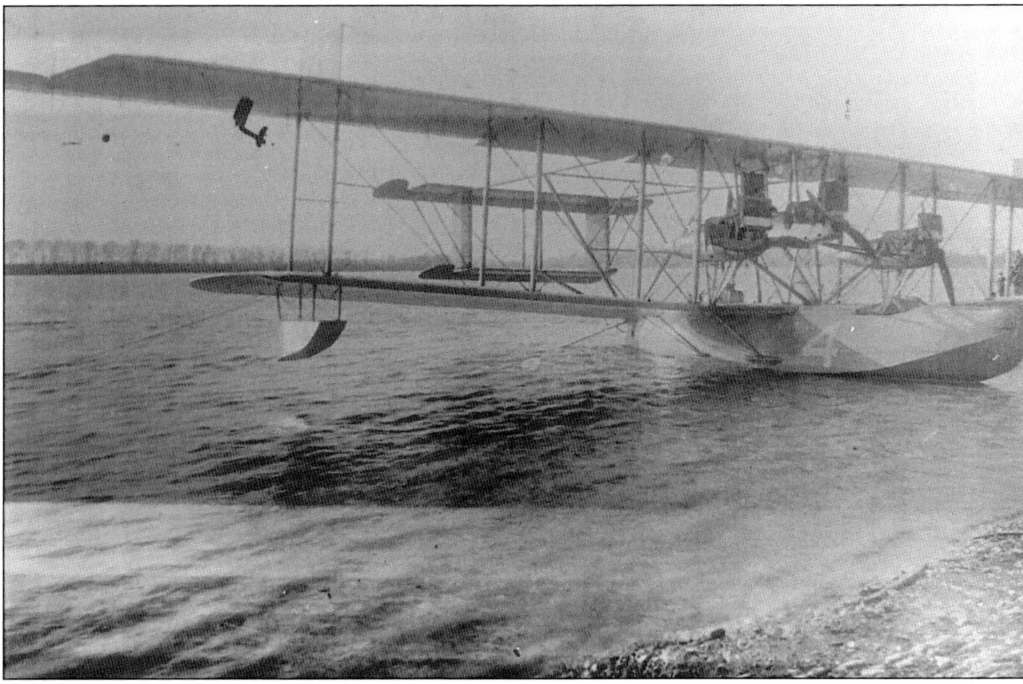

This NC–4 (Navy Curtiss) flying boat stopped in Evansville in mid-1919 on a triumphal tour of cities on the Ohio and Mississippi Rivers. On May 28, 1919, it landed at Lisbon, Portugal, completing the first trans-Atlantic flight. One of four built during the war by Glenn Curtiss, it was 68 feet long and had a wingspan of 126 feet. It could reach a speed of 91 miles per hour. (Courtesy of Willard Library.)

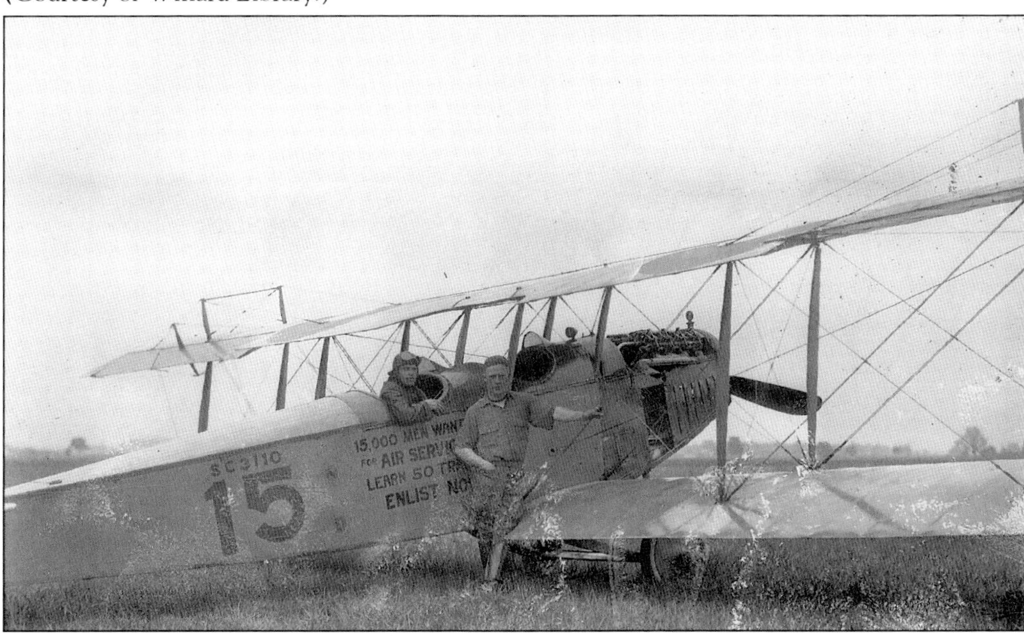

Pilots of an Army Sopwith Camel visited Evansville and other southern Indiana communities on a promotional tour of the country in 1919. The Army was, at the time, seeking 15,000 men to enlist in its new air corps. (Courtesy of USI.)

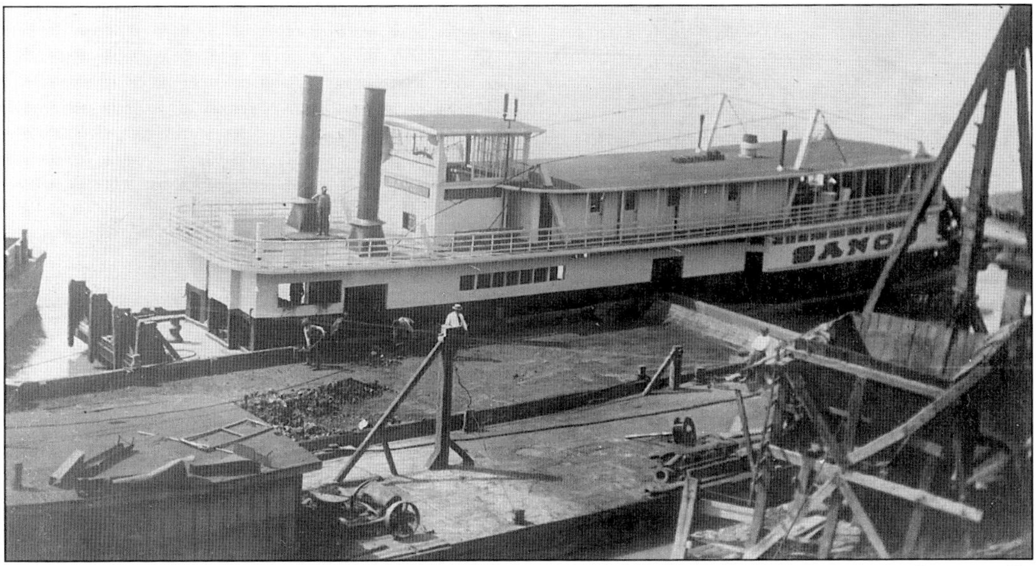

The *Sanco*, built in Evansville in 1920, was a new breed of riverboat. After 1910, and especially due to the need to improve river transport during World War I, diesel tows like these came to dominate barge traffic on the inland waters. (Courtesy of USI.)

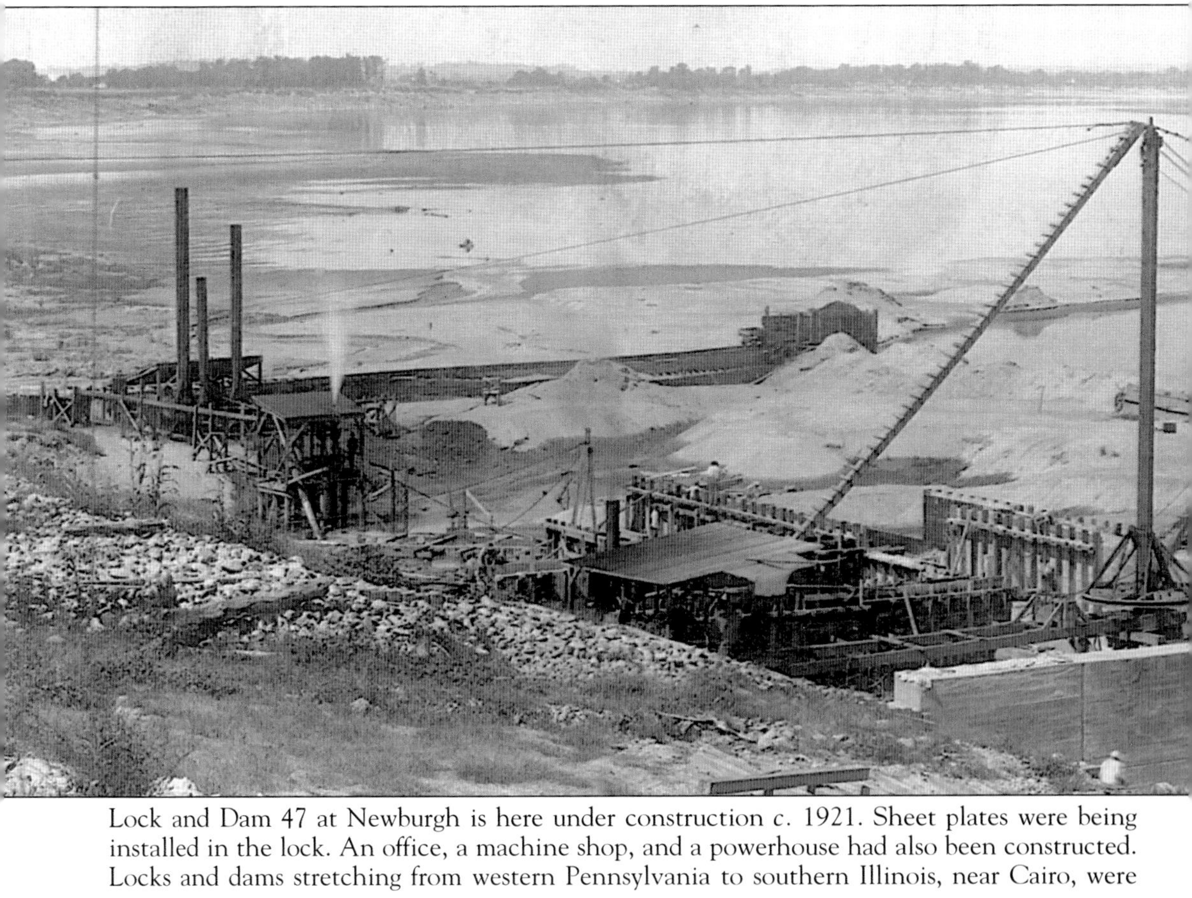

Lock and Dam 47 at Newburgh is here under construction *c*. 1921. Sheet plates were being installed in the lock. An office, a machine shop, and a powerhouse had also been constructed. Locks and dams stretching from western Pennsylvania to southern Illinois, near Cairo, were

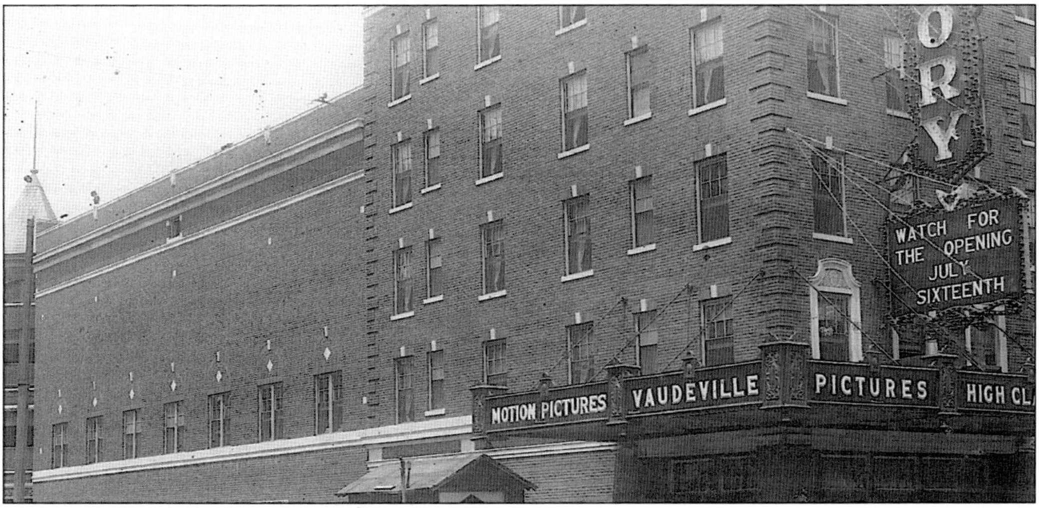

The Victory Theater at Sixth and Main in Evansville is shown before opening (July 1921). The most luxurious in the city, it seated 2,500 in "temperature controlled" comfort. It symbolized the impact of movies on mass culture. The theater also offered vaudeville and had an orchestra pit and a huge organ. The Hotel Sonntag occupied most of the building. In 1926, the Victory became part of the Loews chain. (Courtesy of Willard Library.)

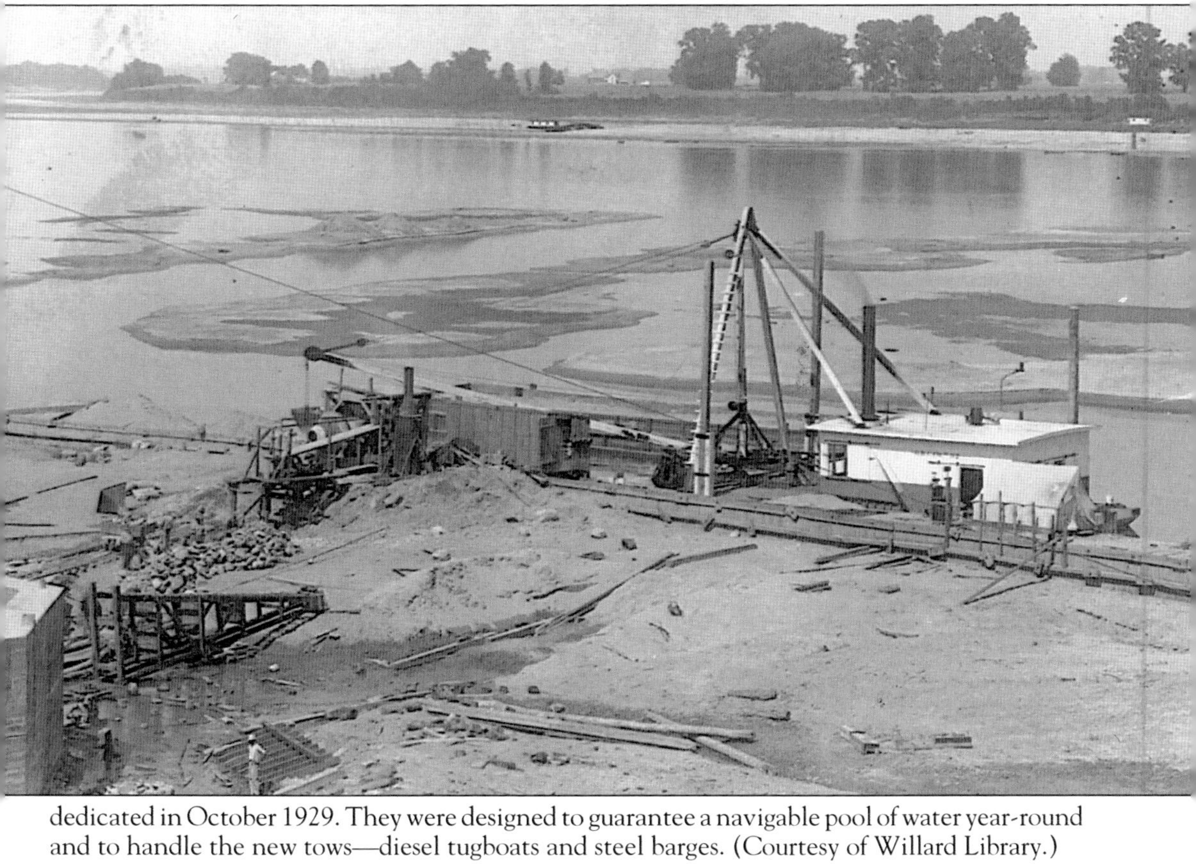

dedicated in October 1929. They were designed to guarantee a navigable pool of water year-round and to handle the new tows—diesel tugboats and steel barges. (Courtesy of Willard Library.)

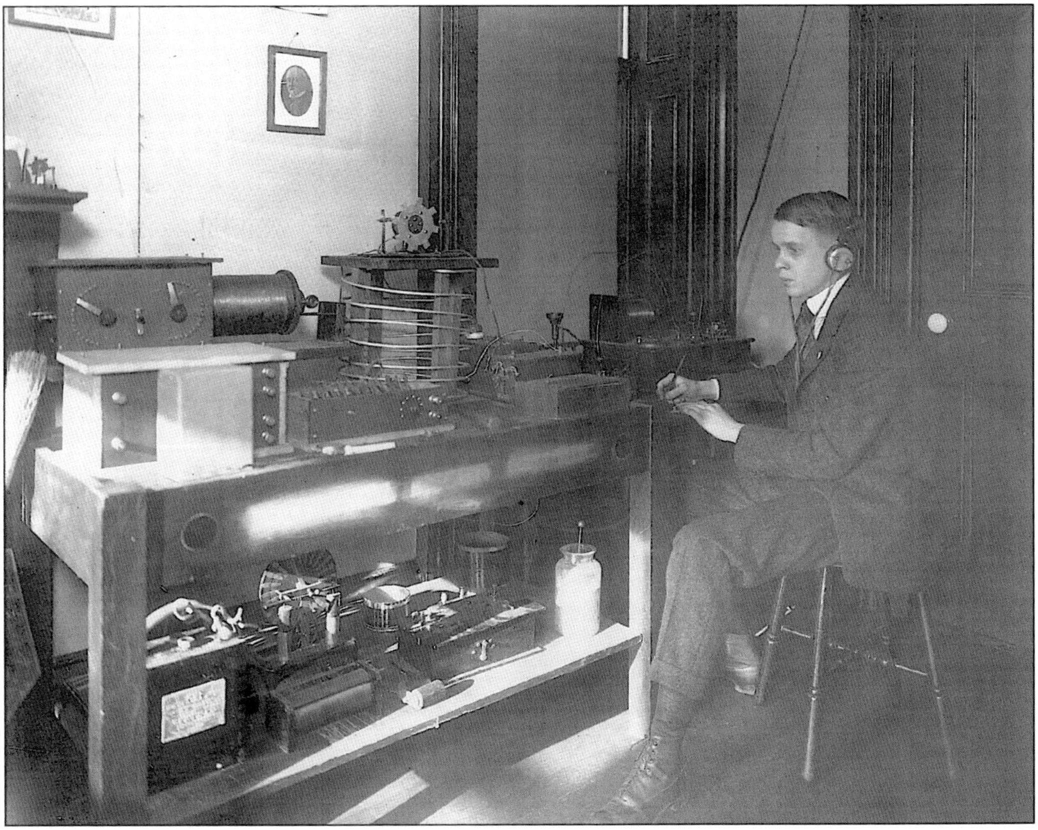

James Clifford, son of prominent Evansville civic leader George Clifford, is shown here with his ham radio set in 1912. In many respects he, like young persons in the 1990s who heralded "the information age," was on the cutting edge of the age of radio, which produced its first commercial station in the United States in 1921. (Courtesy of Willard Library.)